TWELVE STEPS
FOR
WHITE AMERICA

TWELVE STEPS

FOR

WHITE AMERICA

for a **UNITED STATES** *of* **AMERICA**

WILLIAM WATSON

Copyright © 2023 by William Watson. All rights reserved. No part of this publication may be reprinted, reproduced, transmitted, or utilized in any form or by any electronic, mechanical, or other means, now known or hereafter invented, including photocopying, microfilming, and recording, or in any information retrieval system without the written permission of Cognella, Inc.

Trademark Notice: Product or corporate names may be trademarks or registered trademarks, and are used only for identification and explanation without intent to infringe.

Cover image copyright © 2019 iStockphoto LP/CRobertson.

Selections from *Alcoholics Anonymous, Alcoholics Anonymous: The Story of How Many Thousands of Men and Women Have Recovered from Alcoholism*, 3rd ed., pp. 85, 449. Copyright © 1976 by Alcoholics Anonymous World Services, Inc.

Selections from *Alcoholics Anonymous, Twelve Steps and Twelve Traditions*, pp. 75, 106–107, 184. Copyright © 1989 by Alcoholics Anonymous World Services, Inc.

Selections from *Alcoholics Anonymous, Alcoholics Anonymous: The Story of How Many Thousands of Men and Women Have Recovered from Alcoholism*, 1st ed., pp. 70–72, 84, 88, 95–97, Alcoholics Anonymous World Services, Inc., 1939.

Printed in the United States of America.

Call

The only thing white people have that black people need, or should want, is power—and no one holds power forever. White people cannot, in the generality, be taken as models of how to live. Rather, the white man is himself in sore need of new standards, which will release him from his confusion and place him once again in fruitful communion with the depths of his own being.

James Baldwin
The Fire Next Time

Response

May Twelve Steps for White America *provide standards that place White Americans once again in fruitful communion with the depths of our being.*

William Watson

STATEMENT ON ALCOHOLICS ANONYMOUS AND THE SPIRITUAL FOUNDATION OF ANONYMITY

Application of the Underlying Problem-Solving Principles

The principles that form the foundation of the 12 steps presented in Alcoholics Anonymous (AA), are basic problem-solving principles universal to the human condition. Humanity survives because we learn and practice and continuously transfer problem-solving principles that enable us to adapt and survive. Universal problem-solving principles, fundamental to the human condition, pre-date AA. They are catalogued and presented by AA as a revolution in the treatment of alcoholism.

The AA presentation of these underlying problem-solving principles in the form of 12 steps revolutionized the treatment of alcoholism in the 20th century. When referred to throughout this work, the AA 12 steps are sourced appropriately. While AA presents those universal problem-solving principles as a treatment plan for the *dysfunction/disorder of alcoholism*, I present those universal problem-solving principles as a treatment plan for the *national dysfunction/disorder of rigged advantage*, which threatens our democracy.

Anonymity

I share only what is mine to share—my lived experience of practicing recovery principles in all my affairs. I do not speak for Alcoholics

Anonymous. I do not represent AA in any way. I am not identifying as a "member" of AA. I do not share anything in this book as if I am a "member" of AA. I should not be considered as an example of what an AA member was, is, or could be. First copyrighted in 1952 by A.A. Grapevine, Inc. and Alcoholics Anonymous Publishing (now known as Alcoholics Anonymous World Services), the *Twelfth Tradition*[1] (different from the *Twelfth Step*) is a hallowed principle that mitigated a stigma in the early and mid-20th century that may be nearly unimaginable to 21st-century sensibilities. Still, today, it is remains as important as it was then.

Anonymity is the spiritual foundation of all our traditions, ever reminding us to place principles before personalities.[2]

BRIEF CONTENTS

Dedication in Memory   xv
Acknowledgments   xxi
How to Use This Book: Skipping This Part Is Not Recommended   xxiii

PART I TRUTH 1

Chapter 1 Step 1: We Admit Our Problem—Rigged Advantage   18

Chapter 2 Step 2: We Believe Something Can Be Done   31

Chapter 3 Step 3: We Decide to Act   40

Chapter 4 Step 4: We Detail the Problem   49

PART II RECONCILIATION 71

Chapter 5 Step 5: We Present the Problem   85

Chapter 6 Step 6: We Resolve to Change   91

Chapter 7 Step 7: We Humbly Turn Toward Change   98

Chapter 8 Step 8: We Identify the Harm   106

PART III RENEWAL 121

Chapter 9 Step 9: We Repair the Harm   133

Chapter 10 Step 10: We Remain Vigilant   147

| Chapter 11 | Step 11: We Choose Reverence   161 |
| Chapter 12 | Step 12: We Consecrate Liberty Free From Rigged Advantage   189 |

Notes   203
Bibliography   217
Index   235

DETAILED CONTENTS

Dedication in Memory   xv
Acknowledgments   xxi
How to Use This Book: Skipping This Part Is Not Recommended   xxiii

PART I   **TRUTH** 1

Introduction to Steps 1–4   2

CHAPTER 1   Step 1: We Admit Our Problem—Rigged Advantage   18

What I Learned From Alcoholics About the First Step of AA   19

What of This May We Apply to Our Problem, Rigged Advantage?   22

Learning Outcome   30

CHAPTER 2   Step 2: We Believe Something Can Be Done   31

What I Learned From Alcoholics About the Second Step of AA   32

What of This May We Apply to Our Problem, Rigged Advantage?   33

Learning Outcome   39

CHAPTER 3   Step 3: We Decide to Act   40

What I Learned From Alcoholics About the Third Step of AA   41

What of This May We Apply to Our Problem, Rigged Advantage?   45

Very Important Note   48

Learning Outcome   48

CHAPTER 4 Step 4: We Detail the Problem 49

What I Learned From Alcoholics About the Fourth Step of AA 50

What of This May We Apply to Our Problem, Rigged Advantage? 53

Rigged Advantage Theory: What's the Problem? 61

Discussion 66

Learning Outcome 70

PART II **RECONCILIATION** 71

Introduction to Steps 5–8 72

CHAPTER 5 Step 5: We Present the Problem 85

What I Learned From Alcoholics About the Fifth Step of AA 86

What of This May We Apply to Our Problem, Rigged Advantage? 87

Learning Outcome 90

CHAPTER 6 Step 6: We Resolve to Change 91

What I Learned From Alcoholics About the Sixth Step of AA 92

What of This May We Apply to Our Problem, Rigged Advantage? 93

Learning Outcome 97

CHAPTER 7 Step 7: We Humbly Turn Toward Change 98

What I Learned From Alcoholics About the Seventh Step of AA 99

What of This May We Apply to Our Problem, Rigged Advantage? 100

Learning Outcome 105

CHAPTER 8 Step 8: We Identify the Harm 106

What I Learned From Alcoholics About the Eighth Step of AA 107

What of This May We Apply to Our Problem,
Rigged Advantage?   111

Learning Outcome   120

PART III   RENEWAL 121

Revisit Governing and Complementary Steps
to Strengthen Learning   126

Tipping Point of Resolve   132

CHAPTER 9   Step 9: We Repair the Harm   133

What I Learned From Alcoholics About the Ninth
Step of AA   134

What of This May We Apply to Our Problem,
Rigged Advantage?   136

Learning Outcome   146

CHAPTER 10   Step 10: We Remain Vigilant   147

What I Learned From Alcoholics About the Tenth
Step of AA   148

What of This May We Apply to Our Problem,
Rigged Advantage?   154

Learning Outcome   160

CHAPTER 11   Step 11: We Choose Reverence   161

What I Learned From Alcoholics About the Eleventh
Step of AA   162

What of This May We Apply to Our Problem,
Rigged Advantage?   167

Telescoping   169

We Versus Me: What Is True for Us May Not Be True for Me. Something Not True About Me Can Still Be True About Us   171

Ahimsa (Nonviolence) and Asteya (Nonstealing)   172

Drawing the Circle   184

The Crucible of Loving Kindness Meditation   187

Learning Outcome   188

CHAPTER 12 Step 12: We Consecrate Liberty Free From
Rigged Advantage   189

What I Learned From Alcoholics About the Twelfth
Step of AA   190

What of This May We Apply to Our Problem,
Rigged Advantage?   194

Learning Outcome   202

Notes   203
Bibliography   217
Index   235

Nutshell Graphic Review of Table of Contents

Use the following graphic to review the Table of Contents. This will provide you with a visual to contextualize the material within each of the three parts of the book. If at any point in the book you feel you have lost the point, this graphic can steer you back on course.

Image 0.1

DEDICATION IN MEMORY

In Memory of Helga Burnham Watson and Hubert Watson

Twelve Steps for White America is dedicated to
The Honorable Constance Slaughter-Harvey

Twelve Steps for White America is dedicated to a living legend. The Honorable Constance Slaughter-Harvey is an iconic Mississippi civil rights attorney lauded alongside Fannie Lou Hamer and Leontyne Price as one of 10 notable Mississippi women of the 20th century.[1] Constance Slaughter-Harvey ascended to unimaginable heights of political achievement in an era when integrating the University of Mississippi (known as "Ole Miss," a term for the "mistress" of a slavery plantation)[2] precipitated the intervention of the U.S. Supreme Court, the Kennedy administration, and a federalized National Guard for James Meredith to enroll amid rioting.

Mississippi Governor Ross Barnett taunted Attorney General Robert Kennedy and President Kennedy, pontificating that this was "our greatest crisis since the war between the states."[3] The governor's crisis was a Black man enrolling at Ole Miss—not the backlash riot. James Meredith's 1962 televised trail-blazing required a military-style occupation of the Ole Miss college town, Oxford, Mississippi. Rowan Oak, William Faulkner's home in Oxford, remains a literary tourist attraction.[4] Faulkner's nephew, a captain in the federalized Mississippi National Guard, protected Meredith from the mob of violent White insurrectionists, defending their way of life from democracy's march forward.[5]

Constance Slaughter followed this "greatest crisis since the war between the states"[6] to enroll at the University of Mississippi School of Law. An unabashed pantheon of White patriarchal supremacy, the Ole Miss law school reigned as a reliable status quo progenitor of racialized hatred in Mississippi.[7] In that world, Constance Slaughter triumphed as the first African American woman to earn a law degree from the University of Mississippi School of Law, where the Confederate rebel and Confederate flag were mascot and banner. Her courageous and inspiring career produced a domino effect of firsts across Mississippi history becoming the first African American woman judge and then the first African American assistant secretary of state/general counsel, serving for 12 years.

Early on, I only knew "Connie" as the daughter of that nice lady owner of the Six Cees Superette, Mrs. Olivia Kelly Slaughter, who quoted Shakespeare. Connie's father, Mr. W. L. Slaughter, was an esteemed educational administrator and Forest, Mississippi, alderman, who earned a master's degree from the University of California, Los Angeles (UCLA) after losing his left hand in WWII.[8] When you could buy gas at the Six Cees Superette for 32 cents per gallon,[9] my country parents and the impressive and accomplished Slaughters worked for local change when Connie (one of the six Slaughter daughters of the Superette's six "Cees")[10] was becoming a historical juggernaut for justice. "Local change" is my euphemism for my parents' life-risking voter registration drives, community organizing with the Scott County Improvement Association, and working with Mississippi Action for Progress to launch Head Start in Lauderdale, Scott, and Neshoba Counties. Freedom Summer's Chaney, Goodman, and Schwerner had recently been murdered there by the KKK colluding with law enforcement,[11] events portrayed in the film *Mississippi Burning*.[12]

Years later in Oakland, California, I met Black Panther Party cofounder, Bobby Seale, who delivered the commencement address where I was a college vice president. He spoke as an elder statesman recalling the Black Panther Party's Free Breakfast Program for school children and voter registration drives. Afterward, in our brief encounter, I referenced his address saying that in the '60s, Mother and Daddy had worked in voter registration drives in Mississippi. This legendary Black Panther raised his knowing eyebrows and said, "They were some brave people."

His empathic words broke open my soul. Cloaked in academic doctoral regalia, I might as well have been 10 years old, barefooted on a dirt road, twitchy after the Klan threatened to kill us. Triggered raw, faded fear flooded me. I cried hot tears to heaven on the way home, praying, "I hope y'all heard that—the cofounder of the Black Panther Party said y'all were brave." Short but so sweet; it was an extraordinary source of validation uttered for my parents. They worked exposed and threatened, largely uncredited for their sacrifice, shrouded in a tamping Whiteness that settles even the Civil War as simply "the late unpleasantness."[13]

As I grew older, I appreciated Constance Slaughter beyond family friend Connie, whom my parents adored. I came to know her better after I graduated from high school, and, as one does, dropped out of university to enter a psychiatric hospital diagnosed with depression (undiagnosed alcoholism, actually). Surely out of love and sympathy for my parents' grasping for what to do, Connie hired me to do some office work, where, early in her career, she had founded East Mississippi Legal Services as executive director. Through my haze of psychiatric meds, I can hardly remember any of it. What I do know is that her dignity and investment in my future mitigated my nightmare of alcoholism and depression, lighting a way forward beyond my immediate demoralization at a teetering time of life. Grateful, I became a fan of the history-making Constance Slaughter. Mother and I attended her wedding celebration at LeFleur's Restaurant in Jackson,

Mississippi. Thereafter, she became known to history as Constance Slaughter-Harvey.

I learned more about my parents' affections for Connie and appreciated the mutuality of their relationship when she eulogized my father in 2007 and later visited my mother regularly in nursing care until she passed in 2013. It was a great honor for someone of Constance Slaughter-Harvey's status to eulogize my father. The son of outhouse-poor racist sharecroppers, he ran away from his life before completing high school. Proffered by an African American civil rights legend in a southern White country church pulpit, the transcendent symbolism of just her presence credited sacrifice to a man who once told me, "You can go to church with them racist som-bitches if you want to—I'd rather go to hell." Laughter erupts easily at a southern funeral as it did when Connie referenced his well-known obsession with "them goddam Republicans." In retrospect, it was funnier as obsession then, than as prophecy now.

A few years later at Mother's funeral, Connie revealed to me that Mother was already a member of the NAACP "when Medgar was killed." Those were hallowed words of respect from Connie, who, inspired by Medgar Evers, marched in his tragic funeral procession only 10 days after she met him.[14] The day Mother died, the Mississippi House of Representatives adjourned in her honor. I knew who made that happen. The Democratic Party's Resolution hailed Mother as "Lady Warrior."[15] This was the fiercely moral social justice mother I knew—not the sweet old quirky lady from her "White"-washed eulogy.

After Mother's funeral, waiting at Reagan International to board a flight home to San Francisco, I opened my wallet to give my credit card to a café's chatty, sweet server. Surprised by the unexpected, she said, "I hope you don't mind me asking, but I noticed the NAACP membership card in your wallet and I'm just curious." I explained, "Every time I open my wallet, it reminds me of who I am and where

I'm from. Mother was a Yellow-Dog Democrat who would expect me to be a card-carrying member. She was already a member of the NAACP 'when Medgar was killed.'"

Even now, as an "expat" of Mississippi for many years, the stifling inching of Mississippi time, the Slaughters, the Watsons, the NAACP "making democracy work since 1909," the voter registration drives, MAP Head Start, James Meredith-Ole Miss, twitchy bare feet on dirt roads, my precarious coming of age, and the Honorable Constance Slaughter-Harvey all burnish in sagas of memory—a legacy of the price already paid and the debt still due. As Faulkner wrote in *Requiem for a Nun*,

> "The past is never dead. It's not even past."

ACKNOWLEDGMENTS

August 14, 1987, Winfried L. took me to Loyola University in the New Orleans Garden District for an AA Big Book study with notable AA teachers, Joe M. and Charlie P. I had just lost the Big Book I started out with a few months earlier. So at Loyola, I bought a new version of the third edition, which has been with me ever since. It is raggedy and splotchy. The cover is long gone. The yellowed pages are filled with spectacular notes that captured the insights of the Joe and Charlie duo known throughout the recovery world for their illuminating insights into AA history and practical application of the steps.

Winfried (Vin-freed) would put his German accent face within about 6 inches of my face with his pointed finger in between to "tell me a thing or two" about how I was not going to stay sober doing x, y, and z. Of course, I couldn't stand him—and, of course, that was irrelevant. The entire recovery experience has been something I can't stand! But, to get sober, you have to "act yourself into the right way of thinking," not the other way around. Putting up with Winfried left me with a Joe and Charlie–filled Big Book I still study 35 years later and used to write this book. We lost touch years ago, but, while writing this book, I learned that Winfried had passed away. I couldn't stand him, and I am so grateful to him for what he contributed to my sobriety.

Thank you to Lauren Sneed at San Francisco State University for her years of professional support, and for introducing me to Rebecca Toporek, professor and department chair of counseling at San Francisco State University. Dr. Toporek's discussions with me about this work in the earliest stages proved very valuable.

Thank you to the iconic honorable Constance Slaughter-Harvey, Hubert and Helga's beloved Connie.

Thank you to Dr. Christine Sleeter for her luminous integrity, a how-to-live masterclass.

Thank you to Yogacharya Ellen Grace O'Brian, whose *Jewel of Abundance* was the text for my early days pandemic-stillness spirit quest, which launched the writing of this book.

Thank you to Nicole Anderson, Heather Smith Bettini, Dr. Joi Lin Blake, Adolfo Leiva, Dr. Anne Palmer, and my colleagues in the Aspen Presidential Fellowship for being great human beings!

Thank you to James Ball for 21 years and to Ella Rose for joy every day.

Thank you to a great team at Cognella Press for this opportunity.

HOW TO USE THIS BOOK

Skipping This Part Is Not Recommended

Thank you for reading these words. You give me an opportunity to assure you that I have anticipated your experience as a reader. I offer you my guarantee that I intend to serve you with respect and compassion. That is my *how*—my method of operation. Selfishly, I practice hoping *for you* the good I hope *for myself* and my loved ones, since my spirituality dictates that I am not entitled to what I cannot hope for you. In fact, you now know my secret—my *why*—my motivation to put this out into the world.

Question: How do I approach this work?
Answer: I treat you with respect and compassion as I present a treatment plan for democracy, a hope recipe comprised of ingredients mostly repurposed from other sources.

Question: Why am I writing this book? What is the "agenda"?
Answer: I am practicing my 12th step, which I learned from recovering alcoholics: *Having had a **spiritual** awakening as a result of these steps, we tried to carry this **message** to alcoholics, and to **practice** these principles in all our affairs.*[1]

- My *spirituality* as I define it is this: Since I only have a daily reprieve from alcoholism depending on my spiritual condition, and since I have been sober over 35 years, that which has kept me sober is how I define my spiritual condition/awakening.

- *Message*: The problem-solving principles that comprise my spiritual practice are the spiritual tools that have kept me sober.
- *Practice*: My program of recovery addresses two things at once: both the specific condition of alcoholism and the larger context of how to live. **I mitigate my collusion with rigged advantage for my sobriety's sake**. My spirituality (which keeps me sober) cannot afford to live deluded off the backs of marginalized others.

This is what I share with you in this book.

I pray that, if you do not already do this, you treat all incoming information on a to-be determined (TBD) basis. You are entitled to demand the following:

- an assurance that what is presented to you is well-intentioned for your benefit
- clarity regarding what motivates the provider.

What exactly do I mean by that? Bear with me as I use an example from my distant past. I may have watched thousands of cigarette ads on television when I was growing up (yes, that was a thing!). If you are too young to have ever heard it, you can search the Winston cigarette song.[2]

If we apply your entitlement to TBD, instead of singing along to

"Winston taste good, like a cigarette should"

You would translate that to

Buy and smoke our cigarettes! Our industry launched plantation slavery. Our business model addicts you, ruins *your* health (and *others* secondhand). We burden the health care system, but it is 100% preventable. We trap a lot of you who can't afford it. Remember Joe Camel for the kids? We get 'em young knowing that right now high school and middle school students are smoking. We absolutely know it can kill you. We sell it and profit from it anyway. Thanks to all of you who didn't realize your 401(k)'s mutual funds invest in us! (Fast-talking caveat at the end could say, "Regulated by the U.S. Food and Drug Administration").

The catchy Winston song did not say all that, did it?

The point is, what is presented may or may not differ from what something is. This phenomenon ranges from advertising to bamboozling, to sadistic exploitation. Since advertising is so fundamental to the market that makes up our economy, there is a certain amount of this presentation game that we accept. We wink at it because we usually know it is happening. *Usually* is a loaded word here. The implications are fatal individually and nationally. Stay with me.

Let the buyer beware is a long-held principle in contract law, which governs agreements.

> *Caveat emptor, quia ignorare non debuit quod jus alienum* translates to "let a purchaser beware, for he ought not to be ignorant of the nature of the property which he is buying from another party."[3]

Commerce and democracy have this in common. Both require *you* to do your work in advance. Beware before your purchase. Beware before your vote. Too many, for too long, have been sold a bill of goods that shortchanges our great nation.

You already have my guarantee of compassion and respect. With that as a safety net, let us practice some truth telling here early on. If the following disrupts our progress already, the rest of the book is going to be difficult for you. In fact, this may enrage you enough to take off your earrings to fight but let us "go there" early on to illustrate caveat emptor. Please do not give up yet. Think of this as a doctor poking and asking if this hurts. We can use this sample as a measured introduction for something good if you let it.

Gird your loins. Ready?

What can possibly be controversial about

> too much sugar and cheaply produced corn byproducts, which replace calories from whole food may generate a

big profit margin. It is profitable for agri-business if you buy it; but is it good for you?

A storm of controversy hailed down upon Michelle Obama for her White House gardens and fitness campaigns for precisely this reason: *If you control your mouth regarding what you eat, you may also control your mouth regarding what you say with your vote.* For the "pusher" in both cases, it is more profitable for them to keep you triggered to buy their junk food and to buy their junk policies. For the "pusher," it is better to keep you triggered like a junkyard dog to fight intruders that may rob the "pusher's junk"—in other words, the sellers' profit and power. As they laugh all the way to the bank, you are left in frenzy and despair. It is good for them? Is it good for you?

Remember, we just tried a quick example such as the doctor might poke around to see where it hurts. In this case, I gave you a heads up and asked you if we could just try a little poking. I just poked at Michelle Obama's White House garden to ask you if that hurt.

What went off in your head?

What conclusions, pontifications, and resentments rolled around in your head, rent free?

Here, I am not even suggesting that you change a thing about it.

But ask yourself, how disciplined are you at exercising your entitlement that all incoming information is a TBD basis. Do you ask, "This may be good for them: Is it good for me?"

You are free to think what you want. Thinking what you want is about *content*.

The following question is not about content. This question is about *process*. Have you been free? Or do you generally let names, concepts, and recollections trigger you. Content comes and goes. Your process of responding to content is more stable than content. Sometimes that "process stability" is more judgmentally referred to as stubbornness, habit, conditioning, or even brainwashing. How you typically respond to content may say more about you than it does about the comings and goings of content. Special interest groups have a vested agenda in cultivating your tendency toward "process stability" to ensure that you predictably act in their best interests, even if that action counters your best interests.

I write this as an alcoholic who has known what it means to be debased and nearly destroyed for the profit of companies who care more about shareholder value than they care about me. Know this: To be sober for over 30 years, I have become proficient at my entitlement to determine if "incoming" is good for *them* or if "incoming" is good for *me*. Resentments or any other "digital cookie" that may try to take root in my psyche are promptly eliminated. Despite any onslaught of what may debase and demoralize me, I cannot afford to be a host for the agenda/profit of another. By extension, I cannot want for myself what I cannot want for the American people.

I was taught to love the American people. I love us too much to tolerate such debased exploitation. This book developed from an addiction recovery model. This book lifts up a hope for the American people that none of us be trapped or entangled, commodified as a means to sustain rigged advantage. **Step 12 of this book aims for us to consecrate liberty free from the rigged advantage that hijacks and addicts the American people for others' profit and power. May we all be truly happy and free.**

With this book as an offering, I work for your freedom to sustain my freedom. I practice hoping for you the good I hope for myself and my loved ones. I know I am not entitled to what I cannot hope for you. I share with you my experience because it has been a bounty for me that I need to reinvest for my future harvest. *It is more blessed to give than to receive* was not something taught to me; I just grew up with it all around me.

Most people are short-changed into believing that this "giving" teaching is promoting charity for others for goodness' sake. While that may be a secondary outcome, the teaching is more potentiated than that. More powerful than the simple "one-way" reception of gift value, the giver is gifted in both action and reaction. A creator and the created are more than the created. This illuminates the biblical teaching "But to all who received him, who believed in his name, he gave power to become children of God."[4] The idea of "gifted" here is not to have simply received something of value; "gifted" means to be potentiated for even greater future value (to become children of God, to be and do the work of God among us).

Don't worry. I don't need to proselytize you. But I am clear how it works for me. That may be too deep too quickly! It is not necessary that I derail you so early. Just stay with me, for now.

Consider how the country people who raised me modeled this seeming abstraction, give to receive. Mother would give you (you could even be among the KKK that sent a bomb threat to our house last week) the shirt off *my* back if it were still nice enough.

Rags for others?

Why would someone else want what I didn't want?

I am no better than anyone else.

Clothes for charity must be clean and wearable. The rest is trash. Do not give trash to human beings. If you do, expect to be treated as trash. She was not trying to teach me something; she was just being herself. Similarly, being a civil rights worker was not some noble cause she adopted; it was who she was. Her mother, my Mama Burnham, would give you the food bound for my plate if you arrived unannounced and that was the last of supper. We could usually "get a bite" later, but not always.

Mother was embarrassed when times were tough enough that the bite we got came from a brown rectangle cardboard box of "pasteurized process cheddar cheese" from the U.S. Department of Agriculture. Mother may have struggled to get food on the table at times, but she is the ultimate angel investor in this book. The pebbles of justice Mother cast onto an unforgiving pond reverberate long after she passed in 2013. By example, she demonstrated that Karma is not so much a "bitch" as it is a long game. Karma is neither your enemy nor your friend but an investment system. My best life is made possible by this *investment system*, and I learned it from country people while growing up in Mississippi: What I put out can return to me manifold.

Since I have experienced this investment system to be effective, I am selfishly invested in serving you well. These beloved country people formed in me a backbone of dignity, determination, and dedication to others where no one is greater or less than me. They taught me that God's love for others is at least as immense as I experience it for myself—a love as strong in a Saturday night juke joint or honky-tonk as it is in a Sunday morning sanctuary. Behold the people. Behold the universe. I am that. *Aham Brahmasmi*. God Immanuel. In serving you, I serve myself.

We may share this in common: When I try something new and the returns exceed my expectations, at first, I feel some relief that I am not disappointed. Then, when that return adds value to my life, I feel so blessed and grateful. Some of the books I have read have enriched my life so profoundly that I am forever changed, and my life transcends previous limits. Hopefully, with no more than the idea of applying the 12-step tradition to our democratic future, you have already received enough from these pages to count this book as at least more than a waste of time. My blessing will come if I can create an opportunity for you to experience an even richer return than you may have anticipated.

Twelve Steps for White America does not pose as objective scholarship. This work flows from my experience. This work authentically represents what I have learned from the school of life. I am expressing the urgency I feel from a positionality of poverty: "What if this is my only chance to tell this truth?" Caveat emptor: As you may have already realized, this truth is not watered down to make it palatable for the easily triggered (no "don't upset White people" here). What I write about has not only saved my life, but it has also catapulted my life beyond what I could have once dreamed. I hope that you can glean what is potentiated here for yourself so that you and your family, community, and our nation may thrive in a safe, merit-competitive, and contributing future for our world.

These lessons and experiences, forged in Nebuchadnezzar's fire, may at times rub you the wrong way. If you get your "feathers ruffled" just know I "came by it honestly." I have lived a daily reprieve from alcoholism, depending on my spiritual condition, for over 35 years, a table prepared for me in the presence of my enemies. This seems like so much food on my table not to ask you to join me. If this is not for you, if you are not hungry, if our nation doesn't need it, just pass on it. You need not spend another minute on it. If you are not hungry for it, but still, you stick around to trash it, ask yourself, why? Whom does that serve? Why are you at their service? It is, after all, a choice you make to dirty your hands for someone else's bidding.

Finally, there are so many people greater than I, who are theorists, writers, self-help gurus, educators, speakers, and influencers. How could I presume to write anything at all? What could I say that has not been said already? As great as any in the pantheon may be, here we are, still, democracy teetering with no guarantee. While many are greater, fewer are those who fit the categorical boxes checked with Southern, country, "dirt-road" poor, White, man, 1960s Mississippi civil rights legacies, psychotherapist, San Francisco social justice doctorate, gay, alcoholic more than 3 decades sober, whose spirituality is a daily reprieve needed to survive. Like so many who were aghast in rage and sorrow at the public execution of Mr. George Floyd, I searched my soul. Out of what is only mine to give, what could I say if I had the chance? The amalgam of me, forged from love, prayer, teaching, and the sacrifice of all who invested in me, and the lessons hard-won through survival, creates a voice that is mine alone. With that voice, with this opportunity, I have a responsibility to step up. I have an opportunity to plants seeds for harvest. How could I not? So here, I step up. To God Immanuel, I leave the rest.

How To Use This Book: Part One—The Messenger

In this spirit, I present *four domains* of experience and expertise that inform how you may experience this work. Throughout the book, listen for which domain's voice speaks to you.

Alcoholic

Spiritual Awakening

Educator

Teaching and Learning

Psychotherapist

Tools for Insight and Change

Southern White

Firsthand Knowledge and Experience

Here are considerations for each of these four domains.

Domain 1—Alcoholic: Crooked Path to Spiritual Awakening

For more than 35 years I have practiced 12-step recovery principles one day at a time. Each day of recovery has been a bonus—a gift to which I do not feel entitled. "Bonnie," my childhood friend from first grade, died years ago from what nearly killed me. Bonnie has a headstone in the cemetery where most of my deceased family is buried, so I visit her when I visit the family already passed. In the 1st grade, Bonnie and I were princess and prince at the school's Harvest Festival. Bonnie did not survive alcoholism but, so far, I have. This simple fact of the two of us, then, little children, trajected to both face something that would kill only one of us, still leaves my soul quickened. As the survivor, guilt has become something reconciled that in her memory, life must be lived to the fullest. It needs to matter. It is not a possession I am entitled to squander since my life is interconnected with all that has come before me. In honor of sacrifice that leaves me still standing, I am privileged to be alive. Something destined to kill me has now blessed every day as a gift. For half my life now, I have incarnated a bonus life to which I am not entitled. Every horrible struggling day full of incessant failure and disappointment, is lived in the context of gratitude that it is a day of being alive I may not have been granted.

When someone does not feel entitled (e.g., to sobriety), chaos, depression, disruption, and disaster can ebb and flow, painfully, but with less affront than to someone who feels entitled to be above the fray. Through inevitably difficult days, I am free to experience teetering at the edge of the abyss less as dread and more as instruction for liberation. Through struggles to meet life on life's terms, I have cultivated a lesson that informs this book. That lesson is inferred from the seminal text of Alcoholics Anonymous commonly referred to as "The Big Book."

> It is easy to let up on the spiritual program of action and rest on our laurels. We are headed for trouble if we do, for alcohol is a subtle foe. We are not cured of alcoholism. **What we really have is a daily reprieve contingent on the maintenance of our spiritual condition.**[5]

I cull a very important lesson from this. My spirituality is not an abstract piety to be appreciated when I am in the mood for it. It is urgently practical right now, synonymous with the possibility of a daily reprieve free from an alcoholic death spiral.

But I do love an abstract piety! It tickles my brain. Because of my philosophy studies in college, I am always delighted to "ponder how many angels can dance on the head of a pin!" In other words, I love intellectualizing nearly anything to death. Intellectualizing has become a defense mechanism luxury I can rarely afford. I cannot play games with what works for me to enjoy the promises of living sober. One area where I must refuse to play intellectualizing games is choking over what something is named or whether my name for something is as "sanctioned" as your name for it. It does not mean I am not respectful regarding what you want to call something. It is just not a deal breaker that prevents me from the treasure within. My process and any related names for it may not resonate with you. For your comfort (and mine), I am not attached to how the process of successfully living sober is narrated. I leave any proselytizing to others.

"Take what you need and leave the rest" is heard often around recovery tables.

We can test this now. Try this approach as you read the Big Chris story.

(Take note: This story proves too challenging for some readers. But you can decide ahead of time to just read it without losing your serenity! Here is a practice for you to observe yourself and determine how you "process" "content.")

THE BIG CHRIS STORY (LOVE LIFTED ME)

Early in recovery, I was desperately learning some much needed detachment from argument and "intellectualizing." That lesson flared up after an AA meeting where I nit-picked recovery over Shoney's coffee with Big Chris. Before you think I'm being disrespectful, know that "Hey y'all. I'm Big Chris" is how she introduced herself. At about the second cup of coffee, Big Chris got tired of hearing me "prattle on." She shot me down. She reduced my elocutions to nothing but "stinkin' thinkin' gonna get me drunk." Big Chris was a statuesque lesbian truck driver who still had most of her teeth. That night in Shoney's in Hattiesburg, Mississippi,

(Continued)

her company, some will-do coffee poured by a kiss-my-grits bouffant stranger who called me sweetie, and the near or far-muffled utensil clinking of other nighthawk[6] rednecks, kept me sober through a long night of white-knuckling past a drink.

It felt pivotal, like if I couldn't make it through this night, I wouldn't make it at all. Even though I thought I was better than Big Chris, Shoney's, and nighthawk utensil-clinking rednecks, everything in that situation saved me, loved me despite me, and helped me make it through the night. Love lifted me.

Love lifted me is the name of a hymn, one of Mother's favorites. She would see it listed in the church bulletin, and she would get excited about it. When the time came for the congregation to rise and sing, her anticipation would uncork, and she would belt it out loud off-key, unintentionally but cringingly disturbing the congregational peace. Heads unmoved, side eyes glanced as if to wonder unspoken, "Can she not hear herself?"

I was sinking deep in sin,

Far from the peaceful shore,

Very deeply stained within,

Sinking to rise no more;

But the Master of the sea,

Heard my despairing cry,

From the waters lifted me -

Now safe am I.[7]

Mother loved it as much as she loved Hank Williams's "I Saw the Light," released in 1947. She sang "I Saw the Light" as proud and loud as "Love Lifted Me." All these years later, I can only imagine how welcome a redemption song might have been to her. Only 6 years earlier, she lost friends in the attack on Pearl Harbor, while she sat in church, December 7, 1941. She would have been 19 years old at the time, still a teenager. She had already survived the Great Depression and graduated valedictorian at Harperville High School—now the second World War enters her life during Sunday School at the Harperville Baptist Church. Years later, if she thought of it all, she may have felt that if she could find her will to sing, she could sing loud off-key if she wanted to. Hymns or civil rights, she just did not care what you thought. It was not a decision not to care. You simply were not on her radar.

James Rowe and Howard Smith, "Love Lifted Me," 1912.

I could endlessly discuss and debate it, but I have no need to quibble about notions of sin or stain sung about in "Love Lifted Me." I simply get the point of the song. I am becoming more like Mother as I age. I care less about what you think. Love (regardless of what I thought it should look and sound like) has since rescued me so many times. My immense gratitude for it now surpasses any need to quibble details. I offer this to you in hopes that while reading this book, you may likewise transcend your triggers and be lifted higher. Let these 12 steps help us make it through our national night. Be loved even when love may not look like you expected. Even if you cannot help but "Other" me and this book like I "Othered" Big Chris(t), then just white-knuckle it if you must. There is so much more for you, and our nation, if together, we can just get through this night.

So ends this story illustrated for the principle: *Take what you need and leave the rest*.

What did you find objectionable in this story?

My haughtiness amid despair, off-key singing, images of "Oh Brother Where Art Thou," rednecks clinking utensils, a truck-driving lesbian presenting the saving grace of God, poor dental care, revivalist hymns, grits and bouffants?

Could you get past judgmental triggers and find the treasure? For whatever you cannot like about the story, can you receive the love in it? Can you appreciate the profound gratitude in it? Can *you* see the light?

Love will save us if we let it.

Remember this "Big Chris(t)" story when reading the rest of the book: *Take what you need* and leave the rest. This alone will take you far into the first step of this book.

Okay, at ease! You made it.

These decades of practicing 12-step recovery principles to stay sober (working my program) has a specific result mentioned in the 12th step itself:

> *Having had a spiritual awakening as a result of these steps, we tried to carry this message to alcoholics and to practice these principles on all our affairs.*

My personal program of recovery works like an operating system for a computer. While it is essential to practice recovery principles to stay sober specifically, practicing recovery principles permeates a way of life across all matters of life, which becomes undifferentiated from sobriety. Applying recovery principles to the challenges of a nation may seem like a novel idea (even naïve) to some. To veterans of a daily reprieve from alcoholism depending on one's spiritual condition, the application is not only *not* novel, it is specifically how we work our program of sobriety. The extent to which this practice had permeated my life came into sharp focus through the gift of an extraordinary professional development experience.

Many years into recovery, I was granted a year-long fellowship with the Aspen Institute in partnership with the Stanford Educational Leadership Initiative to prepare select higher education leaders for a college presidency. This fellowship cohort of 39 new colleagues was unlike anything I could have imagined. They represent the strongest concentration of educational excellence in a room that I had ever experienced. The privileges of being among them included validation, camaraderie, expanded visioning, shared commitments and declarations, potentiation and, medicinally, that sense of home one finds so rarely and only among those who can truly understand. This setting of rare and concentrated enrichment provided an opportunity to reflect on their feedback. Some of that feedback explored how my capacity for equity and social justice had been constructed. (This was especially interesting for some to learn about how capacity for equity and social justice had been constructed for a southern white man complete with accent! I have learned through the years that sometimes people are not being offensive; they are grappling with a juxtaposition that is unfamiliar.)

Reflecting on their feedback, it became apparent to me just how fundamental recovery principles had become to my position in the world. Despite a civil rights legacy from rural Mississippi, a doctoral degree rooted in social justice and equity, and several years of experience as an equity-minded practitioner in higher education, I realized that recovery principles informed my *practice* regarding race more than other experience or expertise. In fact, it is precisely because I practice recovery principles in all my affairs that I assume responsibility for dismantling rigged advantage which relies on White supremacy and anti-Blackness.

I do not practice social justice and equity because it is needed by others; I practice social justice and equity because I need it. I need this practice because it is fundamentally compatible with a spiritual condition sufficient to sustain a daily reprieve from alcoholism. A spiritual condition burdened by colluding in rigged advantage off the backs of marginalized others is insufficient to sustain my sobriety. Anything less is incompatible with my daily reprieve from alcoholism, which depends on my spiritual condition. Intentional or unintentional collusion has different karmic weight, but my sobriety, my spiritual condition, cannot afford any weight, tethers, or repeating templates.

The steps that lead to a spiritual awakening in aggregated overview are as follows:

- turn away from dysfunctional ingrained behavior (*truth, repentance*); Part I of this book
- account for intra-personal and inter-personal consequences (*reconciliation, atonement*); Part II of this book
- repair the harm (*renewal, redemption*) inflicted whether I intended harm or not; Part III of this book.

Recovery reduces the nit-picking of details such as frequency, recency, intention, and affrontery as deadweight excuse making, nothing more than games played by "those ... who cannot or will not completely give themselves to this simple program, usually men and women who are constitutionally incapable of being honest with themselves."[8]

> A spiritual condition burdened by colluding in rigged advantage off the backs of marginalized others is insufficient to sustain my sobriety.

Increasingly, more individuals, organizations, and companies in the United States now understand that White Americans (not Black Americans, nor any other People of Color) must assume this responsibility for dismantling rigged advantage. However, there is often a wide gap in what one ought to do and what one has the capacity to do. A eureka moment came for me when I realized that more White Americans, beyond just those in recovery, need to know how to apply recovery principles to issues of race in America. As always in recovery, while the work we do may embed remedy for wrongs to others, the reason we do the work is for our own recovery. We do others no favor getting sober. We follow the necessary steps leading to a spiritual awakening *for our own sakes*.

While eureka moments may appear out of nowhere, they usually result from a long plodding progression of spiritual growth. My eureka insight for all White Americans to apply recovery principles to issues of race is the result of a long process of growth. This growth tracks on a continuum from "judgment and prosecution" to the "transcendence of loving kindness" (a level of mastery elusive to most of us), where my own liberation is tethered to liberation for all.

While, of course, justice must be realized, I am not the prosecutor. *Prosecution is not the purpose of this book.* My liberation is found in our collective redemption. Because of loving kindness replacing judgment and prosecution, I became able to extend the hopes of my spiritual condition onto White America en masse and ultimately our nation.

It is only in the miraculous extension of loving kindness that I could envision a path to remedy:

- First for a national sobriety of truth (*repentance unshackling the past*);

- then reconciliation (*atonement making things right*);
- followed by renewal (*redemption needed to make way for all so our best days are ahead*).

> Democracy and sobriety, both fragile, have in common a daily reprieve depending on our spiritual condition. For our house to stand, we must plumb depths of justice, then liberty, which we have yet to realize. This book, *Twelve Steps for White America*, outlines a pathway of twelve steps to accomplish just that.

Domain 2—Educator: Teaching and Learning

In educational design, I practice scaffolding, a way to create tools and concepts introduced incrementally to facilitate successive approximations in learning. I approach students nonjudgmentally as a facilitator capitalizing on students' strengths. The following would be antithetical to my practice as an educator: hostility, stereotyping, shaming, condescension, contempt, low expectations, presumption of incompetence, and scapegoating and blame. As an educator, I am committed to reflecting on my practice to situate deficits in the learning process in my performance as an educator, not in the student.

I apply this same approach as an educator in authoring this book. You would be incorrect if you assume that I begin with contempt that is filled with animosity and condemnation. What kind of educator could I be? As a result, you can expect that I am committed to serving you consistent with my values as an educator.

With this integrity intact, it means I will respect you enough to tell the truth. I will presume your competence to acquire and process information, which requires of you critical thinking skills in reflection and formation and reformulation of concepts. I will uphold with you a mutual embrace of rigorous honesty. I will expect of you the same dignity and respect to which you are entitled. As always in recovery, the dignity of others is an interpersonal commitment one makes for one's own sake. Plainly, trashing you is incompatible with my sobriety.

One of my colleagues urged me to consider softening the truth to prevent alienating "easily triggered" White Americans. Her concern was

"Who would be left to read my book?"

I appreciate her prompt because intention is very important. I had yet to answer that question.

So, for whom is the book intended?

The question created some clarity for me. I seek to write this book from the bounty of intersectionalities I have experienced across my lifetime. This bounty sets the parameters for what I may personally contribute to the zeitgeist of our nation. I need to write the book that only I can write because it is so personally crafted from my lived experience and truth. In fact, this reflects my karmic ethics. I am responsible to faithfully do the work. I, not being God, am not responsible for the results. While that may mean that a considerable portion of White America may pass, I can be fulfilled knowing that I have been faithful to the work. I have written the book that the unique amalgam of my history and becoming enables me to write.

This facilitates at least a couple of considerations for your information. Like my mother's example, I work for the sake of the work. I do not work in anticipation of results, including your approval. I do not seek your approval and I likewise do not seek to offend you. Again, like my mother's example, I do not intend to be offensive when I say it is just not about you. It is more specifically about my duty. It is about my responsibility to be faithful. One implication is that you won't be able to dismiss the truth with a false accusation of disrespectful or other agendized dynamics. You may not like the truth, but you won't be able to dismiss the truth because of me. What you do with this is therefore your responsibility. I fulfill my responsibility in crafting the material.

> My hope is that, together, we can identify deeply ingrained beliefs, intentions, attitudes, and behaviors that do not serve you, your community, or our nation and replace them with justice then liberty loving commitments that can ensure for all that our best days are ahead.

Domain 3—Psychotherapist: Tools for Insight and Change

Possibly before I was ready in my own recovery, I found employment working with others with substance use disorders. *Medice, cura te ipsum* (physician, heal thyself) could have been wise counsel. David Sedaris could have counseled that I may have *talked too pretty one day* too early in recovery and got a job before I was ready. Still, I may have needed the blanket of 24/7 recovery, which enveloped my life professionally and personally. That placed me on a career track. Career advancement would depend on earning a master's degree. Working full-time with classes at night, I slowly accumulated enough credits to earn a Master of Science degree in counseling psychology to get better jobs in the recovery business as a psychotherapist.

Fondly, I remember toward the end of my master's program I was receiving little feedback from my clinical supervisor who was revered by many. I became concerned and approached him about it saying I would like to get an idea of what he might tell future employers checking on references. He said, "William, I'm gonna tell 'em if you played football, you would be Joe Montana." Unsure of the reference, I could tell it was good, so I looked it up later to discover that his exaggeration was intended to be complimentary. In my defense, this was before I lived in San Francisco, home of the Forty-Niners where Joe Montana is venerated as one of the greatest quarterbacks in professional football history.

My supervisor's analogy may have been "a bit" inflated but looking back over that and other feedback he provided, I now see he was referencing my clinical ethos—a combination of empathy, love, and a discipline for rigorous change and/or resolution. I hope this book reflects that ethos as well. The rigor that change demands must be matched by proportional empathy, reminiscent of what Carl Rogers would have called "unconditional positive regard." Rigor, however, may not be so unconditional. There are requirements that are non-negotiable for recovery but loving kindness in supporting those benchmarks should be embedded in the process.

As a psychotherapist, I earned a clinical reputation for being supportive and nice until the overwhelming reality of recovery's requirements set in. Alcoholics who wanted an easier softer way presumed I was the ideal counselor for that—until the rigor of it all became clear. "What an order! I can't go through with it!" is an exclamation right out of the Big Book of Alcoholics Anonymous.[9] Alcoholics reach the "can't-do-it" milestone rather predictably. Between week 2 and 3 of inpatient rehab, alcoholics would usually show up in my office feeling shattered. They would inevitably say something along the lines of "I'm falling apart. I can't take it." Certain that I would tenderly understand their horror and sorrow, 100% of them were stunned when I celebrated, blew on a kazoo, and gave them a little trinket I called the falling apart award. It was shocking to them. Once they got past "WTF," they began to understand viscerally that they could not survive in the alcoholic house they had built. Some demolition may be desirably unsettling. See where I am going here … demolition of rigged advantage … unsettling, anybody?! I certainly appreciate the gravity of our times. Our nation teeter's at the edge of fascism supplanting democracy and the rule of law. But often, amid the handwringing from those who should know/lead/report/teach better, I wish I could blow a kazoo loud enough for a "WTF" nation to hear. Once stunned, I would present the USA falling apart award to a nation who can begin to understand viscerally that we cannot survive in this house, divided against itself, that rigged advantage built. Democracy, like sobriety, is a reconstruction project—fitting since our first Reconstruction proved inadequate against the White supremacy and anti-Blackness rigged advantage relies upon.

Years of building the infrastructure it takes to house an addiction stronger than the survival instinct itself is practically shatter proof. Anyone's recovery is a miracle to me. The contortion of lies we desperately tell ourselves and others to rationalize what is happening to us is debasing and convincing at the same time. Even while what we believe about ourselves is deadly to us and soul crushing to those still around who love us, we persist.

When patients ran into my office exclaiming that this addiction house was on fire, I could tell them the good news. That sense of falling apart was accurate. It means rehab is working. The sick and contorted infrastructure of addiction, which had become synonymous with their identity, must cascade away to be replaced with a solid and sober foundation. So much of what we feel is falling apart about our nation signals to me that we could well be between week 2 and 3 of rehab. Some of what we experience is the pain of reconstruction. A rehab that is desperately needed. That means that instead of labeling 100% of national disorder as destruction, we remain disciplined and alert to those parts of the messiness which may in fact be answered prayer.

> The elements of our national identity rooted in rigged advantage for some, while marginalizing the vast majority of everyone else, is an infrastructure at odds with democracy that must crumble for the pillars of our aspirations to steady the edifice of justice then liberty for all.

Domain 4—White, Southern: Deep Knowledge and Experience of White America

Born into a black-and-white TV era, exactly 40 weeks after the Kennedy inauguration (math, anybody?!), I learned that "normal" at our house on a dirt road 10 miles from the nearest town, was politely considered "eccentric on Negro rights." The era was glamorously known as Camelot in the White House; but, in my community, this side of Tallabogue Creek near Harperville (historically recorded for an 1898 race war), an elderly Black man named Bryant Harper blared Motown on the Saturday night jukebox at his illegal juke joint. Mr. Harper let Daddy in on the business. Daddy "put in" a quarter-game pool table and a shiny, mouth-watering window rotisserie chicken machine to make a little *extry* on the side.

In the southern countryside then, "supervised children" was not a thing. Free-range children got home before dark. During the week, "Bryant" would give me a "yahoo Mt. Dew" if I walked the mile and a half to his juke joint in the sweltering heat. At the time, I thought he let me call him Bryant as an intimacy since he was one of my favorite adults. While that may have been true, I would learn later I was also practicing a legacy of slavery, that African American elders were not entitled to honorifics such as Mr. and Mrs.

When I was still too young to understand segregation (and because my parents didn't practice segregation in our home), I once blithely sat in "Bryant's" lap on the juke joint's gray-weathered plank steps. You could see through to the bald red clay below where chickens pecked. I put my little blonde-hair white-hand against his hand and said to him, "You're Black." I wasn't referring to a race. I was observing and referring a particularly dark skin color. In retrospect, I can understand why Mr. Harper chuckled at the innocence of it. He said, "Nah, baby, I'm blue-Black. I'm so Black, I'm blue."

Despite how complexly cringe-worthy retrospection may be to an adult, Mr. Harper's kindness toward me as a child remains a loving icebox delight of sepia-colored memory from my early years trampling in and out of shotgun shacks and juke joints. With the delight of that kindness also comes a truth about my coming of age in the

American South, the snarled complexity of how I and all White America still wander in and out of racialized legacies from the plantation should make us tremble, fearing the retribution of some wrathful God whose chosen are not exclusively White in Canaan-land. Stunningly, nearly inexplicably (but this book explains it), too many White Americans cannot find a racist bone in their bodies (nor in their household wealth, health, education, social and economic mobility, and engagement with the so-called justice system). Before racists bones in bodies may be identified, the capacity to see what we have never been required to see must be cultivated. How do I explain whiteness to people whose whiteness by operational definition entitles them not to perceive their whiteness. Regarding this conditioned entitlement to not see whiteness, it is nearly a useless question to wonder if you are racist or not before the scales of whiteness fall from your eyes. "My socially constructed entitlements mean I don't have to see or navigate my whiteness" is first in the order of operations before a question regarding racism can have much affect. More about this later.

Although it was later named Watson Drive, the dirt road we lived on was just Rural Route Four in Beat Five of Scott County when I lived there. My maternal family's land had been deeded to an in-law branch of my family by Martin Van Buren after the 1830 Treaty of Dancing Rabbit Creek. "The land" was nearly as sacred as life itself. One of the trauma sagas of my childhood was Mother's near frenzied resolve to ensure that our poverty did not force us lose her portion of that inherited land. Sacred? Hallowed? Divine pact? I do not know exactly but its importance to her was palpable.

Losing the land would be tragic, like an amputation. Her land-love grew Black-eyed and Texas cream zipper peas, and she knew the number of trees in the large yard surrounded by woods. "Don't cut the trees!" Since I had to mow around all the trees in the yard, I knew the number as well, 113. To a visitor, it would have been hard to tell when the yard became the woods and the fields.

I am keenly aware of the recency of slavery, so I am always baffled when white Americans want to just get on with it since *"that"* was so long ago. It was not so long ago. I know because "it" is alive in me, in my memories of my family. The family that raised my Mother's Father fought for the Confederate States of America, but my Mother later fought for civil rights. In me, here, now, I have inherited both slavery and its resistance and both live in my accent, my memories, my food and music, my idiosyncrasies, my mythology, and ideology all in the present. I am living proof that the recency of slavery permeates our present lives. At the family home of my grandparents where I played as a child, my then still living Granddaddy Burnham had been raised by a father and uncles who fought for Mississippi as one of the Confederate States of America, which had seceded from the United States of America as its enemy in the Civil War.

Answering the questions "Who am I?" "Where do I come from?" and "What am I made of?" are abundant treasure troves. It may be the most southern thing about me that I regularly plumb this gnarly rootbound tangle of my past, which lives on in my present like DNA. I am not always thinking about my DNA, but it is working within me, nonetheless. When I hear White Americans assert with absolute assurance that they have no racist bone in their bodies, I marvel at how ignorant people can be. Like I marvel how atheists can conclude definitively about the vastness of even the presently known universe. I marvel at how they can know such a thing so definitively.

Something important that alcoholism and 4 degrees past high school have taught me is that the question may be more important than the answer. An important question, along with the "yes, and" edict of an improvisational actor determined to keep a scene alive, informs the vitality of my life.

> Rather than a knee-jerk reaction to proclaim how "not racist" I am, I ask myself in what way does my cultural inheritance inform how and what I think, intend, and do. How does it proliferate or extinguish the racism that is in me, on me, and around me in both covert and overt ways? For my freedom, I must work these steps every day.

We have just reviewed four domains of my experience which inform *Twelve Steps for White America*:

Alcoholic

Educator

Psychotherapist

White Southern

I hope that describing these four domains of my relevant personal experience informs and enriches how you establish a relationship with the work presented in this book and the accompanying workbook. In any teaching and learning dynamic, both the message and the messenger are relevant.

How to Use This Book: Part Two—The Message

Now that you have information about the *messenger*, I will provide some introductory information about the *message* of this book.

To begin, let's review important recommendations about how to approach the material in this book:

- Read each section (even the dedication? yes)
- Read each section in order from beginning to end
- You can always go back, but don't go forward (with working the next step) until you have progressed through each part, section, and step.

Here are some examples and suggestions about how to digest material if it is helpful for you. I always take in a quick overview scan of an entire work to see the big picture. I want to know where I am headed. I read the front and back covers and flaps when applicable. I read the Table of Contents, and I quickly scan notes and references to see whose research has informed the book. I flip through each page just to have seen it and then, before I dive in, I place large sticky notes at the beginning of every chapter. That way, as I read along, I can make a note on the "sticky" and get a sense of the progress I am making. (Of course, this general approach can be digitized for e-readers.)

I am constantly confirming an author's or presenter's point and determining if someone else has expressed this better, simpler, or in a way that is more suited for my ear. (I have bought different textbooks for classes!) Why suffer because of someone else's selection?!

The intellectual property of another person may be intimidating. Their work presents a power dynamic where they "present something you have not yet read" or you would not be engaging with their material. They are in control of what they present. But I am in control of how I receive it and manage it. After 22 years of degrees, I have grown comfortable saying I do not know what you are talking about. What do you mean? Where did you get that from? How do you know that?

Most people in the room presume that the presenter, author, or content expert is "above them" in some way. They presume that if something is unclear, they must be the problem. Who would want to look ignorant by asking a question or challenging a point? I would. I always do. And I hope you will as well. Far from a resistant challenge, I perceive others' speaking up as a gift of engagement—an opportunity to hone my craft, to improve it, to see the world from yet another perspective.

If you speak up with the intention of seeking clarity and the questioned person is not grateful for the opportunity, allow that to *inform* your assessment of the material. Their material may be as narrow as they are. Do not allow that to *mis-inform* you about your information processing, much less your value. (However, being disrespectful is never acceptable. I can usually tell if you are otherwise "agendized." I will shut that down.)

Especially after swallowing the firehose of information that is a doctoral program (and paying thousands of dollars for the privilege), I refuse to suffer fools gladly. Some come with years of highly compensated expertise. I do not disrespect them because of it, but neither do I have any patience with having to suffer at their hand! I do not care if I appear ignorant and uneducated. I have looked behind the green curtain to see that presentation is constructed! That does not necessarily mean it is "made up" as if untrue. It just means that, in its manufacture, it may not have been best suited for my consumption. At this point, if I don't get it, I trust that I *may* not be the problem. It could be that the material may have been presented better.

Finally, please understand this about information and your attention. Both are commodities. Profit and propaganda interests are competing for your attention to provide you with information because it is their business model. I rarely fault others' business models since usually the consumer can take it or leave it. As the Vicar of Christ said about gay marriage, "Who am I to judge?"[10] However, as we learned over the years watching big tobacco, insidious manipulation of human beings to profit over their death is (to me) an unacceptable business model.

Who are we to judge? Americans with an allegiance to the republic. The republic may facilitate commerce, but the republic is not for sale.

No less abhorrent than the tobacco industry is a sexy trendy social media company, who profits from how triggered you can become. Democracy be damned, as long as you click. The more you click, the more they present you with what made you click. Crack dealers have a worse reputation, but I do not see a crack dealer tearing down the halls of democracy. The tobacco industry (the industry that brought you colonial slavery) is still in the business of delivering a product whose logical end is your disease and death for their profits (at an enormous cost to society). Decades in, we have made some progress against the strong headwinds of big tobacco. But are we already too late in perceiving the cost of the totally preventable manipulation by social media companies whose business model is clicks by as many triggered domestic enemies of the U.S. Constitution as possible? The documentary, *The Social Dilemma*[11] provides clarity about what is happening.

Pregnant women smoking used to be a thing. Drinking and driving had some proponents. Inhaling secondhand smoke on a plane was all about freedom and smoker's rights. How are those who treat me like a commodity because it is human nature to look at roadkill any different from a crack dealer? I usually hear crickets over this, especially in Silicon Valley.

I walk you through that for two reasons that have to do with external locus of control:

1. I am modeling for you to question incoming information (delivered to you from an external locus of control) and showing you how I do it and why.
2. Our economy depends on an external locus of control influencing your behavior (advertising works using information to trigger your choice that results in a behavior profitable to the external locus of control).

Alcoholism is such an external locus of control despite your initial control over alcohol. This book compares the loss of control over alcohol to our dysfunctional relationship with the external locus of control of so-called market forces. Those market forces are not as purely competitive as is the ideal of American democracy and capitalism. In fact, the system is rigged.[12] Advantage unfairly rigged for some at the expense of others is the problem operationalized in this book. Fair competition is not rigged. Fair competition is about merit.

Fair competition is the exact result envisioned by the 12th step of this book: "We consecrate liberty free from rigged advantage." So, it is incorrect to say that this work is anticapitalist in that sense. If for you rigged advantage is fundamental to capitalism, then it is correct to say that this book is antirigged advantage. Those who have rigged it defend it at all costs. They need you to confuse a critique of unfair rigged advantage with a critique of a meritocracy where competition generates innovation and accelerates human progress. This book is a critique of rigged advantage. This critique may threaten the so-called freedom of the few who benefit from unfair rigged advantage as curtailing their freedom to pillage and plunder. In the way that sobriety is freedom from the death grip of alcoholism, this book proposes 12 steps that White America (and its witting and unwitting affiliates of all colors) can take to relinquish the death grip of rigged advantage.

I am not trying to interfere with your favored process of locating and digesting information. However, the actual work of the steps is sequential and foundational.

You will struggle if you have not sufficiently worked a previous step.

Each section builds on the previous section.

If you jump ahead, if you skip sections (even those you have always skipped when reading a book, such as the dedication), you will have less foundation on which to construct your learning. At each stage, scaffolding (like a painter would use to paint a taller building) has been carefully considered to aid you in deconstructing and constructing anew the knowledge and plan of action you need to learn and work these steps to

- unshackle the past with truth (repentance);
- strengthen U.S. security and global competitiveness with reconciliation (atonement); and
- make way for all so our best days are yet to come with renewal (redemption).

For example, consider that you skipped the dedication section. You missed out on Faulkner, the first insurrection in my lifetime, Medgar Evers, civil rights parents working where Chaney, Goodman, and Schwerner were killed, Ku Klux Klan threats, voter registration drives, and "goddam Republicans" at the Harperville Baptist Church. That is quite a bit of information that you would know nothing about if you barged right in at step 1!

If you barge right in at step 1, you will have missed the four domains that inform how you may expect me to support you. If you skip the James Baldwin quote excerpted from his seminal work, *The Fire Next Time,* you will have missed a very important arc of this work that could give you greater vision for this work and what you may accomplish individually and for our nation. To remind you of the literary lineage, which inspires this book, I will provide that quote again here to be followed by instructional advice:

> The only thing white people have that black people need, or should want, is power—and no one holds power forever. White people cannot, in the generality, be taken as models of how to live. Rather, the white man is himself in sore need of new standards, which will release him from his confusion and place him once again in fruitful communion with the depths of his own being.
>
> **James Baldwin, *The Fire Next Time*[13]**

From this quote by James Baldwin (and my related blessing, which followed the quote earlier in the book, a small section of the book that you may have initially skipped), you are able to frame the entirety of the personal and national experience potentiated within *Twelve Steps for White America.*

To complete the arc of intention, I followed this quote with the following blessing:

How to Use This Book | liii

May Twelve Steps for White America *provide standards that place White Americans in fruitful communion with the depths of our being.*

If you hastily skipped this important material, you would barge on without having already established the following:

1. This book answers the call of James Baldwin who proclaimed both a need and a hope for White people:
   a. **Need**: The sore need for new standards for White people
   b. **Hope**: Release White people from confusion to be placed in fruitful communion with the depths of their own being.
2. Baldwin's suggested "new standards" are proposed in this book as so-called recovery principles transferred from my lived experience of the spiritual awakening promised by working the 12 steps of Alcoholics Anonymous to achieve sobriety.
3. The arc of this spiritual awakening includes a three-part (four steps each) approach to living (as evidenced from the Table of Contents):
   a. Truth, repentance (turning from; steps 1–4)
   b. Reconciliation, atonement (making right; steps 5–8)
   c. Redemption, renewal (living democracy's promise; steps 9–12)

Image 0.2

Something extraordinary is happening in the United States. If we can survive this dark night of the soul, we could in the morning discover the United States as the potentiated promised land (*for all*) it can become.

> Democracy has not failed so much as we have not tried it yet.

Our tipping point has arrived. Democracy can no longer masquerade as thinly veiled rigged advantage for the few who exploit the rest. I am wildly optimistic that our best days are ahead *if* we do the work that the urgency of now[14] demands.

Embedded within this country's structure is the potential for something so glorious—expanded peace and prosperity rooted in justice then liberty for all. But our structure is burdened by rigged advantage for some, and our potential is yet unrealized by too many Americans. The integrity of the great America that is *idealized* and treasured, and the great America that is *realized* do not align. For our best days ahead, the integrity of what is idealized and what is realized must match.

That match is fundamental to integrity. Without integrity, a house divided against itself cannot stand. This is a national security priority because our racialized fault lines expose us to external manipulation and control, while, domestically, rigged advantage robs us of our integrity now and erodes our future competitiveness in a global diverse world.

Actualizing the American ideal is obstructed by White Americans living within rigged advantage (intentionally and unintentionally), who must

- unshackle the past,
- strengthen U.S. security and global competitiveness, and
- make way for all so our best days are yet to come.

Admittedly grand (and possibly even grandiose), *Twelve Steps for White America* outlines the "new standards" Baldwin called for so that White Americans can experience "fruitful communion with the depths of our being." Like alcoholics in recovery, White Americans must do their work for their own sakes so that the American family may know the promises of liberty consecrated free from rigged advantage.

So far, we have learned about the messenger and message of this book, along with some advice for using the step, then the next-step approach (no skipping around), which the book is built on. As we begin the next section on what to expect, I want to make something explicit that may already be implicit. While *Twelve Steps for White America* draws on the Alcoholics Anonymous 12-step program of recovery, it is not the exact step that transfers to this book. What transfers is the fundamental principle behind each step, which is more universal. It is so universal in fact, that later in the book (and especially in the accompanying workbook), **I will demonstrate that you already have the skills and abilities to work these steps because you already do it every day, every time a problem needs a solution.** What may be lacking (and precisely why this book is relevant and potentiated) is the knowledge of how to transfer these problem-solving skills and abilities onto the larger issue of rigged advantage in the United States.

This big-picture perspective on this book's intention will strengthen your ability to finely hone the particulars of working the steps. To that end, this next section will explore specific tools along with recommendations for working the steps and expectations you may anticipate for outcomes. I introduce the following three tool sets as an overview to frame the work ahead:

1. 12-step practice mandala
2. Governing (steps 1–6) and complementary steps (steps 7–12)
3. Learning outcomes

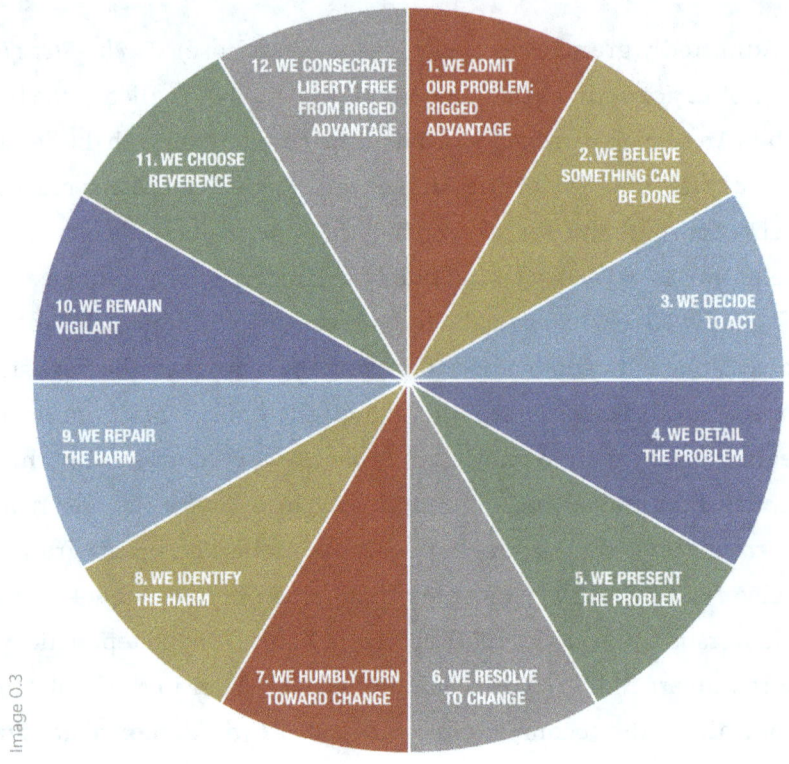

Image 0.3

Practice Mandala

To support your work throughout the book and accompanying workbook, I encourage you to learn the steps well enough to recall them from memory. The steps need to be available by recall for you to practice them throughout your daily life. As you learn the 12 steps, it may be helpful for you to use the blank practice mandala provided in the workbook.

(Tip: You could make copies of the blank mandala to complete from memory every few days until the steps are easily recalled.)

The mandala will be useful to you for at least two reasons:

1. The "clock face" nature of the 12-sided mandala will support your imagery in recalling each step.
2. This 12-sided mandala will also enable to you have an experience of what I have termed governing and complementary steps.

Governing and Complementary Steps

Imagine that the mandala represents a 12-sided pavilion in a park.

Walk up the steps into the pavilion and stand in governing step 1.

While reciting governing step 1, look across the pavilion to see complementary step 7.

Next, walk across this imaginary pavilion to complementary step 7 and recite it while looking back at governing step 1.

Stand in the relationship between the steps and evaluate your work to date exploring for opportunities for continuous improvement.

More on Governing and Complementary Steps

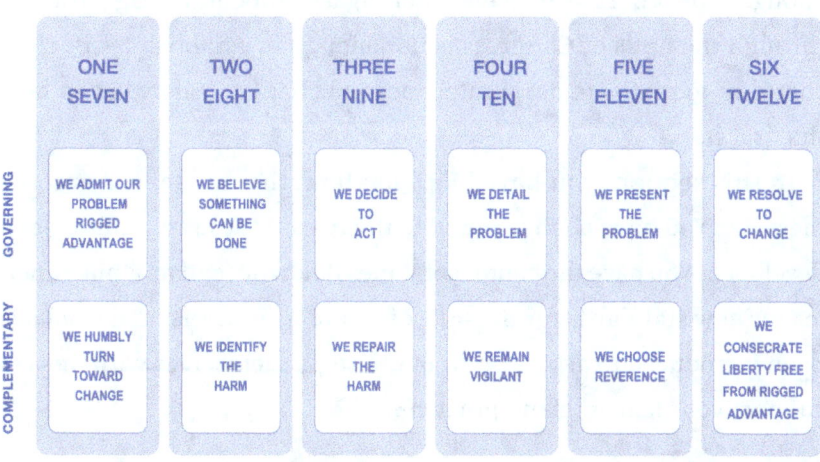

Image 0.4

Steps 1–6 each govern complementary steps 7–12. Each complementary step is enabled or limited by the proficiency of its governing step. Looking at the graphic, start at the left with 1 over 7.

We have all heard that taking the first step on any journey is the hardest or the most important. Solutions to any given problem would have never happened without that first step of exploration. Any recovering alcoholic will tell you that the rigor employed to grapple with the first step will set the parameters for all that is to follow. Some alcoholics talk about "hitting bottom." The idea is that unless you have become thoroughly convinced there is a problem, you are not ready to undertake the (possibly) harrowing rigor required for the program to work.

Looking at the graphic for each of the pairs of governing and complementary steps, ask yourself, "In what way does the complementary step rely on its governing step?" For example, you can readily see that one will hardly "humbly turn toward change," step 7, to solve a problem that one has not really admitted exists. On the national stage, you can see that, for some, George Floyd's public execution was not enough. For others, even insurrection violating our nation's Capitol while a branch of government fulfills its constitutionally defined duty is not enough. For others still, even watching a Confederate flag parading through the halls of Congress is not enough to establish a sufficient "bottom" to motivate desperately needed change. Only you can take the first step.

In this section, you have learned about the messenger and the message. You have been exposed to the reason these steps have been developed. You have the context of James Baldwin's call to White America for new standards for the sake of White Americans, and you have been introduced to an overview of the steps themselves with tools to support your learning and practice.

About Learning Outcomes

Lastly, before you get started, it is helpful for you to understand the outcome you may expect from each step to ensure you are on track. This work is designed to support at least the stated learning outcome that is associated with each step. As you make progress through each step, you can review the learning outcome (keeping the end in mind from the beginning), learn the step and its relationship to either its complementary or governing step, and assess for yourself the progress you believe you are making. Each step builds on the previous step.

STEP 1 LEARNING OUTCOME
Identify the gap between presented and realized democracy in the United States.

STEP 2 LEARNING OUTCOME
Recognize the potential for personally impacting democracy's promise.

STEP 3 LEARNING OUTCOME
Determine the need for a personal program of liberation for the common good.

STEP 4 LEARNING OUTCOME
Identify, analyze, and categorize specific knowledge, skills, and abilities rooted in Whiteness-affiliated rigged advantage.

STEP 5 LEARNING OUTCOME
Recognize, describe, and present specific knowledge, skills, and abilities rooted in Whiteness-affiliated rigged advantage.

STEP 6 LEARNING OUTCOME
Contrast intentional versus unintentional beliefs and behaviors that reproduce rigged advantage, then dedicate self to a merit-rich democracy.

STEP 7 LEARNING OUTCOME
Relinquish Whiteness-affiliated rigged advantage to habituate justice, then liberty for all.

STEP 8 LEARNING OUTCOME
For peace and prosperity, formulate remedies that eliminate disparities in socio-economic outcomes.

STEP 9 LEARNING OUTCOME
For peace and prosperity, implement remedies that eliminate disparities in socioeconomic outcomes.

STEP 10 LEARNING OUTCOME
Habituate rigorous self-assessment to sustain justice then liberty, replacing periodic remission of rigged advantage with its eradication.

STEP 11 LEARNING OUTCOME
Synthesize personal spiritual discipline as the pathway to relinquish rigged advantage for the common good.

STEP 12 LEARNING OUTCOME
Dismantle rigged advantage for an integral democracy where competition thrives from race-neutral merit.

PART I

01

TRUTH

12 STEPS *for* WHITE AMERICA
IN A NUTSHELL

PART ONE STEPS 1 - 4	PART TWO STEPS 5 - 8	PART THREE STEPS 9 - 12
TRUTH	RECONCILIATION	RENEWAL
REPENTENCE	ATONEMENT	REDEMPTION
Stop, turn.	*Make things right.*	*Live democracy's promise.*
Unshackle the past.	Strengthen U.S. security & global competitiveness.	Make way for all so our best days are ahead of us.

Image I.1

Unshackle the Past

Introduction to Steps 1–4

Collection of the Smithsonian National Museum of African American History and Culture

Description: Shackles consist of an iron bolt with a pair of loops slid onto it through a hole in each end of the loop. One end of the bar is fixed closed by an integral metal flange large enough to prevent the loops from being removed. The other end of the bar ends in an "eye" and is locked by a large lock washer inserted at the time the shackles were applied.

In steps 1 through 4, we admit there is a problem. We believe something can be done about the problem. We decide to do something about the problem. We get specific about the details of the problem. These are the problem-solving steps we take every day when we apply them to both the complex and the mundane. Throughout our lives, the content of problems differs, but problem solving has elements in common. The process is repeatable in many languages across the human condition. As we progress through this book, it will become clear that, in fact, we already know *how* to do what needs to be done for a United States of America. We actually already know a great deal of *what* needs to be done. Each of us has a part to play. In each of us, part of the problem and part of the solution is already manifest, whether we intend it or not, whether we given it a second thought, or whether it concerns us at all.

For solving problems in any language across the human condition, we start by telling the truth. Then, we stop and turn from (known since ancient history as repentance) what does not work toward what works. We cut ties to what does not work to capitalize on what works and manage the risk of unnecessary repetition, which threatens evolving progress. For the problem of cutting ties to rigged advantage in a divided United States, I use the potent and painful language that we must unshackle the past. Part I prepares us to cut these ties. Actually, cutting the ties comes later, but for now, we take this one step at a time.

This is very simple:

Tell the truth (be honest).

Stop, turn (quit doing it).

Unshackle the past (move on).

This is not easy, is it?

While it may not be easy, it truly *is not complicated*.

If it is simple, not complicated, and we solve problems every day, *what about this particular problem proves resistant?*

We need to be clear about this. This book is my attempt to tell you what I have learned and practiced in answer to this question. Since there are greater scholars, writers, thinkers, and talking heads making a living answering this question, it seems nearly absurd that this book is necessary at all. While perhaps I offer something of an innovative recipe, no ingredient here is new. I take no credit for new ingredients. I wince to walk out onto this stage in the theater of the absurd. I only dare to tread forth when I weigh my responsibility and opportunity to sow what *I* have reaped.

Two considerations finally determined my resolve to write:

1. I am reminded that if all the illustrious minds already on this absurd stage were sufficient, the problem would have been solved.
2. Their contributions cannot substitute what is mine to give. Even if mine is a mere "widow's mite" it is mine to give, and I am responsible for giving it.

Since the process of problem solving is truly "not complicated," how do we begin to answer the question, "What about this problem proves resistant?" Let us venture into telling the truth. A psychotherapist may work with an individual to understand how one's present life is shaped by past experience. Getting to the truth of how we developed ignites a process (truth -> reconciliation -> renewal) to set us free from dysfunctional patterns that impact our behavior but may elude our conscious awareness. True, there is little point digging around in the past unless it can inform our present in order to achieve targeted outcomes. At its worst, "past digging" can be somewhat like trying to remodel the kitchen when the living room is on fire. At its best, an inventory enables us to account for our liabilities and assets to inform both our *vision* for progress and identify the steps and tools needed for the *mission* ahead of us.

Treating alcoholism is an example. Talking about your resentments while continuing to drink does little to put out the fire of alcoholism. "First things first" is one of the most important mantras an alcoholic new to recovery will learn. Dismantling any dysfunction involves prioritizing sequence. "Get a jumper off the ledge" first is all that matters. "Keep a jumper off the ledge" next time is a more nuanced matter. After the initial triage, understanding what is causing the problem becomes an essential part of mitigation; it informs the recovery treatment plan.

Consider this: No alcoholic takes the first drink thinking, "Let me toy with my own self-destruction." The person who becomes an alcoholic drinks initially because of what alcohol can do for the drinker. For a plethora of situations and experiences, it works. Drinking works so predictably well that drinking is repeated. You can predict and rely on the desired effect. Then, that reliance becomes a habit, while other skills recede and physical tolerance grows, where more is needed to achieve the same results. (I can drink you under the table is *not* a good thing!) Before a threat is even realized, the drinker becomes trapped, addicted.

In the way that dreams protect sleep, psychological defense mechanisms protect a skewed reality that enables the addiction to persist without disruption. Codependent others are coopted and exploited to sustain the drinking despite the alcoholic's devolving capabilities. The physical, psychological, social, and spiritual decline is predictable—the same story in a million tales. Without disruption, alcoholism will destroy its host. But remember, at the beginning of drinking, it worked so well it was worth repeating, a solution of great reward.

Reiterating that there is little point digging around in the past unless it can inform the present, let us grant that, at its best, knowledge may serve us like the discovery of hidden treasure. It can be the treasure of truth that unlocks an abundant future of reconciliation and renewal for both individuals and a nation.

> The premise of this book is that alcoholism and rigged advantage have etiological elements in common and therefore may share problem-solving principles in common.

To this end, let us transfer our understanding of alcoholism's etiology to the etiology of racialized fault lines in the United States.

The beginning of this section of the book features an image of actual shackles that once enslaved a human being. As disturbing as it may be to view, 21st-century White Americans need to have seen these shackles, which trapped human beings and exploited their labor to produce wealth from White-owned plantations. The reality of these shackles can quicken our consciousness about the depraved system that produced them. If we can allow it, this quickened consciousness can awaken our senses to identify legacies of slavery persisting into the present.

Symptomatically, too many 21st-century White Americans have not seen these extant tools of slavery. We are more likely to pass a monument to secessionist enemies of the United States of America than to have seen shackles or a monument marking the locations of slave auction blocks. Why? Because the victors write and rewrite history. Before you argue that secessionist enemies were defeated, consider how one is more likely to have seen a Confederate monument than shackles. Aspects of what was not defeated live on. Telling the truth about it is simple. But, as firestorms about telling the truth prove, telling the truth is not easy.

For our best days to lie ahead of us, history as justification to venerate power must cede to history as reckoning with the truth. Confronting an alcoholic with intervention is a greater love than coddling their progressive disease. Likewise,

> it is greater patriotism to yearn for the fulfillment of America's democratic promise for justice, then liberty for all, than collude with an entrenched power minority to sustain their rigged (and growing) advantage at the expense of democracy.

A minority of entrenched power Whites protect their interests while bamboozling the hordes of other Whites who are exploited to do their bidding and sustain rigged advantage. This bamboozling Whiteness collusion surges now as hysteria about what gets taught to "our" children. Legacy victors see the handwriting on the wall in the form of demographic inevitabilities. They fear that if minority rule by White Americans no longer holds, *what could become of rigged advantage?*—not *what could become of the USA?*

For these exploited White Americans, rigged advantage is conditioned as synonymous with the United States of America. Aghast, if the United States were to no longer to equate with rigged advantage, they screech a cry to "take their country back" from "those" vandals at the gate: "Others" who threaten their rigged advantage. These fading victors rail against the truth of history because it threatens their con—a ruse of tamping Whiteness that settles even the Civil War as "the late unpleasantness." Some of these White Americans, who feel aggrieved, are so triggered and exploited it becomes difficult to realize whom their anger and resentments serve. Sadly, they feel the truth of their exploitation, but they are trained to displace the blame for that exploitation onto "Others"; vote against their own interests; and despair the loss of a social contract that their Whiteness would guarantee a future they thought was rigged for all Whites, not just elite Whites in power.

This tamping Whiteness represents the work of those who exalt patriotism as long as the United States is equated with rigged advantage; as soon as that equation is challenged, they are prepared to squander the constitution of the United States and the entire democratic republic. The cacophony of their bamboozling bombast cannot erase history which, so far in the United States, has been doomed to repeat itself.

The nutshell of this is simple. England's colonial ventures in the New World were unprofitable until enslaved labor prospered tobacco plantations. Agricultural success meant colonial success for Elizabeth I and the Virgin Queen's colony, Virginia. This system proved so successful that the economic formula would transfer to additional crops, cotton and sugar. The history of the United States (and indeed global capitalism) is represented in these crops (tobacco, cotton, sugar) and today, corn. The plantation system that rooted in Virginia became economic propulsion for the prosperity of colonial America, a replicable catalytic. Then, as now, however horrific and antidemocratic it may be, it is essential to understand that while it may exploit and marginalize many and even most, our present system works extremely well for a few, just as it did for its progenitor.

Before you conveniently dismiss the U.S. slavery economy as ancient history, best left tamped down in the dust bins of polite society, please comprehend its recency. My grandfather (Granddaddy Burnham, b. 1888, who always announced my arrival from down the dirt road as "It's just Helga's boy; thought it was somebody") came of age with a father and uncles who had fought as enemies of the United States for the Confederate States of America to enslave human beings. If my ancestors and "their cause" had succeeded, enslaved human beings would have remained property—tools for economic prosperity for a few wealthy Southern White secessionists who needed the exploited collusion of most other Southern Whites (who did not enslave human beings) to sustain their "White way of life." I grew up hearing people asserting "I am not responsible for slavery"; "slavery ended with the Civil War"; "no need to relitigate the past"; and "it's a free country."

Nostalgia for a Confederate past, the so-called "lost cause" movement to re-present Confederates from the Civil War in the best possible light, loomed larger in my childhood consciousness than did the actual history I have had to work diligently to replace it with. The *Encyclopedia Virginia* lists six assertions that counted for my early historical understanding of the Civil War:

1. Secession, not slavery, caused the Civil War.
2. African Americans were "faithful slaves," loyal to their masters and the confederate cause and unprepared for the responsibilities of freedom.

3. The Confederacy was defeated militarily only because of the Union's overwhelming advantages in men and resources.
4. Confederate soldiers were heroic and saintly.
5. The most heroic and saintly of all Confederates, perhaps of all Americans, was Robert E. Lee.
6. Southern women were loyal to the Confederate cause and sanctified by the sacrifice of their loved ones.[1]

It was a point of pride to revere the Confederate flag, believe that the South will rise again, and tap a foot to "A southern man don't need him (Neil Young) around anyhow."[2] Well into grade school, I remember being shocked to learn that so many African American men had served in the Mississippi legislature during Reconstruction as such a thing was "unimaginable" to my historically "White-washed" mind. And "my mind" grew up in a household of civil rights workers! It reminds me hearing once about a child with two daddies who came home from school repeating homophobic comments he had picked up at school!

I grew up hearing stories about what happened at Granddaddy's and Mama Burnham's homeplace during (Union General William Tecumseh) Sherman's *March to the Sea*. Sherman burned nearby former Scott County seat Hillsboro to the ground. These stories linger.

Tobacco, cotton, and sugar remain among us. Our language, with our multiple accents, remains among us. Recipes, traditions, folkways, and mythologies remain among us. Slavery legacies remain among us. Never uprooted, these legacies sprout again and again as templates that prevent our truth, reconciliation, and renewal. I will write more

> Minority rule, a legacy of plantation control of enslaved human beings, lives on in our Senate, where a minority of states from the former Confederate States of America exert a will (especially with judicial appointments) contrary the majority of voters across the United States of America.

about this later, but take this as an example for now: The systemic structure, which enabled a few Whites on a plantation to control many more enslaved persons on that plantation, persists today as a systemic structure referred to as minority rule.

The use of violence as a tool of degradation and whereabouts control (including vigilante "slave catchers") was enshrined in U.S. law, and the Supreme Court said there was nothing Dred Scot could do about it because he was not a citizen. It remains enshrined in muscle memory as a presumption to the White American entitlement of whereabouts authority over Black American bodies. Not only were slave patrols legal in the South, but the Fugitive Slave Act also demanded that those living in the North cooperate with "slave catchers" and return fugitives, who were regulated by law as the property of slave owners. While the 13th Amendment purports to end this practice, this legacy lives on today in the self-granted White entitlement to question the whereabouts of people of color—while driving, sleeping in a dorm, walking home with Skittles, cooking out in an Oakland park, selling cigarettes on the sidewalk, jogging in the neighborhood, driving with a child in the back seat, birding in Central Park, even "presidenting."

In one of the most notorious recent examples, the late George Floyd, a purchase at a neighborhood convenience store risks an "officer of the law" putting his knee on your neck for over 9 minutes, snuffing the life out of you while being visually recorded for all the world to see. How can we as a people tolerate this excruciating inhumanity and expect a future for coming generations?

> White Americans, en masse, must pursue a zero-tolerance policy against "slave catching" in the 21st century. This truth is simple. Hearing it may be difficult. Living it is worse.

Not only do the legacies of slavery's shackles persist to deny Black Americans (and by extension other People of Color) full citizenship in the United States today, the enmeshment of how any White American was required to uphold a system of slave patrols lingers. In the same way that domestic abuse can transfer generationally, and, in the same way that alcoholism is a codependent system enmeshing the family, slavery legacies linger in our laws, policies, institutions, behaviors, traditions, norms, and entitlements. If you think it shames White children to learn about this, does it matter to you that Black children have to live it?

Only a few elite Whites in power owned plantations, but it required that most other Whites collude with the system that benefitted a few plantation owners to make an entire slavery economy work for a powerful minority. This pattern is a legacy of slavery alive today, threatening the future of a great nation teetering on these racialized fault lines. An unimaginably wealthy elite few benefit from a system that exploits a majority of nonelite White Americans to ensure a Whiteness coalition to sustain rigged advantage.

Systemic collusion by the many for the few is a repeating template that still operationalizes our nation to this day. The few powerful elites operate this template to horde and sustain its benefits for themselves. They pledge allegiance to the American flag as long as the flag represents their interests. This template corrodes the realization of democracy and compromises our integrity and our potential sacrificed on the fault lines of slavery legacies. These fault lines fuel growing inequality off the backs of most of us, including exploited White Americans, who are bamboozled in a collusion of Whiteness to support a political agenda that sustains power and wealth for the few. Today, these exploited White Americans comprise a voting block that sustains wealth for the few, even when such votes counter their own interests.

Like weeds in the garden of democracy, this smoldering exploitation of Whiteness is dry kindling that erupts into a raging fire under the right conditions. Consider the manipulation by a mentally disordered megalomaniac narcissist who wields the corporate power of social media (itself an unchecked trigger of baser extremes) to titillate mass hysteria with lies in order to overthrow democracy in a coup d'état. Those who understood the persistence of slavery legacies knew exactly what was happening. For a strong United States well into the future, fewer Americans must become shocked to witness the enemy flag of the Confederate States of America marching through the Capitol of the United States of America on January 6, 2021. On cue, bamboozled, hysterical, triggered marauders were readily whipped into a frenzy to perform insurrection against the United States.

Hardly a new phenomenon, this is not the first insurrection in my lifetime (see James Meredith, Ole Miss). These bamboozled, hysterical, triggered marauders are the intentional design of a system built to benefit some while the rest are corralled into the distraction of fighting amongst themselves and the few continue to prosper. Punishment for crimes? Of course. In addition to punishment due, the healing enterprise of love will need to extend to both the exploited and marginalized others for the sake of a United States of America.

> Our present and future are compromised because we (the United States of America, including White Americans), are shackled to the past. Not only do Black Americans and other people of color live as second-class citizens, but a mass of White Americans also collude in minority rule to support the wealth of a few in power even while it shakes the foundations of our democracy. It is past time to heed ancient wisdom: a house divided against itself cannot stand. White Americans must do the excruciating work necessary to unshackle the past. *Twelve Steps for White America* outlines a path forward.

During the months writing this book, a U.S. culture war erupted (same story, different day!) over a somewhat dusty 40-year-old blast from my academic past, critical race theory (CRT). In my wildest imagination, I could never have predicted what would spark societal interest versus what will quietly fade away. Accustomed to being in the minority of an opinion poll, a common condition during my first 30 years growing up in Mississippi, I learned the hard way not to use me as a focus group of one to gauge public opinion. Something as "intellectually obtuse" as CRT, born of critical legal theory, within the larger studies of social theory, seems like pretty wet kindling to me.

Having grown up in the bamboozling culture of southern segregation, a survival skill learned early was recognizing bamboozling. The first rule of bamboozling in the culture war fight club is "Turn 'em on each other so we keep our hands clean." In this scenario, those keeping their hands clean above the fray includes anyone who benefits from a United States at odds with itself. Those benefitting from the fray include "enemies" foreign and domestic. Some domestic enemies do not look like enemies at all. They look like us. They say what we say. They appear to like what we like. We see them among us in our communities. They appear to hold to the same values, but there is a catch.

The catch is they hold the same values as long as those values benefit rigged advantage as intended. "Vandals at the gate" is a tool of hysteria in the culture war toolbox used to avert the scrutiny of those who could object to this rigged advantage. The people's focused attention could disrupt the status quo benefits for those in power bloated from absconding wealth off the backs of the bamboozled in the culture war fight club.

From the Dedication in Memory section of this book (it is important not to skip sections of the book; the material scaffolds your learning to support your understanding), you learned that my consciousness about race was cultivated differently from most little White boys in 1960 rural Mississippi. Most little White boys grew up spending little time on "being White." That is included in the privileged membership package they are born into. In stark contrast, I had to learn early on that "membership privileges" were socially constructed and situational; it is granted, and it is taken away. (My words for it came later but I had to "get it" at the time to survive.)

My parents were working for civil rights in voter registration drives, election campaigns, and community organizing, launching Head Start where Freedom Summer's Chaney, Goodman, and Schwerner were murdered by the KKK in collusion with local law enforcement. Usually, I could be just another dusty-legged White kid until other Whites in the larger community realized I was Hubert and Helga's boy. I had no words for it then, but the language I acquired later on helped me reflect on Whiteness. At times my Whiteness wonder cloak worked for me like it worked for all dusty-legged White kids. At other times, like Joseph's coat of many colors, my Whiteness wonder cloak was snatched away, usually with spitting hate-filled racial slanders.

The land mines of segregation were not intuitive to me since my parents sent me out into my rural Mississippi community without teaching me the rules of segregation. I learned the hard way. To avoid race-hate consequences when possible, cultivating a hypersensitive "Race consciousness" became urgent to avoid harm. Most little white kids just absorb "how it is" from their families' behavior. Since my parents didn't practice segregation in our home, I didn't absorb the rules of segregation. Here is an example of how I had to learn it in real time.

Once, while waiting at the doctor's office in the "White" section, I could see through the passageway Keith Patrick waiting in the "Colored" section visible on the other side of the somewhat open floor plan. I wanted to yell out to him and go over to see why he was there since I knew him, played basketball with him at his house, and our parents worked on campaigns together. Mother was furious with me, insisting I stay put and be quiet—like a church lady's covert pinching. I thought it was rude not to speak to him. In the car on the way home, she explained to me that the wife of a KKK member was in the White's only waiting room with us and I needed to learn when and where I could "be myself" in public. She and Keith's mother had acted like they did not know each other. I needed to learn that for Keith's sake, rude now was better than what could come for him later.

Since race consciousness has been ingrained in me from childhood, it is natural for me to consider in what way race matters across society. What role did race play in the founding of our nation? In what way has race informed patterns of behavior transferred across generations? What laws and policies have a racial legacy both apparent and obscure? What are present-day consequences of the past, where remedies for wrongs have been lacking, minimized, or even misrepresented?

There are some things from the plantation economy of the past that live on in the present. We need to know the truth about these plantation slavery legacies, which live on in our present. By design, it is intentionally hard to do this when we are bamboozled in the culture war fight club. It is hard to do this when we are socially constructed with the privilege to live above any race consciousness. It is hard to do this when the very foundations of rigged advantage depend on you not asking important questions that lead to the truth. That would challenge a system where an autocracy (the few who benefit the most from a divided United States) now hoard the wealth and hopes of democracy's promise of a great nation for a great people.

Make no mistake, the work is not optional. *The arc of the moral universe bends slowly, but it bends toward justice.* As the aspirations for justice and liberty are realized more fully, it should come as no surprise that proportional to progress comes proportional opposition.

16 | Twelve Steps for White America

As you learned from this book's Dedication in Memory, insurrection is a template from my history. (In 1962, James Meredith integrates the University of Mississippi at Oxford, while Mississippi Governor Ross Barnett bloviates that "this is the worst crisis since the war between the states.") Because we have not sufficiently uprooted legacies of slavery to this day, insurrection is a U.S. security risk template repeating in the present (obstructing a constitutionally mandated certification of a presidential election the day after Georgia elects its first African American and Jewish senators, January 6, 2021, U.S. Capitol).

While the example of multiple insurrections is a glaring example of historical templates repeating, how many others act like weeds in our garden of democracy, trimmed for immediate pacification, but lurking still rooted to sprout benefit for rigged advantage to sustain the status quo? We must get rigorously honest about this. We need to know. This accounting of our inventory is a matter of truth and reconciliation that enables us individually and nationally to course correct.

For our future greatness, we turn from repeating templates ("turn from" is a simple definition of "repentance"). Repentance enables reconciliation to see and tell the truth, then repair where needed ("repair" is a simple definition of "atonement"). Given the historical contribution of religion to American identity, bedrock principles of truth, repentance, reconciliation, and atonement become essential guideposts for our best days ahead. Interestingly, these bedrock principles inform the very recovery principles that facilitate sobriety for millions whose repeating templates were nearly fatal.

I am not surprised by the demonization of any set of analytical tools that account for repeating racialized templates in our history. Demonization of inquiry is a bamboozle technique from the Culture War Fight Club. Truth is not for sale. I refuse to be manipulated and bamboozled by enemies both foreign and domestic who may rant about saving America because it suits a rigged advantage agenda. But, as soon as America means the United States of America where justice then liberty for all fulfill democracy's promise, they would rather burn the house down. In the "vandals at the gate" hysteria over CRT, it is but another sprouted weed in the long line of "Othering" intended to choke out hopes for our best days ahead so a few can retain wealth and power.

The teaching is not the "truth shall make them free"; the teaching is the "truth shall make you/us free." While I believe this book may have many applications, it is a tool that White Americans can use to reckon with the truth of our past, which lingers in our present. While that will surely accrue long-term benefits to Black Americans and other people of color, the truth is a treasure of great price, which for our sakes we seek in order to be free and in order that the American experiment with democracy shall be long lived. Free people who know the truth cannot bow to a rigged advantage master forever.

Image Credit

IMG I.2: Source: https://www.si.edu/object/set-wrought-iron-leg-shackles: nmaahc_2008.10.4.

CHAPTER 1

STEP 1

WE ADMIT OUR PROBLEM—RIGGED ADVANTAGE

> This book does not begin here! Start with "Dedication in Memory" and "How to Use This Book," and then read the introduction to Part I. You will be glad you did. It's the equivalent of "reading the instructions" before assembly. These steps may be simple; however, what they require of you is too rigorous for cutting corners. The result of working these steps can be extraordinary for you and our nation. Please allow me to walk you through it, step by step.

Step 1 Governs Step 7: We Humbly Turn Toward Change

Key Words: **Surrender, Hitting bottom, Consequences, Turning point**

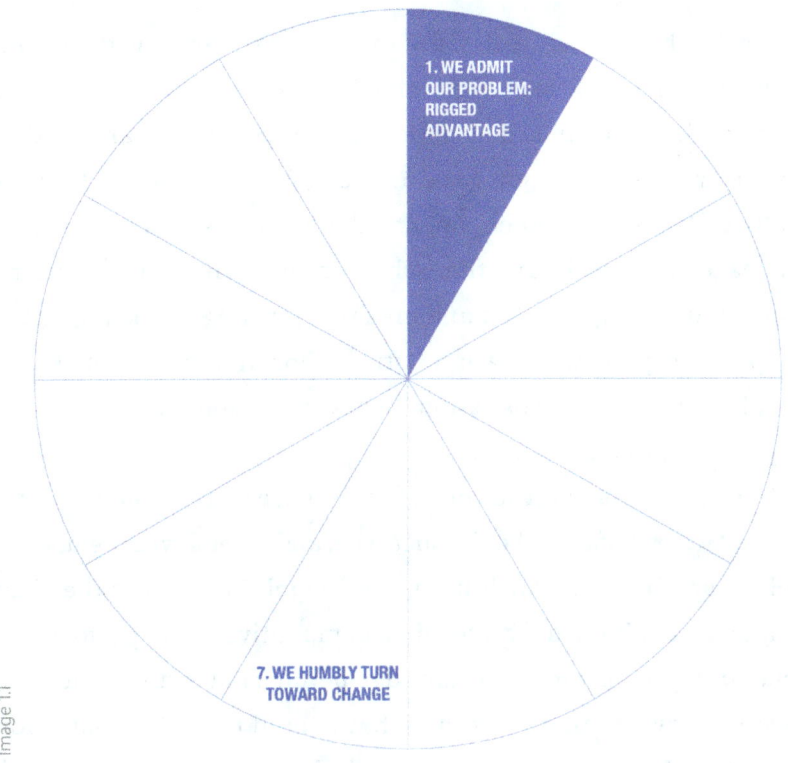

Image 1.1

What I Learned From Alcoholics About the First Step of AA

"We admitted we were powerless over alcohol—that our lives had become unmanageable."[1]

Most alcoholics take the first step after life has somehow bludgeoned and beaten[2] them into no other choice. Consequences become the bricklayer's bricks, stacking us into a walled tomb of the inevitable "locked up" or "covered up." The stranglehold grip of alcohol addiction entangles existence. Life becomes rootbound with alcoholism.

I am one of those alcoholics whose genetic kindling fast-forwarded my demoralization. I started drinking at around age 12. By the young age of 25, I had already teetered at the edge of the abyss with an Emergency Room overdose in high school and several weeks on a psych unit partially diagnosed as depressed, since an 18-year-old, then, was nearly never thought to be an alcoholic. Still, surely, I was not as "bad off" as those other patients: the "Pentecostal sex addict," the "teenage cutter girl," and the "schizophrenic wife beater," but they came and went while staff and my family wrung hands together to keep me hospitalized. It was a Catholic hospital, but for my snarky self, I renamed it the Mississippi Institute for Hopeful Futures since hope, there, remained elusive.

One cascade of many to come, that episode started months earlier with a Mozart Sonata, Chopin Nocturne, and a Gershwin prelude—my ticket out of the red-clay hills of Mississippi. These were the pieces of music I auditioned with to win a competitive piano performance scholarship to university. It started hopefully. But instead of it finally changing everything, I learned that I could toy with suicide long enough that I could lose my choice. Suicide began to come for me. The protection of psychiatric hospitalization nearly proved inadequate to save me. There are some who can arrive at recovery less dramatically; but drama is more likely than not. Bewildered, exhausted, demoralized, and hopeless amid an avalanche of consequences in nearly every corner of life, these are common themes among alcoholics who share their story. After the "Hopeful Futures" debacle, I would face 6 more years of catastrophic episodes, with addiction burning bridges. Few were left who thought I would be alive past my 20s. Even I was relieved it would surely all be over by then.

The cruel twist is that in the beginning, drinking worked. Drinking was a solution—a powerful and predictable solution, in fact. If I was uncomfortable, drink. If I was a bit anxious in a social setting, drink. If I tried to build a community of friends in common, drink. Grief and loss, drink. It becomes trusted and reliable—until it is too late.

Controlling its predictability to produce a desired effect was precisely the original allure.

This is the cruel twist I hear from nearly every alcoholic I have ever known. Before we realize what is happening, the habit, built out of trusted predictability, cedes to addiction, where we are no longer in control, and it is no longer predictable. By that point, who we thought we were has been gone for a long time. We are physically trapped. We are psychologically trapped. We become embroiled in twisted defense mechanisms. We coopt others (codependency) to compensate for the skills we lose while overrelying on alcohol. We are spiritually tortured by self-loathing. We mask resentments regarding what's wrong with anyone or anything but us.

While every alcoholic's story is an individual's story, the condition presents common elements. Telling our common story to each other begins to dig us out of the deep well of isolation. We see and learn from our success and failures revealed in our stories. Most of us come to learn that

> unless we are absolutely convinced that life and alcohol are incompatible, we have little chance of getting sober, much less staying sober. The person we became is trapped defending a way of life, making excuses, denying culpability, finding fault in others. It's all a house of cards that must come down for a recovering identity to have a chance.

The degree to which the drinking identity is replaced with a sober identity may predict sobriety itself. If you haven't uprooted your drinking identity, it will sprout again. Relapse is virtually inevitable since when a person is stressed, ingrained behavior supplants more recently developed replacement behavior. This is where we are as a nation. We are stressed. Ingrained patterns supplant recent gains we may have prematurely concluded would continue toward a more inclusive and perfect union.

What of This May We Apply to Our Problem, Rigged Advantage?

Let us begin with some rigorous honesty. Before alcoholism became deadly, alcohol itself worked so well it was repeated with predictable reliability. What began as a solution turned into a problem. To fix the problem alcoholism inevitably becomes, we must get honest about what it was solving when it turned deadly.

Before that can happen, you have to admit things are not working. Unless a problem is sufficiently consequential, you have not bottomed out enough to relinquish desperate delusions. The stove you touch is not hot enough for you to learn. While the current teetering of American democracy is nail-biting, I know that unless the stove is hot enough for us to pull back, what we have always done will be what we always do.

As a nation, we are in a psych unit, and our company consists of Pentecostal sex addicts, teenage cutters, and schizophrenic wife abusers. The question is not complicated. Can this be our bottom? Can this be our wake-up call? I know it can get worse, but how much worse can it get and still retain a hope for intervention?

A person making an extraordinary contribution to American culture is Henry Louis Gates, Jr., Harvard professor and PBS host of *Finding Your Roots*. His showcase of ancestral discovery illustrates how transformative knowing our roots can be in liberating our future's potential. Gates provided an analysis in an interview with Lee Hawkins of the *Wall Street Journal*, which foretold something true about this book, *Twelve Steps for White America: For a United States of America*. The transcript reads:

> Traditionally in America, the white working class has been baited, in such a way, to identify economically, with people whom they have nothing in common—wealthier white people instead of just looking across the tracks, across the river, down the road, and seeing their black working-class counterparts. That is the union that should

have been affected so often in the history of America. Slavery itself was race and class fused. A slave is a living economic commodity. A slave in America was a Black person who was not a human being. It was a a commodity like the pigs, and the horses and the chickens on the census record. So, slavery was race and class fused. Race and class have always been fused in the United States and Martin Luther King realized this after the passage of the Civil Rights Act in 1964 and the Voting Rights Act of 1965. He began to move toward an economic analysis and that was when he was assassinated. I heard Calvin Butts say on a stage in New York that "when you go up against the empire, that's when you get crushed." This was a month ago. He was talking about people who in part move against the system with an economic analysis, because that's where the rubber hits the road. ... Race is not the most important thing that divides us, it is class. It is always about the money. The history of the West is about the money. ... I tell my students, the floorboard of Western culture has a river running under it. If you lift up those floorboards, you know what you see? There is a stream called anti-Semitism. What's that about? Class justified in the name of religion. Look down there and anti-black racism. Is that about race? No. It is about class justified in the name of racial difference.[3]

As alcohol was a solution that turned into alcoholism, so was slavery an economic solution to sustain rigged advantage. It worked insomuch as it generated great wealth, making Virginia a prosperous colony for England. Legacies of plantation economy persist to this day. As long as there has been a White majority, rigged advantage could masquerade as compatible with the American ideal. With demographic realities on

---

Henry Louis Gates, "Henry Louis Gates Discusses Ideological Divides Among Black Americans," *Wall Street Journal*. Copyright © 2016 by Dow Jones & Company, Inc.

the horizon heralding a new era for America's future, rigged advantage must rely on plantation legacies structured in our operations, particularly minority rule. A plantation could not exist without the control of a minority. Overt and covert violence held the system intact. On a continuum into the present that started before the fugitive slave act, the presumption of whereabouts authority (PWA)[4] persists as an entitlement of Whiteness.

- An essential part of slavery on plantations was absolute authority over the whereabouts of enslaved people who were legally considered to be the property of the plantation owner.
- Violent retribution was the price to be paid if a slave was found *out of bounds*. Fugitive slave patrols were legally sanctioned. Whites in free Northern states were legally required to cooperate.
- A minority (the owner and employees such as an overseer) ruled over the majority (the enslaved people who in most cases outnumbered the owners and employees).

Examples of Plantation Behavior and Ideology in Modern Life

- Plantation slavery race habits[5] continued after the Civil War *and persist in our present-day lives.*
- Presumption of whereabouts authority (PWA) over Black bodies was reimagined and sustained:
    - Legislation and judicial opinions such as *Plessy v. Ferguson*
    - Segregation of schools, transportation, and lunch counters
    - Miscegenation
    - Overt domestic terrorism (e.g., the Ku Klux Klan)
    - Minority rule
    - Poll taxes
    - Trumped-up charges to produce incarcerated labor
    - Sun-down towns
    - Redlined neighborhoods
    - Tulsa, Wilmington, Thibodaux, Harperville
    - Limited economic participation
    - Fugitive slave patrols masquerading as law enforcement
    - Covert domestic terrorism: Symbolic veneration of White Americans who had fought to own Black Americans, Confederate monuments

- Since plantation slavery, the United States struggles with whereabouts authority constantly resprouting in current events:
  - Police brutality
  - Charlottesville
  - Insurrection with the Confederate flag in our Capitol overtaken by people shouting, "We own this, We own you"
  - Karens in Central Park
  - Suspicious "May I help you?" personnel in retail

It should not be surprising today that the former Confederate States of America, a minority of the American population, use the Electoral College and the Senate to control judicial appointments, including to the Supreme Court, to protect their interests, even though they hold minority opinions at odds with the majority opinions of the American people. The moneyed interests who benefit from the rigged advantage sustained by minority rule have waged an extraordinary campaign of socially constructing race to begin with, then perpetuating racism, marginalization, bamboozling, patriotic bamboozling, Whiteness collusions, White supremacy, anti-Blackness, and Othering, all to sever naturally occurring multiracial class alliances. Sufficient numbers of culled and exploited White Americans support a rigged advantage agenda for the few who already benefit from the status quo.

Let us step back to review for whom this book is written.

Before you conclude this is a funny question in the tradition of "Who is buried in Grant's Tomb" let's just say, it's complicated! Obviously, the category "White" is in the title of the book, but let's talk about that briefly now. "The book is intended for White Americans" is *an* answer but *the* answer is more complex.

The *Twelve Steps for White America* are about dismantling rigged advantage, which requires more than just a group of individual White Americans. White American individuals are necessary but insufficient to dismantle rigged advantage.

This work to dismantle rigged advantage involves an entire culture of organizations, traditions, laws, systems, beliefs, habits, and more.

However, the book emphasizes "White America" for a reason. The book assumes that since the category we refer to as White America has benefitted from rigged advantage, White Americans should work categorically to dismantle rigged advantage. The burden for dismantling rigged advantage should not be placed on the very backs of those whom the system is rigged against.

That said, this is an American condition, which demands at least an American solution. We must ask ourselves questions to achieve clarity of purpose.

1. "Who is White?" and "How does White work?"
   - Who: Throughout American history, "Who is White?" has evolved from no one was categorized as White in the early history of Virginia to today, where the category White includes more people than the category included even at the end of the 19th century.
   - How: Since median household wealth in the United States is eight times higher for White households than Black households, "how White works" is a dysfunction that the future of a United States of America cannot afford to remain competitive or secure in the world.
2. Since most White Americans share the same interests with "other" Americans regarding what they need to thrive,
   - Why do "many Whites" align with the interests of a few elite Whites against "many Whites'" self-interest?
   - Who does this manufactured alignment serve?
   - Who does not want me to answer these questions?

john a. powell is the Haas Chancellor's Chair in Equity and Inclusion and is a Professor of Law, African American Studies, and Ethnic Studies at UC Berkeley. Professor powell writes,

> Most people who identify as white and are phenotypically white, are really the middle players. They do not put

white supremacy in place, not are they always a beneficiary of it. It is true that there is a psychological benefit to being affiliated with whiteness and its relationship to non-whites, but there is an incredible cost that is ignored. The material benefits associated with whiteness have been in decline for several years, but the benefits have not been extended to people of color by and large, with few exceptions. It is the elites that benefit the most from the ideology of whiteness or othering in a given society. This is important because in order to challenge white supremacy, it is not enough to challenge white people. You must challenge the white supremacist ideology and those who benefit the most from whiteness, which mutates over time. The benefit is often in the form of a transfer of wealth and power from people of color, working class and middle-class whites themselves. They also can use the ideology of white supremacy, which is bound up with religion, particularly Christianity, as a justification for imperialism. Imperialism and whiteness were never solely about one's religious affiliation or one's color, but also the arrangement of power and distribution of privilege. In terms of power, elites have been given a disproportionate share, but do not have all of it and can never have all of it.[6]

3. Since "who" is white may feel so complicated, let's oversimplify this for now to say what is still a mouthful:
   Your personal struggle may actually feel rigged but not in your favor. That may absolutely true for you personally. Please understand that at no point does this book say that you personally have not and do not struggle against unfair conditions. In fact, I suspect that is highly likely.

You can be different from your category. The category of all White America is rigged *for an elite portion of White America* who exploits your White affinity to sustain their elite advantage.

> **Me Versus We**
>
> What is true for "my group"
>
> may or may not
>
> be true for "me."
>
> **MY GROUP, FOR EXAMPLE**
>
> White American households may be eight times
>
> wealthier than Black American households.
>
> **VERSUS ME, FOR EXAMPLE**
>
> My White household may be struggling, and
>
> the Black CEO where I work is a multimillionaire.

We will more fully cover rigged advantage theory in step 4. Here is a quick introduction to the problem we are trying to admit.

image 1.2

Whiteness masquerades as solidarity but masks within-group exploitation. Power Whites collude in Whiteness to co-opt exploited Whites' power in exchange for derivative and tenuous value, embedded in social constructs of race.[7]

> The delusional mechanism enabling exploited Whites to experience the value[8] of whiteness versus their subjective exploitation, persists through two strategies:
> - White supremacy: Social reinforcement for the value of Whiteness
> - Anti-Blackness: Displacement of exploitation onto Black, Indigenous, and People of Color
>
> Strategy mechanisms include racelighting,[9] voter-suppression, and legacies of slavery, including minority rule, state-sanctioned violence, disproportionate incarceration, disparate outcomes in education, generational wealth, health, and economic social mobility.

Rigged advantage for the few is normalized, excused, evaded, or mythologized, while any status quo challenge is bamboozled and demonized. The few who benefit from rigged advantage need the rest of us distracted and turned against each other. Our historical fault lines of race prove ideal fodder. However, throughout our history, there are times when the rigged advantage few "overplay their hand" and the rest of us find "desperation makes strange bedfellows" for such a time as this.

Increasingly, strange bedfellows hold two things to be true at the same time:

1. We love our country—especially for what it aspires to be.
2. We know that our country's aspirations are more realizable for some than others.

That's both un-American (as an ideal) but so American (in the lived experience of far too many, including many White Americans).

Our time feels especially tumultuous, but I argue that the tumult is proportional to the change that is needed. Tenaciously, I believe we are in the crucible our ancestors hoped for us. Out of this crucible, the United States of America can become a meritocracy where justice, then liberty, for all ensures our best days ahead.

This transition will not be easy, nor will it be guaranteed. Autocracy concentrates power in the hands of the few, and they experience an almost divine right-of-kings entitlement to their inheritance. The rigged advantage few would rather burn the house down than cede any ground. They can bamboozle the rest of us to turn on each other to sustain their entitlement for only so long.

This insidious rigged advantage has masqueraded as a great "America" for too long; but rest assured, there are legions of us who love the aspirational America enough to protect her from all enemies, foreign and domestic. The rest of us are becomingly increasingly equipped to ensure that our country's aspirations are finally realized.

Democracy has not failed as much as we have not tried it yet.

The time for American awakening has come. The United States is a democracy ideally becoming a more perfect union where race will not predict the outcomes of democracy. It is not a country that some White Americans own and need to take back from another group. Citizenship works fervently toward the democratic goals that all Americans are created equal and entitled to certain inalienable rights.

For Black Americans to increasingly take their seat at the table of democratic citizenship means that the United States will evolve more perfectly, things will get better, and the country will be competitive and secure on the world stage for generations to come.

Any White American who seeks to limit that seat at the table curtails justice and liberty and forecasts the demise of the American experiment with democracy.

Those White Americans are in fact the thing they fear and project: a threat to the United States.

Learning Outcome

Identify the gap between presented and realized democracy in the United States.

CHAPTER 2

STEP 2
WE BELIEVE SOMETHING CAN BE DONE

Step 2 Governs Step 8: We Identify the Harm

Key Words: **Delusion, Hope, Sanity**

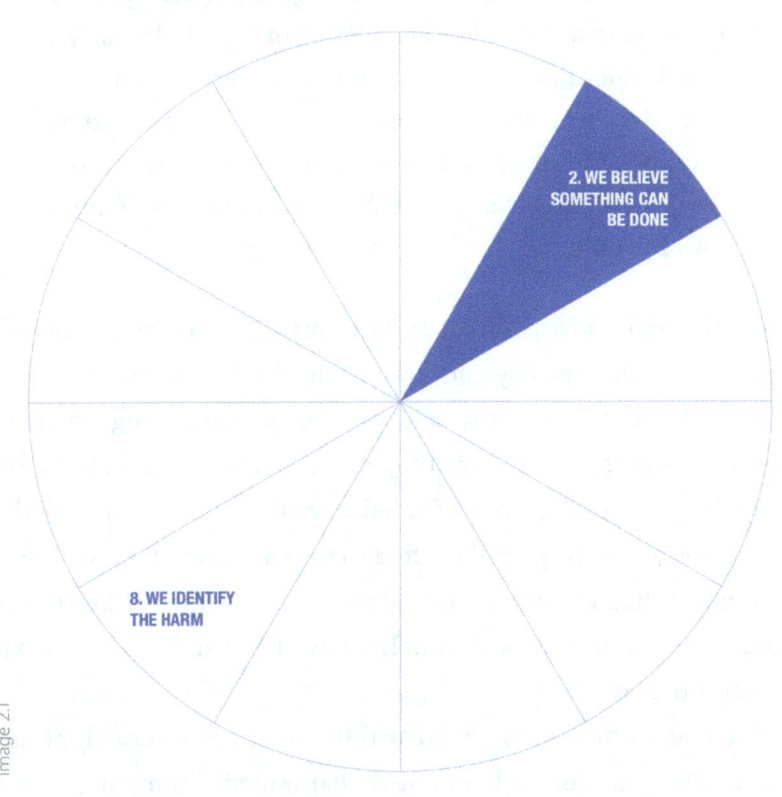

Image 2.1

What I Learned From Alcoholics About the Second Step of AA

> *"Came to believe that a Power greater than ourselves could restore us to sanity."*[1]

We are a nation that seems to not understand the difference between a meritocracy in a democratic republic versus a system of rigged advantage. We could learn from alcoholics.

> Some will be willing to term themselves "problem drinkers" but cannot endure the suggestion that they are in fact mentally ill. They are abetted in the blindness by a world which does not understand the difference between sane drinking and alcoholism. "Sanity" is defined as soundness of mind. Yet no alcoholic, soberly analyzing his destructive behavior … can claim soundness of mind for himself.[2]

We alcoholics are a defiant and resentful lot. To you, we become "buck-up" babies one day and "hair of the dog" masochists the next. You may begin to wonder which one of us you are going to get. You may look us in the eye and see the twinkle of the good life, but we are crumbling inside. A fortress of defenses both attractive and repellant comprises a cloaking spell crafted to manage you while we obsess over controlling everything else since we are losing the battle to an external locus of control. Alcoholics have been stabbed in the back by a best friend.

Bleeding, we devolve to survive within a solution that cruelly became deadly. That was not the bargain. We bargained to remain in control of when and how much, like anyone else. When our drinking patterns began, alcohol worked so well that we could predict and control its reward. This solution worked so well that alternate response skills atrophied over time. Like a runner whose injury may be severe enough that even walking is prohibitive for months, you may still have an identity as a runner, but your capacity reveals otherwise until you recover your former capacity.

Similarly with the alcoholic, the river between identity and capacity is wide. A naturally occurring range of skills is used less and less. They deteriorate. They atrophy from disuse. What you don't use you lose. No one intends this. It is something devastating—even deadly—that happens covertly until the trap door shuts and there is no return.

What of This May We Apply to Our Problem, Rigged Advantage?

What predictably unfolds between the time that alcohol is at first a solution but later turns into a deadly problem is worth understanding because this parallels our nation. Our nation now mirrors a certain point in the alcoholic life cycle. Like holy water thrown at the possessed in horror movies, we can go to great lengths to resist change. Earlier in the process, we can employ elegant strategies such as denial, justification, or rationalization.

But as the impairment metastasizes, the reactivity to any system challenge becomes proportionally more severe:

- Projection (I'm not the problem: you're the problem)
- Displacement (those people are the problem)

The alcoholic has rotted within; but, trapped and hopeless, the mind games the alcoholic must play just to get through the day can spiral into to a spectacle of dysfunction on fire. You can see fire, but the alcoholic cannot smell smoke. Crazy? Yes. But in a very specific way. The process is well understood and has been for a long time. While science has added greatly to our understanding of addiction, especially understanding genetic predisposition, the psychological components of relapse, and innovations in treatment, what needs to be done about it is at least as old as when Bill W. and Dr. Bob fatefully met and A.A. was born.

Treatment providers, sponsors, and loved ones with recovery principles intact have zero tolerance for the dysfunctional fire, whether the alcoholic can smell smoke or not. In the same way you would not leave a person in the street run over by a car even if their head injury makes them think they are okay, the "world view" of an untreated alcoholic is recognized for what it is. We love the person enough to do the right thing despite protestations or any other thing that is used as smokescreen.

As alcoholism progresses, the smokescreen can be propagated by co-opted others with a vested interest in sustaining the alcoholic's condition. Maybe they are drinking buddies justifying their condition as well. They see good times, unable to see that good-time Charlie's got the blues. Maybe others have been beaten (sometimes figuratively, sometimes literally) into a state that psychologically requires the similar defense mechanism the alcoholic uses, so they ally as birds of a feather. This dysfunction in common can become codependency. One of the parties may not be addicted to alcohol, but the entire system becomes fueled by common determinants. As the alcoholic loses capacity, the capacities of those relating to the alcoholic are co-opted and exploited for their capacities to minimize consequences, which in turn become more justification for denying the problem.

As we learn more from addiction research, time evolves the technical definition of alcoholism, but recovering alcoholics presume to know it when they see it![3] With as much pop psychology as America has consumed for generations, what most people actually understand about mental illness is still scant at best. About mental illness, far too many people "can't see the forest through the trees." People presume norms when they see deviance even when they sense something is just "not right."

Sometimes "That's crazy" is offensive.

Sometimes "That's crazy" is a mental disorder that masqueraded past you without you realizing what just happened.

Sometimes "That's crazy" is an actual mental disorder, which, out of the ignorance of impacted unfortunates, got a pass at best, and went untreated to the consequence of millions as a worst-case scenario now too familiar, unfortunately.

Regarding the latter, the Goldwater rule must be mentioned here.[4] Presidential candidate Barry Goldwater sued *Fact* magazine, who publicly presented opinions regarding Goldwater's unfitness for office. He won the libel suit. Thereafter, the American Psychiatric Association's medical ethics considers it unethical to provide an opinion on the psychiatric fitness of an individual who has not been personally evaluated.[5] Later, *Tarasoff v. Regents of Univ. of Cal.* (1976) would determine

> Once a therapist determines, or under applicable professional standards reasonably should have determined, that a patient poses a serious danger of violence to others, he bears a duty to exercise reasonable care to protect the foreseeable victim of that danger. While the discharge of this duty of due care will necessarily vary with the facts of each case, in each instance the adequacy of the therapist's conduct must be measured against the traditional negligence standard of the rendition of reasonable care under the circumstances.[6]

In the case of our national trauma, the Goldwater rule muzzled Tarasoff's duty to warn. The APA Goldwater rule was established in an era when the proliferation of video footage and social media record of diagnosable behavior now available was unimaginable. Nassir Ghaemi, MD, MPH, professor of psychiatry at Tufts University and lecturer in psychiatry at Harvard Medical School argues that

> The Goldwater Rule exists for two reasons. First, psychiatrists are ethically forbidden from revealing diagnoses without the consent of a patient, and second, it's not professionally sound to diagnose a patient without directly examining that individual. Neither justification makes sense for public figures, though. ... In a democracy, the public has a right to know about its leaders' medical health. Why should psychiatric conditions be excluded?[7]

Presuming mental health in the face of mental illness colludes with its dysfunction. What we call alcoholism is defined as substance use disorder (SUD) in the fifth edition of *the Diagnostic and Statistical Manual of Mental Disorders* (the psychiatric bible of diagnoses.) Other diagnoses in the DSM-5 include the personality disorders. Here, especially, the public fails to appreciate the forest through the trees. I believe the name "personality disorder" does no favor to the public since this nomenclature both confuses and diffuses. Since a diversity of personality is as common as the number of individuals you may know, too many people conflate a natural diversity of human personality with personality disorder, an actual mental disorder.[8]

A chicken or egg first analysis emerges when trying to determine if existing mental disorders predispose SUD or if SUD predisposes other mental disorders. In these cases of so-called comorbidity or dual diagnoses, an individual's addiction can progress to the point where triage becomes vital. If my kitchen is on fire, discussing a living room remodel becomes ludicrous. In some cases, harm reduction is merciful until more intervention is possible. Getting a homeless person off the street, even if they are still using, may reduce potential harm and increase the chances for the onset of recovery. Clean needles to prevent HIV spread were initially controversial, mostly to those far removed from lived realities.

This book attempts to draw parallels between the complexities of SUD and the societal dysfunction of racial oppression as a tool to sustain rigged advantage. While the elements of those complexities of course vary, I am proposing that what is common across these dysfunctions leads us to what is common across the principles of recovering from each. As deaths of despair[9] and opioid addiction ravage our nation at the same time that White supremacy and anti-Blackness surge, we must come to terms with some analysis of what is happening to us, what has worked for others faced with desperate circumstances, and get specific on a treatment plan that holds promise for a recovery from what threatens our stability and our future.

Our nation feels so dysfunctional because technology accelerates and permeates across all society what was formerly managed *covertly* and *compartmentally* within the norm of rigged advantage. While the extent of this permeating process is a new phenomenon, the content is not new. Where and how much and against whom are new. White Americans are becoming aware of how rigged advantage threatens them. "White cold = Black flu" is no longer contained within the norm of rigged advantage. As the pandemic has made abundantly clear, something that affects some of us can surely affect all of us.

White Americans are increasingly aware that not only Black, Indigenous, and other People of Color pay the price for rigged advantage (which relies on White supremacy and anti-Blackness). Too many White Americans, just trying to make ends meet, trust power White elites who scapegoat "Others" as the real problem. Exploited and bamboozled, that trust is killing us. We are experiencing, "deaths of despair" at alarming rates. The work of this book is not something White Americans need to do for "others." White Americans need to save themselves so that a United States of America—for all—can thrive in a secure and competitive future. Burning down our House does not work.

Now that our national dysfunction is "overwhelmingly in our (meaning White America's) face" there is an increasing urgency that something must be done about it. We then realize that "it" has been overwhelmingly in the face of Black America all along. We can only get through it if there is a sufficient tipping point of understanding the problem to change it. As the middle class continues to shrink and the next generation's promise is compromised, more White Americans realize that the membership they pay for Whiteness is too great. Rigged advantage for some = bad for all. It is not just bad for others.

Coming to terms with the overwhelming nature of step 2, especially as we comprehend the toll that dysfunction has taken on us individually and, on our nation, is perhaps a fitting way to end this section with some consolation. The recovery tradition honors the famous prayer by theologian Reinhold Niebuhr referred to as the serenity prayer.[10] I have heard and uttered the serenity prayer many times. Like so many tools used to support recovery, the serenity prayer is simple but so difficult.

God, Grant me the serenity

To accept the things, I cannot change:

Courage to change the things I can;

And wisdom to know the difference.

Courage may grow out of the clarity and assurance that consolation's serenity provides. The serenity prayer calls for courage to change what you can. In the middle of complex intellectualizing, I was always taught to hold my hand up in front of my face and remember the following: Most of what I can change is on my side of the hand. Most of

---

Reinhold Niebuhr, "Serenity Prayer," 1943.

what I cannot change is on the other side of my hand. But herein lies an extraordinary thing about spirituality. I can be the change I wish to see in the world. In fact, it is the most powerful tool at my disposal—to change me.

When we change, it reverberates beyond our immediacy. As overwhelming as step 2 may seem, it is, in the end, very simple. You have already admitted there is a problem. Now, step 2 simply requires you to believe something can be done about the problem. In step 2, there is not a single thing you need to do but look within your self and determine that a better way is possible.

Learning Outcome

Recognize the potential for personally impacting democracy's promise.

CHAPTER 3

STEP 3
WE DECIDE TO ACT

Step 3 Governs Step 9: We Repair the Harm

Key Words: **Willingness, Key, Earnest, Brave desperation**

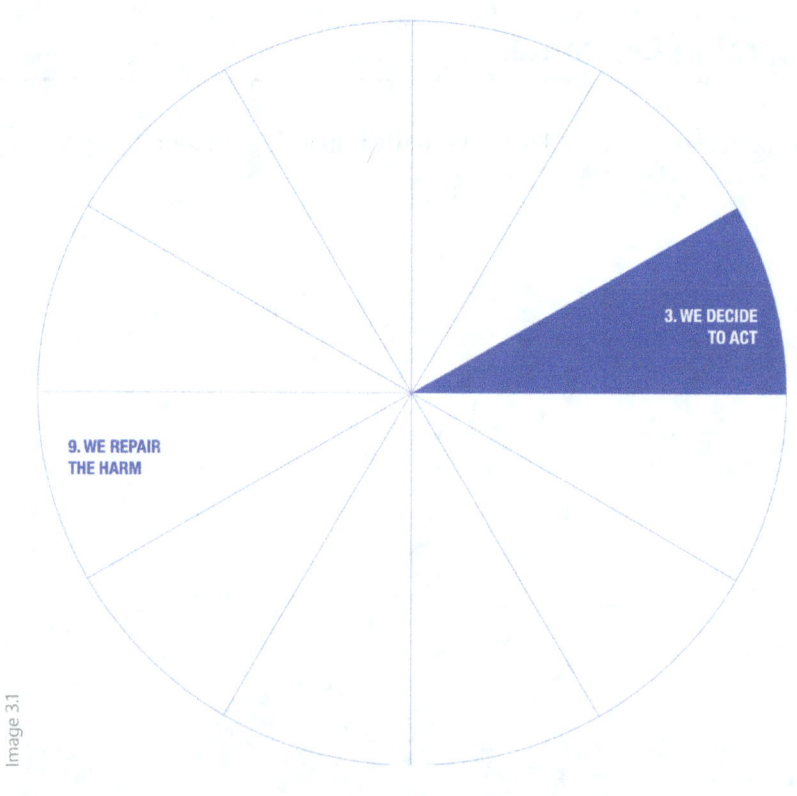

Image 3.1

What I Learned From Alcoholics About the Third Step of AA

> *"Made a decision to turn our will and our lives over to the care of God as we understood Him."*[1]

In the *Twelve Steps and Twelve Traditions of Alcoholics Anonymous*, the cofounder writes, "the effectiveness of the whole A.A. program will rest upon how well and earnestly we have tried to come to a decision to turn our will and lives over to the care of God as we understood him."[2] Before you choke on too much religiosity, understand that many thousands of alcoholics have wrestled at the same choking point. Step 3 is not step 1 for a very good reason.

Before we wrestle the mighty step 3, we must be thoroughly convinced that

- there is a problem (step 1) and
- believe that something can be done about the problem (step 2)

Why *make a decision* (step 3) to evacuate a coastal city without a trusted warning that a hurricane is inching closer (a step 1 action: there is a problem) and believe that an attempt to run for cover could reduce harm (a step 2 action: something can be done about the problem)? After step 1 and step 2, step 3 becomes more surmountable—brave desperation.

Mississippians of a certain age think of one thing when they hear the name Camille. The 1969 hurricane season wrought storm devastation previously unimaginable to most Americans living at that time. The nation was horrified when Hurricane Camille flattened towns along the Mississippi Gulf Coast, including Pass Christian (pronounced Christy Anne), Long Beach, Gulfport, and Biloxi (pronounced buh-lucksy). If you say "lox" we know you are not "from here." The Mississippi Gulf

Coast (known more as a region than individual towns, even though each has its own personality) is more like New Orleans than most of Mississippi. Not just a drunk day for pre-Lent tourists, the culture of Mardi Gras (a *joie de vivre* hard to imagine unless you have seen a reclining elderly lady you thought could be dead rise up to dance when a second-line parade goes by midday in the middle of the week) extends beyond New Orleans. The range of Mardi Gras culture extends from the Cajun-country capital of Lafayette, Louisiana, along the coast past Mobile, and the Redneck Riviera, all the way down to Panama City.

Several years after Camille, I took some of my undergraduate coursework at the Gulf Park campus of the University of Southern Mississippi on the Gulf of Mexico waterfront in Long Beach. Sitting on campus among the sprawling limbs of the 500-year-old live oak tree, "The Friendship Oak" is unforgettable. Looking out over the Gulf of Mexico at sunset, my romanticized love of southern veranda life bloomed, like camellias and azaleas, showy in fall and spring sunshine, respectively. After almost 30 years in California, I still yearn for *that* romanticized notion of "home."

Home is knowing that if someone soaked overnight the Camellia brand of dried red beans for some Paul Prudhomme red beans and rice (recipe available in the 1983 *Southern Living Cookbook*), that's "gonna be mighty fine, yeah!"—a catch phrase of Cajun cook-humorist Justin Wilson from Tangipahoa Parish. Wilson's brother-in-law was Louisiana Attorney General Bolivar Edwards Kemp, Jr. If you travel there, you may hear the term "registered coon ass" but exercise caution. You should not call either Wilson or Kemp an RCA (fr. connase).[3] When he was about ten years old, one of my Noël cousins from New Orleans proudly proclaimed he was a coon ass at a family funeral in Forest, Mississippi, but I always knew better than to say it myself! His inference was that being a coon ass made him better than just a plain ole redneck like me, something he felt needed to be said at a red-neck funeral.

Before I moved to California, I worked in Baton Rouge at the largest hospital in Louisiana for the Sisters at Our Lady of the Lake Regional Medical Center as a psychotherapist on a behavioral health unit. Sweet and humble Sister "Glenda" was an administrator who welcomed new employees at orientation. The guy next to me in the back of the room fell asleep during her welcome. She told me to rouse him awake. She issued an edict: "Sir, stand up. You're fired. Go sleep at home!" The rest of us better understood the sweet nun Sister Glenda after that.

A family of self-identified Cajuns supported their patriarch in family counseling for alcoholism. I nearly needed a translator, but we made it. Embarrassed that he needed treatment, we were getting started when he proudly exclaimed to me that his daughter was studying in Paris. "She speaks the real Fransh." He signaled some colonial inferiority wrapped in community pride bundled with adoration that his daughter was so accomplished that she was practically Parisian, not just a bayou Cajun like him. White is definitely not monolithic: RCAs, rednecks, hillbillies, country hicks, gentry, proles and preppies, French Quarter White, Garden District White, New England White, Californ-yah White, Irish White, and Italian White. There are big differences, but these are all considered White.

While remembering Camille is mostly reserved for those of a certain age in Mississippi, many more Americans recall Katrina. There's no need to say "Hurricane Katrina" because we just know that Katrina is synonymous with a devastating hurricane that triggered flooding in New Orleans in 2005. Especially since Camille had been so destructive, New Orleanians for years gritted their teeth (worse than when tourists say "N'Awlins") for the day that would surely come. We absolutely knew hurricane categories. We had long feared that a "cat 5" hurricane would destroy New Orleans.

Katrina's wrath actually missed New Orleans to destroy the Mississippi Gulf Coast for the second time in my lifetime. "Only" a proximate cause, Katrina's aftermath flooding broke the New Orleans levee system. When it failed, New Orleans, sitting in a bowl below sea level, began to fill with water overflowing from the Mississippi River, which snakes past the Ninth Ward and the French Quarter, and Lake Pontchartrain, which borders the northern part of the city.

The tragedy was so painful: all those stranded human beings clustered on roof tops, some drowning in their attics trying to escape the inevitable. The Lower Ninth ward was hit so horribly. A professor I worked with in the Bay Area lost her mother this way. I could feel the gash of her woundedness and knew she would never heal from that.

We respond to tragedy uniquely. As a classically trained pianist, I couldn't help but imagine all the pianos underwater, decades old, haunted by jazz past. I grappled with the metaphor of drowned music underwater. We did not know then if New Orleans was totally destroyed. Response to the tragedy was nearly as repugnant as the tragedy itself. While he ranks better by comparison now, George W. Bush could not have been more contemptable to me when he said we couldn't have known a category 5 hurricane could produce such devastation. If you were "from there" you knew it was either inexcusably ignorant or a cruel lie—salt in a horrible wound. When he then said on camera to the incompetent leader of the rescue effort, "Brownie, you're doing a heck of a job" I felt so violated sitting in front of a television in Northern California.

Heartbroken to see a place I loved so much so devastated, it was demoralizing to watch news cycle talking-head pontificators scapegoat a wounded New Orleans as nothing more than an American embarrassment for its "exposed" poverty, laid bare for all the world to see. As one who lectures on inequality to university students, it was not the fact of the poverty that so insulted me (I teach that racial wealth inequality is one of the most egregious fault lines in the United States), it was the scapegoating of New Orleans at a time when it was so hurt. It is a national habit to displace everyone else's racism onto the South since it is so blatant among us there.

Inequality in America is extensive in San Francisco and San José, California—arguably the production center of inequality in the modern age. (I once counted more than 70 billionaires living near the 280 freeway in and between San Francisco and San José.) This is precisely a function of how Whiteness colludes to benefit the wealthiest, that "those racists in poverty-ridden New Orleans" are the problem. Whiplashed, I went from category 5 to second Camille, to citywide flooding, to "We couldn't have known," to "all y'all nasty racists down there." I was broken by it. I could hardly express my sorrow about it all. "Out here" in California, I knew few could "get it" since I have experienced Californians looking oblivious at nothing but Latinos working at the car wash and ask me what it is like to be from such a racist place as the South. Something as romanticized as New Orleans, to me a jewel of culture unique in all of America, was trashed, gone, just a stinking rot of putrid racist poverty.

Psychotherapists reading this may have already concluded that I certainly identify with New Orleans. It is complicated. How can I so deeply love and possess such yearning for such a romanticized notion of home when home can also mean poverty, virulent racism, homophobia, and domestic terrorism? How can it offend me, living in the San Francisco Bay Area for half my life for people to scapegoat New Orleans? All these attachments, familial storehouses, cultural identities, romanticized narratives, folkways, customs, even recipes, idioms, what only those of us "from here" can understand.

What of This May We Apply to Our Problem, Rigged Advantage?

A thing or situation can be more than one thing at a time. New Orleans can be both a jewel of American culture, an object of my affection, and reveal a shocking truth about poverty in modern America, all at the same time. White America may generally hold a romanticized notion of the idealized American experience that chaffs at any criticism. Especially in our tumultuous time of protests, addiction, a global pandemic, and egregious inequality robbing our children's' futures, I can love America and criticize it at the same time.

I ask you to gird your loins. Let us have a quick round of critique that may, like medicine, be hard to swallow.

Power Whites bamboozle exploited Whites to advance a power White agenda using *Otherness*.[4] (We are valued[5] White Americans and not Others; i.e., devalued Black Americans). White supremacy ensures that exploited Whites abhor Otherness (anti-Blackness) and vote against exploited Whites' self-interest to sustain power White advantage. If exploited Whites withdrew from the Whiteness political coalition to vote with other exploited groups, the power White status quo would erode.

- Bamboozling is a time-worn technique alive and well in the 21st century.
- "Bamboozle" is an 18th-century term for self gain through exploiting others with deceit and trickery.
- Its meaning was extended in the 19th century by the context of Jim Crow minstrelsy—anti-Blackness as entertainment.
- The 20th-century version of bamboozling presents as distraction, disinformation, scapegoating, voter suppression, brutality.
- In the 21st century, social media propagates bamboozling in echo chambers that congeal contorted, seemingly unmatched coalitions.
- Minority rule in government perpetuates plantation control over the many by the few to sustain the status quo for power Whites.

I have now lived equal parts of my life in the American South (mostly Mississippi) and in California. This enables me to have a window into each state from the other.

If you feel stuck in the opinion that legacies of slavery are consigned to the past and you struggle to see how then impacts now, let us consider the roles California and Mississippi play in sustaining rigged advantage. These two states illustrate two sides of the same Whiteness coin, glued together with White supremacy for rigged advantage.

As an epicenter of American inequality, San José and San Francisco lead a democracy-threatening transfer of wealth to the very few at the top. Their stellar reputations for being diverse liberal bastions mask how they sustain rigged advantage for power White America. While California's 40 million people have two senators, Mississippi's two senators, representing 3 million people (less than 1/10th of California's 40 million people), consistently vote for power White advantage, even when their own people languish exploited like millions of Californians.

How is this possible?

Two sides of the same Whiteness coin glued together through White supremacy to rig advantage for elite whites (and anyone else who can sustain rigged advantage for those who benefit from it, mostly a small minority of elite White Americans who have nothing in common with the many Whites who validate and ensure the status quo).

This answer is important to understanding the steps White Americans need to take for American democracy. Exploited Whites vote with power Whites because of bamboozled convictions (what Eddie S. Glaude, Jr. calls race habits[6]) habituated in the sticks and carrots of racism.

The stick is

> to avoid anti-blackness: "I may not be rich, but I am White—not one of those subjected and devalued others."

The carrot is

> to reap the benefits of White privilege: "I may not be rich, but I am White. This land was made for me."

It serves power Whites that California displaces its own racism in stereotypes of Mississippi's racism. (This same displacement of subjective exploitation is a core function identified in rigged advantage theory). In truth, a slight realignment of Whiteness affinity in Mississippi (largest Black American population in the United States) could help save America from California.

Very Important Note

You do not need to agree with me to move forward. In fact, *the recovery tradition insists that you take what you need and leave the rest.* You may not agree with my theory of the problem. But I owe it to you. If I am presenting a solution in the form of 12 steps you can take to unshackle the past, strengthen security and competitiveness, and make way for all so that our best days are ahead of us, I owe it to you to tell you my theory of the problem that I propose we solve. If you are this far in the book, you have at least entertained the idea that there is a problem. You may have even entertained the idea that something can be done about the problem. If you disagree with rigged advantage, that may be exactly what you need in the problem-solving process. If you disagree, then it helps you determine what the problem is not, in your opinion. All that is required of you in step 3 is not agreement, but willingness: *We want something to be done about the problem.* Not to worry!

Decide to keep going. There it is: Your step 3 decision gets you to step 4.

Learning Outcome

Commit to a personal program of liberation for the common good.

CHAPTER 4

STEP 4
WE DETAIL THE PROBLEM

Step 4 Governs Step 10: We Remain Vigilant

Key Words: **Rigor, Painstaking, Liabilities, New bedrock**

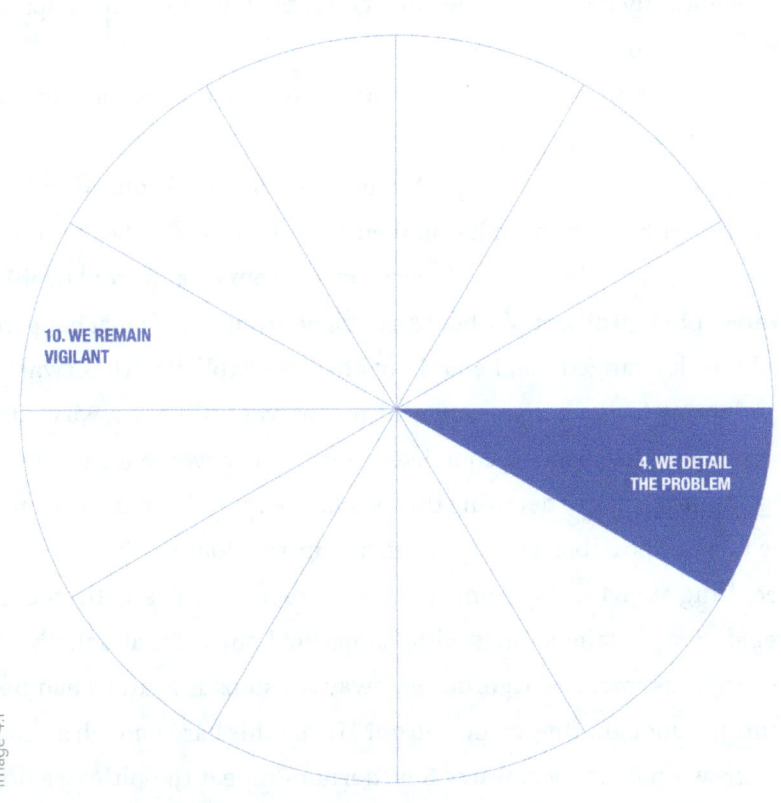

Image 4.1

What I Learned From Alcoholics About the Fourth Step of AA

"Made a searching and fearless moral inventory of ourselves."[1]

An accounting is needed to determine where we are and how we got here. To realize that to which we aspire, we must be rigorously honest about who we are now.

I learned and practiced step 4 in my early recovery: "Made a searching and fearless moral inventory of ourselves."

I had admitted my apparent problem: step 1.

I eventually believed something could be done about my apparent problem: step 2.

I became hopeful enough to want something to be done about my apparent problem: step 3.

So, what *exactly* was the problem? Answering this question is not possible without the foundational building blocks afforded by steps 1, 2, and 3. **Step 4 shifts alcoholism recovery from an apparent problem to an explicit problem.** Without an explicit inventory of what happened and how it changed me, I could not chart an explicit path forward.

Adapting to alcoholism, something that was killing me, was pathological; but it had become completely normal. For everyone in recovery, the daunting task of detailing this problem explicitly presents some of the most impossible, excruciating, and miraculous work of recovery. Recalling step 4 work from early in my recovery, I can still feel the trepidation I felt then, David with a slingshot knowing that Goliath odds were against me. The rigorous gateways of steps 1, 2, and 3 had been daunting enough. How could I go on? Wasn't this hard enough already?

I grew up hearing country Southerners repeat the pithy wisdom, "Don't poke a snake." While that is generally good advice (usually learned the hard way), alcoholism left unprovoked will kill you. Step 4 "pokes" at a Medusa of pathology: the dysfunctional adaptations that alcoholism habituates to persist. Proportional to the problem, the quest of step 4 requires complete abandon, a leap of faith into a fiery pit with nothing but a slim-chance promise to survive it. I shudder, even now, writing about it.

Most days, for over 35 years, I have acknowledged that the present is a blessing. How could even a difficult day, rife with opportunity, be taken for granted. May this be the story of a United States of America that we tell future generations, that we did the work we needed to do to ensure for all that our best days were ahead.

If the past is prologue, we may not make it. There are too many lies and too many "bamboozlers" for a simple accounting of our condition to take place. Lies, myths, and collusions across religion, state, and vested economic interests benefit some at the expense of others. Marginalization is already baked into the cake of who we are. Aspirationally, yes, "We are better than this." But, similar to the deadly dysfunction of alcoholism, a host must rationalize the parasitic threat in order to tolerate the condition. Denial, displacement, projection, and collusion with similar others who provide external confirmation of the rationalization all comprise an entrenched worldview that must be dismantled in order for the parasite/dysfunction to be dismantled. Even though an existing worldview may be deadly, it masquerades as something that is working. Dismantling the dysfunction will feel exactly like what it is: things falling apart.

In my years as as psychotherapist working with patients in hospital behavioral health units, a certain milestone was predictable if treatment was on course. At about the 2-week mark of inpatient treatment, patients would in great distress tell me that this isn't working. I'm falling apart. I think I'm losing it. A well-built psychological structure supported their deadly dysfunctional identity. Since that normal masquerade was killing them, it had to be dismantled step by step in order to build recovery on a new foundation.

Psychically, that dismantling process feels excruciating—even life threatening. Imagine their shock when my response would be celebratory when they are overwrought with crushing desperation. "This is fantastic. I'm so proud of you. How wonderful that the work you have done has gotten you to this excruciating crucible!"

I would explain to them that their exasperation meant something very good, that the structure alcoholism built, was tumbling down so recovery could be built. It was so predictable that I would even have something ready for them to walk away with—a small award of some kind—for them to be reminded that my assessment of their psychic tragedy was "treatment on track; all is well!"

When our nation, built on the backs of marginalized others, quakes under their protests that the nation's promise is yet to be realized for so many, I always remember that crucial phase "I'm falling apart; this is not working," which I predictably heard from patients if progress was real. It was my job as a therapist to facilitate that journey. In the middle of their despair, it was my spiritual honor (and a validation of my own recovery) to already "see them" to hold a vision for them as recovered, whole, living a full life proportional to their potential. The desecrated host before me was beautiful already in my eyes and I would "see" them for them until they could see themselves.

Rigged advantage remains rigged for some White Americans exploiting the rest of White Americans using White supremacy and anti-Blackness. To uproot something so entrenched, we must be explicit about the nature of our apparent problem. Accommodating something that is killing us is pathological; but, for too many, it still remains completely normal. This work is not optional. What we are going through and the ongoing work it will take may feel like we are falling apart. For rigged advantage to unravel, its strategies, White supremacy and anti-Blackness, must be absolutely revealed for all to see. It must be dismantled. We must clear out wreckage. We become something of a construction site. None of that is going to feel safe, secure, mundane. People are going to react according to whatever their dispositions predict. If we have a chance for a United States of America, this is the work that must be done.

> This is the work not only of all White Americans, but all those systems, organizations, and institutions (even those including Black Americans) who wittingly and unwittingly collude with rigged advantage.

So here we go:

Like Shadrach, Meshach and Abednego, we must enter Nebuchadnezzar's fire.[2]

What of This May We Apply to Our Problem, Rigged Advantage?

Cultures use a generally accepted framework of understanding—a narrative—to function. Comprised of many individuals, a culture does not reinvent the framework every day since that would defeat the "making sense of things" purpose of how narratives work. For sense making to be efficient, the story becomes an operating system that functions in the background. I do not have to relearn "door," "map," "internet," "alerts," "medicine" every day. The basics of daily living are already operationalized; they operate in the background as part of the operating code or narrative. This is a necessary learned part of successful survival. This learning extends from basic survival (terms) to how we make meaning of our world (stories). A Russian doll nest of stories within stories, our collective narrative both creates and reflects the sense we make of our world.

Our narrative—what we believe and tell—is powerful. It is formative. Our word is our bond. What we offer as promise in exchange for something valued is our contract with legal protections. We speak our meaning forth, into existence. Genesis begins with what God said. The ancient Hebrews dipped honey onto children's tongues when teaching them, "Sweeter than the honey drippings are the words from the mouth of God." The ancient Greek philosopher Heraclitus taught that the word *logos* was a reasoning or ordering of the universe. Jewish philosopher Philo differentiated between the word spoken and word within. John co-opted and extrapolated this to say that Jesus was this word incarnate, the creating force of the universe that became flesh and dwelt among us. Paramahansa Yogananda extended this idea to Jesus as demonstration of the mastery of universal Christ consciousness—our ultimate God communion.

Since our narrative depends on language, how language lives in us or, more precisely, how we live in language, features among the most fundamental and universal aspects of the human condition. A specific language is not necessarily universal, but the use of language is. If we try to function in another language new to us, we become keenly aware that our first language operates on automatic. Arguably, we cannot remember learning something so fundamental to our survival because we have to have it to remember, at least to think about remembering. Language transmits our cultural framework of understanding—the operating narrative with the terms and stories of our existence. It develops us. It reflects us.

A treasured part of our development is when a child is read a story. Children love to tell a story. In my Southern heritage where generally "children should be seen, not heard" a child could become the center of attention if the story was good enough to take the floor. We have stories about stories—the rules of telling. Children know that "once you say it, you can't take it back." We rationalize that "sticks and stones may break my bones, but words may never hurt me." We say that "the tongue is mightier than the sword." And it cuts both ways. As a tool versus a weapon, what we say can build versus destroy.

Our stories are not limited to words on a page. Exceptionally creative artists are revered precisely because of their ability to create and perpetuate the representational (or an abstractional) story of us, usually from a new perspective, often presented to us for the first time before we are ready for it. At the time, we scoff at artists such as Kandinsky, Duchamp, Frankenthaler, Warhol, and Basquiat. In time, we say they were ahead of their time. We were, in fact, developed by their presentation in order to reach that conclusion. The American experiment with democracy unfolds this way: An additional perspective of inclusion presents before most are ready for it, but "in time" we conclude "ahead of their time." Indeed, time itself (linguistically partitioned into past, present, and future in English) is part of the story we tell ourselves. Lastly, something accepted as a universal truth is considered timeless, outside the bounds of temporal experience.

Stories convey power, healing, and redemption; therefore, *we* who control the narrative have a kind of 3D power: dominance, defense, and deliverance when narrative power is used for good. Any assessment of rigged advantage must grapple with the overwhelming (but often covert by design) ordering that occurs in our narrative, mythology, origins, tenets, doctrines, and the presentation of information.

Let us consider "discoveries" as an example of the power of narrative in culture. Already, a "discovery" becomes about us rather than the discovered since we glory in the extension of us—our "greater-ness"—that the discovery creates. Students of history from elementary school through doctoral studies can imagine a top-10 list of "discoveries" that radically changed our understanding of our world and its relationships.

We now know that the Earth is not the center of the universe. But we still think of "sunrise" and "sunset" as though we are situated while the sun comes up and the sun goes down. Scientifically, we are certain that it takes about 365 days for a complete orbit of Earth to round the sun. However, culturally, we are ego centric, not helio centric. We even have romantically sung notions about "that lucky old sun got nothin' to do but roll around heaven all day." We operate both of these at the same time, depending on our situational positionality not only in the universe, but within our operating narrative.

The fact of our orbit may only minimally change our culturally informed notions about our lived experience. Most people I know (a well-educated lot since I worked in higher education for over 20 years) find it mind-boggling when I ask them to imagine that today's location of Earth in the universe is at least 180,000 miles away from its location 6 months ago (orbitally speaking). Those of us blessed with an address think of ourselves as residing in a fixed location. We have an address from which we go and come. My present address is stable while the Earth is hurtling (orbiting) through the universe at over 60,000 miles per hour. I can be both still writing at this desk today and be far from where I was yesterday.

Let us consider another discovery. It was as recent as 1859 that Louis Pasteur debunked the theory of spontaneous generation—the long-held notion that life could come from inanimate objects. Once, people assumed that because a bag with bread and cheese could later be found with mice, the one produced the other. It is obvious to us today that while there is a relationship between bread, cheese, and mice, we know that mice come from mice, not bread and cheese.

To appreciate our sensitivity to a narrative operating system, let's consider how we react to the following discovery, the "new world." I was taught that Columbus sailed the ocean blue in 1492 to discover America, the New World. That story has explanatory power that informs the story of "our" origins. But it matters who is whom in the story since the "new" world wasn't new to people who had already lived there for thousands of years. It is perhaps more "historically true" to say that the Taíno discovered lost and disease-carrying marauders from Spain who were mistakenly dragged up on the shores of the Bahamian Island of Guanahani.[3] It matters who is telling the story and why.

As a final example of the significance of narrative in our lives, let us imagine our position in the narrative by using an image of Earth taken from Space (possible for the first time in my lifetime). One of my spiritual practices, "zooming perspectives," functions like this: From Space, the beauty of a marbled jewel, blue, ochre, and green is breathtaking. Zoomed in, we know that those colors are produced from geological volatility, photosynthesis, and life cycles that include "tragedy" such as disease and "killing" such as predation.

> Breathtaking beauty at one level of zoom is predation and disease from a different level of zoom. They are both true at the same time. The spiritual practice is to appreciate my positionality related to what I perceive as Other. The spiritual mastery is intentionally changing that position by zooming to a different level or merging formerly perceived separateness into oneness.

From the beautiful and distant perspective of the marbled jewel, we do not see the diversity of culture, language, boundaries. Rather, we see our oceans and lands, but we do not see the geo-political lines drawn as they are on a map. For those places familiar to us without the geo-political lines drawn, we can imagine the lines drawn in. Consider this about those lines: We made them up. That does not mean the lines are made up and therefore not "real." The lines are part of human production.

Without those geo-political lines, we could not have land as property. The concept of land as property is not something that has always existed. Hunters and gatherers who foraged across lands would experience a different value proposition for land than farmers who invested their labor into a particular piece of land for a yield. In our modern world of private enterprise economies, private ownership of land as property (especially real estate) is so essential we hardly consider that the whole system is what law and policy says it is. In that sense, "real" estate is not real at all. It is what we agree to say it is. The zoom perspective at which you are operating matters to how you perceive a given circumstance, condition, reality.

Property is defined and defended subject to law, which is a function of the state/nation. But as our satellite imagery proves, nations and property are only real to the extent that they are devised. In other words, "property" is a concept that includes a complex narrative requiring a large cohesion of agreement. "Who has what" makes up a great deal of human activity. Some people go through life attending to "who has what" as their entire sense of identify and purpose. I don't minimize something's importance by saying it is devised; I just seek the clarifying perspective of knowing the difference between a satellite photo of the Earth and a geo-political mapping of the Earth. Both are the Earth, but they are not the same thing. In a sense, both are true. Knowing about both and understanding which is true from which perspective adds a richness to our ability to appreciate and understand.

Let us consider a final note about property in the United States using my family history of property. My childhood included my grandfather John Raymond Burnham, who was beloved by my "civil rights working" mother. The Burnhams lived on land ceded by the Choctaw in the Treaty of Dancing Rabbit Creek in 1831.[4] This treaty quickly followed the Indian Removal Act passed by the U.S. Congress in 1830. This act had been pursued by Andrew Jackson who needed the Choctaw to cede their land for Whites' agricultural production, which relied on slavery. That land, known for generations as Burnham land, had been granted by President Martin Van Buren to an in-law branch of the family: the Butlers.

Butlers married McCabes, who married Burnhams, and the land has remained within a branch of the Burnham family since it was deeded by Martin Van Buren. "Grandaddy" grew up on that land in a family that included his father, Newton Edney Burnham, and uncles who had fought against the United States of America as soldiers for the Confederate States of America (CSA). A key element of that fight sought to preserve a right to property they defined as slaves, essential to the agricultural economy made possible by Andrew Jackson's horrific Indian Removal campaign, the Trail of Tears. My great grandfather and his brothers fought for the CSA to preserve that "right" to property, that "way of life," that "heritage" that Confederate monuments throughout this country exalt.

Far from being American history of the past, this is immediate family consciousness for me—an author living in the present. Who and what does it serve for us to think of the enslavement of human beings as a part of history but not part of our present? My grandfather was raised by veterans of the Confederate States of America, a secessionist enemy of the United States of America. That same grandfather raised my mother who risked her life in the Civil Rights Movement in Mississippi. This not-so-distant past is present *for* and *in* me as much as my family is present for me and in me. It is present in my accent, my recollections, my recipes, traditions, and folkways and in the laws and policies of the present which evolved from precedent.

Multiply this presence across the living American experience and it becomes evident how twisted the logic becomes in order to relegate American slavery to the past. Precisely because it lives in our present without acknowledgement of its truth, without the remedy of redemption and reconciliation, it metastasizes—an inextricable cancer in a diseased body politic, fragile, shaken, triggered so our international enemies do not have to lift a finger against us. So manipulated, trapped, and desperate are some to sustain the rigged advantage of White America for the few by the colluded many, that without it (without rigged advantage equating to the story of America itself) some White Americans would rather burn the house down than live in a United States of America, which is the promise of our unfolding experiment with democracy.

The immediate experience of family memory for most Black Americans is also far from being ancient history. This immediacy, which represents that journey from *being* property to *having* property for Black Americans, has been painfully wracked by rigged advantage sustained for White Americans, embedded in our nation's historical and ongoing definitions of property. Exploited White Americans, desperate to take back "their country," may have complexly constructed reasons for their longings. However, if taking back "their country" means they intend to ensure that the journey of Black Americans from being property to having property is persistently disrupted well into the future, a reckoning must come. **The potential for American greatness in the future cannot coexist with rigged advantage**. Status quo tendency toward that coexistence compromises the security and competitiveness of the United States of America.

> If a "fight for the soul of America" means we want our country back to a steady state of rigged advantage for an elite few at the exploited expense of most other White Americans, and at the marginalized expense of Black Americans and other People of Color through White supremacy and anti-Blackness, that is a fight agendized by an enemy of a United States of America. Reckoning, past due, means that instead of hand-wringing that another Civil War may come, we realize that the Civil War we had lives on like weeds in the garden of democracy, trimmed but never uprooted by truth, reconciliation, and redemption.

The structures upon which our country was built (including those treasured structures that represent the most extraordinary democratic tools civilization has yet experienced) embed insidious dysfunctions that prevent the fullest realization of our democracy's promise. A rigorous assessment is essential to dismantle threats to the promise of American democracy.[5]

Any book proposing a solution to a problem owes the reader a thorough explication of the problem. Since the book has referenced rigged advantage several times, the solution should map to the problem, and the learning outcomes tied to the solution should provide a specific mapping of what the solution to the problem will encompass.

To that end, here is an explication of rigged advantage.

Rigged Advantage Theory: What's the Problem?

We say things like "the rich get richer, and the poor get poorer" and "you can't fight city hall"; then we conclude, "whatta ya gonna do" and "let sleeping dogs lie." Most of us sense that there are others who "pull the strings," not us; but so many of us "struggle to make ends meet" that all we can do is worry that there "ain't no making it." We may not see it. We may not name it. We may not admit it. We may even be defensive when others may criticize it. This gnawing suppressed reality that the system is rigged lives in our language, as idiom, aphorism, colloquialism, and adage. It reveals to us the truth of it even while habituating its normalcy at the same time.

Rigged advantage for the few is normalized, excused, evaded, or mythologized, while any status quo challenge is bamboozled and demonized. The few who benefit from rigged advantage need the rest of us distracted, turned against each other. Our historical fault lines of race prove to be ideal fodder. However, throughout our history, there are times when the rigged advantage few "overplay their hand" and the many rest of us find "desperation makes strange bedfellows."

Increasingly, strange bedfellows hold two things to be true at the same time:

1. We love our country, especially for what it aspires to be.
2. We know that our country's aspirations are more realizable for some than others. That's both un-American (as an ideal) but so American (in the lived experience of far too many, including many White Americans).

Our time feels especially tumultuous, but the tumult is proportional to what is needed. I believe we are in the crucible our ancestors hoped for us. Out of this crucible, the United States of America will become a meritocracy where justice, then liberty for all, ensures our best days ahead. Autocracy concentrates power in the hands of the few, and they experience an almost divine right-of-kings entitlement to their inheritance. The rigged advantage few would rather burn the house down than cede any ground. They can bamboozle the rest of us to turn on each other to sustain their entitlement for only so long.

This insidious rigged advantage has masqueraded as a great "America" for too long. The masquerade is increasingly revealed for what it is. Many are becoming increasingly equipped to ensure that our country's stated aspirations are finally realized. Democracy has not failed as much as we have not tried it yet. Our awakening has come.

Many of us want to "do something" but we don't know exactly what to do. We sense that the rigged part of things has got to go, but where do we start? It is not the responsibility of those targeted by a rigged system to fix it. Since the few for whom things have been rigged are overwhelmingly White, (even at the expense of many other White Americans) *Twelve Steps for White America* presents steps all White Americans can take to unshackle the past, strengthen global security and U.S. competitiveness, and make way for all so our best days are yet to come.

Since *Twelve Steps for White America* presents steps for a solution, it begs the question, "Exactly what is the problem that needs a solution?"

Rigged Advantage Theory (RAT) details the problem. RAT could be considered a theory of power in a lineage of power theories presented in sociology studies. Traditional theories of power in sociological theory identify who has the upper hand in a given context. Literature reviews of power theories show that race is incidental, if referenced at all. Academia is littered with a whitewash of erudite scholarship that either ignores the elephant in the room or presumes to account for race unnamed within other variables.

Rigged Advantage Theory identifies an interpretation of power specific to the United States of America, which *centers race* in its explication of how power is reproduced.

Rigged Advantage Theory does not ignore the historical fact that all White, Anglo Saxon, property-owning, straight, abled, "religious freedom" men are created equal in our founding aspirational hopes for liberty and the pursuit of happiness. We console ourselves with the idea that we are working toward a more perfect union, while "nattering nabobs of negativism" are marginalized as those who do not love America. That very marginalization is a key strategy of preserving power for those who already have it.

A recent example preposterously drags Critical Race Theory (CRT) out of the academic closet as proof that something bad is happening to America simply by accounting for the role race continues to exert in present power dynamics. To equate an accounting of the role that slave labor had in proliferating colonial and so-called postcolonial prosperity with race-baiting Marxist indoctrination (as is the current hysterical fashion of those whose power feels tenuous) is tortuous at best. At its worst, it is a glaring example of what existing power will do (or exploit others to do) to fend off any threat to its stranglehold. Even to these standard bearers, CRT is a scapegoat for the problem of controlling a narrative that has traditionally sustained status quo rigged advantage.

Today it is CRT, but in my lifetime it has also been Freedom Riders, Martin Luther King, Jr., Malcolm X, hippies, the Student Violent Coordinating Committee, feminists, queers, immigrants—the list is quite long and includes conspiracies that the Catholic Church is the whore of Babylon, the Elders of Zion are secretly running a global cabal manipulating world puppet strings, and the Black Panther Party should be subjected to the FBI's COINTELPRO operation. All this looking at the Other versus looking at the actual problem, has a long history in America illustrated by bamboozling.

Key terms for rigged advantage are defined as follows:

Rigged advantage: By design, the entitlements, rights, benefits, privileges, afforded by American citizenship accrue disproportionately to a select group of people whose wealth and power are self-reproducing and anti-democratic. What is presented as a meritocracy where justice makes peace and liberty makes prosperity is actually an autocracy that sustains its power for elite power Whites through the collusion of exploited whites who must displace their subjective experience of exploitation using White supremacy and anti-Blackness to marginalize dissent and dismantle any threat to the status quo.

Whiteness: The value afforded to perceived inclusion in the socially constructed category of White identity. Whiteness masquerades as solidarity but actualizes within-group exploitation. By colluding in Whiteness, exploited Whites align with power Whites for derivative and tenuous value, which is embedded in social constructs of race.

Power Whites: The elite group of people whose wealth and power self-reproduce are disproportionately White but comprise a very small percentage of all Whites. They depend on exploiting all Whites (including each other) to collude with the presumption that any Whiteness has value even if a majority of White Americans are exploited by power Whites. It is the presumption of value for Whiteness that enables a *power Whites and exploited Whites collusion of Whiteness,* where exploited Whites are co-opted against their self-interest to sustain status quo benefit for power Whites. The tenuous trickle-down value of Whiteness accrues to exploited Whites through mechanisms such as exemption from the marginalization of Othering that operates as White supremacy and anti-Blackness.

Exploited Whites: The majority of White Americans whose socially constructed racial identity aligns them with all whites and includes a shared ideology with power Whites that Whiteness has inherent value. By aligning with power Whites, the sheer number of exploited Whites (e.g., voting block) is co-opted by power Whites to sustain the status quo even when the status quo oppresses exploited Whites.

The delusion enabling exploited whites to experience the value of whiteness versus their subjective exploitation, persists through two strategies:

1. White supremacy
2. anti-Blackness

White supremacy: An ideology that operationalizes social reinforcement for the value of Whiteness. Many people conflate White supremacy and anti-Blackness. In Rigged Advantage Theory, one can think of White supremacy as a noun and anti-Blackness as a verb. White supremacy (noun) is an ideological identity affiliation, which may manifest subconsciously without intent. Actions (verb) that derive from White supremacy can include anti-Blackness.

Anti-Blackness: Consciously unable to identify and acknowledge their own exploitation by power Whites (ego-dystonic), exploited Whites will displace their subjective exploitation onto those perceived as non-White, including Black, Indigenous, and other People of Color. Examples include racelighting, voter suppression, and living legacies of slavery, including minority rule, state-sanctioned violence, disproportionate incarceration, and disparate outcomes in education, generational wealth, health, economic and social mobility.

Discussion

One focus group presented with Rigged Advantage Theory found the concept of "exploited Whites" objectionable since it appears to give cover for unacceptable behaviors. To better understand the concept of exploited Whites in Rigged Advantage Theory, consider, for example, another extreme oppressed/oppressor dynamic, that of domestic violence where a dominant spouse abuses their spouse. In the context of mental health treatment, we do not explore the abuser's family history of growing up in a violent home as an excuse for their inexcusable behavior. We consider it (when applicable) because we are trying to fully understand the problem/disorder to treat it and prevent it. Likewise, when exploited Whites displace their subjective exploitation onto Black, Indigenous, and other People of Color using White supremacy and anti-Blackness, that too is of course inexcusable, but understanding its mechanics can inform what to dismantle and how to do it.

Exploitation is a term used in traditional criticisms of laissez faire capitalism. Further extrapolated is the term *subjective exploitation*, postulated in the paper by Deranty.[6] Deranty's brilliant paper explains exploitation not from the standpoint of the capitalists who are exploiting, and he digs deeper by shifting the analysis to a discussion of the experience of those who are exploited and how they are impacted. Rigged Advantage Theory does not use the term *exploitation*, but specifically the term *subjective exploitation*.

A paper by psychoanalyst Beverly J. Stoute[7] provides an exceptional review of race in psychoanalysis as a profession and details the specifics of displacement in the context of racialized narratives in the United States, especially within her profession.

Her review informs how I differentiate two defense mechanisms, displacement versus projection, in a racialized America:

1. Displacement means that exploited Whites cannot acknowledge their exploitation; therefore, they transmute that reality—what is done to them is done by them to others (othering)—and it is therefore displaced. (Understanding how displacement functions helps to explain why exploited Whites will vote against their own interests to receive the derivative value of Whiteness afforded to them by power Whites.)
2. Different from displacement, where the unacceptable is not even conscious, projection is when the unacceptable reality is conscious but cannot be owned. It is not ego-**syn**tonic. It is ego-**dys**tonic (self distant). In other words, it *is* but it is not me; it is you. That happens often in racist America. However, projection does not explain how the strategies of White supremacy and anti-Blackness operationalize. Rigged Advantage Theory, which proposes that a collusion of Whiteness, where power Whites trigger exploited Whites' need for the displacement of subjective exploitation, has explanatory power for how the rules of White supremacy and anti-Blackness work in America.

In summary, RAT explains how rigged advantage operates, why it operates, who the players are, how Whiteness differs from White supremacy, how a majority of Whites vote against their own self interest, why it feels crazy to many Americans (displacement is a psychological defense mechanism), how it sustains class oppression, and it outlines the economic motivation. Because of rigged advantage, democracy hasn't so much failed as we haven't really tried it yet.

How do we apply what we have operationalized as RAT? How do we as individuals weed our plots in the garden of democracy? Where do we begin to actualize truth, reconciliation, and redemption? We exist together at this point in time, but we did not spontaneously generate. We emerge from our genealogy. Basic genealogy identifies who is in our family tree. That alone enriches our sense of being linked across time. Richer still is understanding that our ancestors were products of their time. The choices they made in the context of their challenges and opportunities are the reason we are here. Our sense-making operating systems by definition include our inheritance from the contextualization of our family trees. This journey of inheritance includes the "baggage" created and used along the way. The story of us is enriched by understanding these elements of context and what sense has been made of the choices our forbearers made in the contexts of challenges and opportunities they faced. Who had/has charge of those stories (narrative operating systems then and now) informs how we interpret our family history.

At this point, many may be overwhelmed, thinking "I have no idea where to start with all of that! I am doing the best I can to get by in extraordinary times, and I would need help." Take heart. Help is the intention of this book. The framework of the book is crafted out of a tradition that acknowledges how overwhelming change can be. That is precisely why we take it "one day at a time." We practice first things first in order to just do the next right thing. Twelve steps are specific digestible actions an individual can work on. The fourth step is admittedly tough for alcoholics in recovery. The fourth step here is admittedly tough for Americans who are committed to putting rigged advantage in context to eliminate it.

Tough though it may be, there are no shortcuts. For alcoholics, taking an easy way out of the fourth step virtually guarantees that the "wreckage of the past" will trigger relapse. Likewise, unless the category of White Americans (which has disproportionately been advantaged in a rigged advantage system) clears out the wreckage of our past through truth, reconciliation, and redemption, we cannot be entitled to expect our best days to be ahead of us.

There is even more reason to take heart regarding the difficult work of the fourth step. This book is written in conjunction with a related workbook. The workbook includes a special feature presented for the first time, the *contextualized family history assessment*.

Developed and presented by the professor and author whose groundbreaking work on critical family history is transforming genealogy, National Academy of Education member Christine Sleeter charts and analyzes lineage using contextualized inquiry.

This inquiry illuminates how power, privilege, and marginalization manifest for individual White Americans (and for the social institutions that serve a Whiteness-colluded agenda) to sustain rigged advantage.

The work of the fourth step is introduced here, but the work is explicitly charted in the related workbook.

> Sleeter writes:
>
> As a white person, I was seeking a conceptual framework that situates one's family and its history within a wider analysis of social power relationships and culture. White people, especially those of middle-class status and above, tend to think of ourselves and our stories in individualistic terms. But since who we are involves not just the work of individuals, but also how individuals' lives were shaped by

local culture and power relationships across generations, I wanted a framework that would illuminate the social contexts of family lives, and that would help to unearth memories we have lost. In a nutshell, critical family history challenges historians to ask about their ancestors: Who else (what other groups) was around, What were the power relationships among groups, How were these relationships maintained or challenged over time, and What does all this have to do with our lives now?[8]

If for no other reason than to manage your work on step 4, I highly recommend that you get the workbook that accompanies this book. The workbook provides tools designed to support your exploration and learning for each step, but that is especially true for step 4. Step 4 for recovering alcoholics is one of the most painstaking and painful but rewarding experiences of the recovery process.

For anyone working on *Twelve Steps for White America*, the workbook will be essential to guide exploration into your family history. You, your circumstances, your family, your community, your nation, all comprise various levels of perspective and engagement. Having all the tools you need will make your work on these steps more manageable at each perspective.

Learning Outcome

Identify, analyze, and categorize specific knowledge, skills, and abilities rooted in Whiteness-affiliated rigged advantage.

PART II
02

RECONCILIATION

12 STEPS for WHITE AMERICA
IN A NUTSHELL

PART ONE STEPS 1 - 4	PART TWO STEPS 5 - 8	PART THREE STEPS 9 - 12
TRUTH	RECONCILIATION	RENEWAL
REPENTENCE	ATONEMENT	REDEMPTION
Stop, turn.	Make things right.	Live democracy's promise.
Unshackle the past.	Strengthen U.S. security & global competitiveness.	Make way for all so our best days are ahead of us.

Strengthen U.S. Security and Global Competitiveness

Introduction to Steps 5–8

In Part I of the book, we reviewed the simplicity of steps 1 through 4.

We admit there is a problem.

We believe something can be done about that problem.

We make a decision to do something about that problem.

We get to know the problem.

Part I demonstrates that we already know *how* to do what needs to be done for a United States of America. Not only do we know how, but we also actually already know a great deal of *what* needs to be done. Because freedom is not free, each of us has a part to play to ensure the promises of our great democratic republic. In each of us, part of the problem and part of the solution manifests, whether we intend it or not, whether we have given it a second thought, or whether it concerns us at all. Ideally, we are free **in** a democracy, not free *from* it. If everyone were a "free-rider" there would be nothing to ride.

Problem solving is universal across human cultures or we would not have made it this far. For solving problems in any language across the spectrum of humanity, we start by telling the truth. Then, we stop and turn from (known since ancient history as repentance) what does not work toward what works. We cut ties to what does not work to utilize what works and manage the risk of unnecessary relearning, which threatens evolving progress. For the problem of cutting ties to rigged advantage in a divided United States, I use the potent and painful language that we must unshackle the past.

This is very simple:

Truth (be honest).

Stop, turn (quit doing it).

Unshackle the past (move on).

Simple but not easy, is it?

While it may not be easy, it truly *is not complicated.*

If it is simple, not complicated, and we solve problems every day, *what about this problem proves resistant?*

Now that you have completed reading about steps 1 through 4, you may be able to see that we are taking on a very big problem by dividing it into pieces. We are literally taking this one step at a time. While the ingredients of this problem-solving process are nothing new, the recipe's directions in this book outline a very important problem-solving process as practiced by recovering alcoholics, human beings whose lives have been trapped, hijacked onto a trajectory of being locked up (prison), or covered up (grave).

PART I, Steps 1–4

Everyday Problem-Solving Process	Application to Rigged Advantage
There is a problem.	1. We admit our problem: rigged advantage.
Something can be done about the problem.	2. We believe something can be done.
I want something to be done about the problem.	3. We decide to act.
What exactly is the problem?	4. We detail the problem.

This summarizes Part I; working steps 1 through 4 is primarily an *inward process of discovery.*

Part II prepares your discovery to *venture outward*.

Here is an overview to the next four steps:

PART II, Steps 5–8

Everyday Problem-Solving Process	Application to Rigged Advantage
Okay. Got it. This is a problem.	5. We present the problem.
Now that I get it, I choose to change it.	6. We resolve to change.
I want to replace the old behavior with the new.	7. We humbly turn toward change.
Others have been impacted.	8. We identify the harm.

Steps 5 through 8 build on the inward discovery and establish a pathway outward toward the "Other," what we perceive to be separate from "us," both as individuals and the group with which we identify.

Step 5 can be thought of as a confessional, coming clean, getting honest, a rehearsal of what you discover, clarifying or refining ideas by hearing them out loud. "Music" to our ears is a saying we have because we more fully learn and understand something when what we have learned is not just an idea, it is something heard and presented back to us. By this extension, it becomes authenticated, validated, and reinforced. We have many expressions related to this phenomenon. We come clean. We get it off our chest. We unburden ourselves. A weight is lifted off our shoulders. Confession is good for the soul.

Step 6 is a resolution about what you do now that you have come this far in the process. As we all know from our years of "New Year resolutions," a resolution represents an intention, something necessary but insufficient. An intention does not achieve the outcome of the resolve, but there is no result without it.

Step 7 is a getting-started step. Step 7 is the first step toward a future now made possible by your progress: (a) truth, (b) belief, (c) will, (d) inventory, (e) expression, (f) resolution, (g) start, (h) account.

Step 8 is where some sobriety arrives and begins for the storm-shelter family we mentioned earlier. Instead of the alcoholic emerging from the storm cellar after a tornado and surveying the damage with the proclamation "Ain't it grand the wind stopped blowing," the alcoholic has worked the steps sufficiently to now ask the question, "Who has been impacted by the wreckage of my stormy life, and how?"

Astute readers will notice that we are already over half-way through the steps, and we are still only preparing to do something: Work toward a solution for the problem of rigged advantage.

While the following quote is often attributed to Mohandas K. Gandhi, he may have not said it, at least not exactly this way. Still, the quote matters here in an important way. "Be the change you wish to see in the world." Earlier, we said that in each of us, part of the problem and part of the solution manifests whether we intend it or not, whether we have given it a second thought, or whether it concerns us at all. Here, we elaborate on what we mean. The title of this book specifically says for a United States of America. The intended result is not an individual result; it is a collective result. While the intended result is a collective result, we get there one individual at a time, one step at a time.

When we consider the problem of rigged advantage, "that" is a problem that may appear to be bigger than me, "this." Here is where the wisdom of "be the change" really matters. For "that" (rigged advantage) to change, I, "this," must change. The steps outlined in the book are provided as a pathway for each of us, "this" to impact "that," so that we strengthen our democracy, make us safer, and ensure our global competitiveness in a very diverse world, far into the future.

Reconciliation may follow forgiveness. When a person has been aggrieved, the long journey to forgiveness, if achieved at all, achieves more for the forgiver than the forgiven. Ultimately, we practice forgiveness that we may be free—free from the burden of cementing the infliction's persistence. Like a ball and chain broken free, forgiveness unlocks the fixation on what happened. It releases the recurring damage that the closed feedback loop perpetuates. Any benefit that

76 | Twelve Steps for White America

> It may be worth an aside here for anyone who has ever wished for more change from White America; the result you may be seeking is step 9 in the process. At this point in the 12 steps of problem solving, we are still working on steps 1 through 8. Look at all the work involved in these eight steps. I am writing the book, so we get results. But I am not underestimating the steps of change needed before the impact of step 9 is realized for a United States of America. For deep and lasting change, the work of these steps must run deep and wide. The greatest chance is if we all have an understanding of the steps that are needed for lasting results.

accrues to the forgiven pales by comparison to the renewal of life forgivers come to know. But before renewal, reconciliation must come; before reconciliation, truth.

Reconciliation, like forgiveness, occurs between at least two parties, a reconciler and the reconciled, two sides of the same coin. Or, put another way, at this intense crossroads in our nation's history, in order for history to not repeat itself, it would be worth remembering Abraham Lincoln's speech to the 1858 Illinois Republican State Convention:

> A house divided against itself, cannot stand.
>
> I believe this government cannot endure permanently half slave and half free.
>
> I do not expect the Union to be dissolved —
>
> I do not expect the house to fall —
>
> but I do expect it will cease to be divided.
>
> It will become all one thing or all the other.

The words of Lincoln (passed through history from Jesus, Augustus, Paine, Hobbes) provide a clarion call to our future as a nation. We have not yet determined which side of the house will stand and endure. We must decide. In our mythology, we say we made that decision. But facts remain. If the American experiment is like a garden growing justice then liberty for all, then the legacies of slavery, including racism, are like weeds whose roots propagate overgrowth choking out the harvest of democracy. Trimming this overgrowth, without uprooting the weeds, never relieves the threat.

Years after the first arrival of enslaved human beings exploited for their labor to fuel an economy of a global power, we must pull the weeds by the roots. More than any *external* threat against which we have rallied, this internal threat is arguably the most existential since it is already here, metastasizing like an untreated cancer. Plantation slavery profited a wealthy few off the backs of slave labor, a system that relied on a collusion of power Whites exploiting other Whites who displaced subjective exploitation using White supremacy and anti-Blackness. Nominally, we no longer operate our economy with plantation slavery, but elements of that operationalization persist to this day. We must tell the truth. Here is precisely where we must ask ourselves, if problem solving is something replicable, something which we do every day,

What about this problem of rigged advantage (which persists from plantation slavery) proves so resistant?

This question necessitates two additional questions, which we must practice throughout the steps:

- *Who benefits from the problem?*
- *How do I wittingly or unwittingly contribute to this problem?*

Many White Americans think of White supremacy as something prevalent in the past and even associate the term with terrorist organizations that have infamously wielded power throughout American history. White Americans of a certain age have seen improvements in representation, improvements toward income equality, and even look to the election of the first biracial president as a major indicator of the progress the nation has experienced. A culture embedded with centuries of rigged advantage leaves too many White Americans ill-equipped to not only estimate even unintentional impact on marginalized others, but also left ill-equipped to estimate the spiritual cost to our own liberation burdened by the karmic debt we carry. What may have seemed normalized in the Whiteness fog of White supremacy is actually a threat to the future of our democracy.

For our own liberation and for the survival of the American experiment with democracy, White America must reckon with reality as the fog lifts more slowly for some than others. Indicators that matter to the pursuit of liberty and justice show that White Americans have a different set of advantages than Black Americans. You personally may not intend that to be the case, but the fact of it remains. This book is a call to our responsibility in these circumstances. It is also a call to grace, which holds promise for your personal liberation from generations gnarled in an oppressed–oppressor dynamic from which you may break free.

Any hint of real change that threatens status quo rigged advantage triggers a "cut White nose off to spite White face" phenomenon, which Heather McGhee illustrates in her book, *The Sum of Us*. Rather than swim in a civic pool with Black Americans, fill in the swimming pool with dirt so no one swims in the pool. That actually happened in my lifetime in Forest, Mississippi, and across the United States.[1] This knee-jerk tendency remains with us, but we must not conclude that the United States is a failed state where democracy did not work. To the contrary, I believe we are closer than we have ever been in perfecting this experiment with democracy. It is precisely because we are edging closer to a meritorious, race-neutral republic that bamboozling is at an all-time high. This is the same backlash at work now across generations. The more potentiated change becomes, the more opposition reverberates across the culture to shut it down.

CASE STUDY: YOU CAN'T HANDLE THE TRUTH!

Rigged Advantage Demands That Critiques Exposing Rigged Advantage Must Be Demonized

Chair of the Joint Chiefs of Staff, Army General Mark Milley, and a congressman at a congressional hearing

A congressman (while under investigation for sex trafficking of a minor)[2] railed against General Milley for so-called woke elements infiltrating and demoralizing our troops. Joint Chiefs of Staff Chair Army Gen. Mark Milley (June 23, 2021) said it was important for service members to understand critical race theory, shooting down assertions by Republican lawmakers that studying the topic was harmful to military cohesion. In an impromptu and passionate statement, Milley at a House Armed Service Committee[3] hearing rejected the assertion that critical race theory and other such teaching could be damaging, telling lawmakers the following:

> First of all, on the issue of critical race theory, et cetera, I'll obviously have to get much smarter on whatever the theory is, but I do think it's important actually for those of us in uniform to be open-minded and be widely read. And the United States Military Academy is a university, and it is important that we train, and we understand. And I want to understand white rage and I'm white, and I want to understand it. So, what is it that caused thousands of people to assault this building and try to overturn the constitution of the United States of America? What caused that? I want to find that out. I want to maintain an open mind here, and I do want to analyze it. It's important that we understand that because our soldiers, sailors, airmen, Marines, and guardians, they come from the American people. So, it is important that the leaders now and, in the future, do understand it.
>
> I've read Karl Marx. I've read Lenin. That doesn't make me a communist. So, what is wrong with understanding, having some situational understanding about the country for which we are here to defend? And I personally find it offensive that we are accusing the United States military, our general officers, our commissioned, non-commissioned officers of being quote "woke" or something else because we're studying some theories that are out there. That was started at Harvard Law School

(Continued)

years ago. And it proposed that there were laws in the United States, antebellum laws prior to the Civil War that led to a power differential with African Americans that were three quarters of a human being when this country was formed. And then we had a Civil War and Emancipation Proclamation to change it. And we brought it up to the Civil Rights Act of 1964. It took another a hundred years to change that. So, look, I do want to know, and I respect your service. And you and I are both Green Berets, but I want to know, and it matters to our military and the discipline and cohesion of this military. And I thank you for the opportunity to make a comment on that.

Analysis

In this riveting exchange during a hearing in Congress with cameras rolling, the congressman parrots the cotemporaneous iteration of culture war roadkill, which may appear to be scraping the bottom of the barrel of distraction until you appreciate what exactly is happening. The topic of this iteration is an academic theory from my doctoral studies over 10 years ago, which was already 30 years old at the time.[4]

The congressman attempts to lure General Milley (both of whom are Green Berets) into the **bamboozle theater**. This is an old tactic.

Don't look at that,

look at this!

It is an abomination that threatens our nation!

This tactic uses blood for sharks to feed upon, while what is really happening persists to benefit a rigged advantage agenda.

In the guise of concern for military cohesion and readiness, the congressman attempts to bait General Milley on the record for how CRT not only teaches White children to hate themselves (one of the accusations that would later help oust a Democrat governor of Virginia and replace him with a Republican governor),[5] but that CRT has infiltrated our military academies where now our troops languish as a result. This blood for sharks is that not only is CRT coming after our children, CRT is ruining our troops. Our children and our troops!

In the bamboozle theater of this congressional hearing, General Milley's poise and eloquence reflect a historical and venerable "American sensibility." The congressman used his position to fuel the hysterical, hateful, and threatening protests against the alleged threat posed by

CRT. (Railing against CRT gets him a better headline than "Sex-Trafficking Investigation.")

With this blood in the cultural water, stoked for political purposes, this CRT threat erupted at school board meetings around the country, eruptions that reflect another "American sensibility."

Both sensibilities reflect the United States of America. We are a country of both of these sensibilities at the same time.

1. We are better than this, aspirationally.
2. We are not better than this, practically.

We are this tumultuous amalgam, which even a Civil War did not settle.

General Milley's posturing says,

The state restricting what can be taught at an institution of higher learning is not the nation that he is defending against enemies foreign and domestic.

The congressman's posturing says,

We will be burn down the house if it doesn't suit the agenda of rigged advantage.

This house divided served the sole purpose of sustaining rigged advantage early in our country's history (the very reason Whiteness was invented), and it lives on in the present today.

CASE STUDY: RESTORATIVE JUSTICE

Bishop Desmond Tutu

In 1984 the Nobel Peace Prize was awarded to Desmond Tutu, archbishop of the Anglican Church in South Africa, for his work in opposition to apartheid. He was the chair of the Truth and Reconciliation Commission, charged with hearing evidence of human rights violations under White rule, and led the Truth and Reconciliation Commission of South Africa.

According to the 1998 Truth and Reconciliation Commission Report,

> One of the main tasks of the Commission was to uncover as much as possible of the truth about past gross violations of human rights—a difficult and often very unpleasant task. The Commission was founded, however, in the belief that this task

(Continued)

was necessary for the promotion of reconciliation and national unity. In other words, the telling of the truth about past gross human rights violations, as viewed from different perspectives, facilitates the process of understanding our divided pasts, whilst the public acknowledgement of 'untold suffering and injustice' (Preamble to the Act) helps to restore the dignity of victims and afford perpetrators the opportunity to come to terms with their own past.[6]

From South Africa to Oakland,[7] restorative justice has elements in common.

According to Zehr,[8] in restorative justice, the questions are as follows:

1. Who has been hurt?
2. What are their needs?
3. Whose obligations are these?
4. What are the causes?
5. Who has a stake in the situation?
6. What is the appropriate process to involve stakeholders in an effort to address causes and put things right?

In contrast, traditional criminal justice asks:

1. What laws have been broken?
2. Who did it?
3. What do the offender(s) deserve?

Analysis

The United States of America has never experienced anything like South Africa's Truth and Reconciliation Commission. For example, many people were just becoming aware of the Tulsa Massacre during the period when I was writing this book. The outrage that White Americans experience when our racial history is exposed knee-jerks the bamboozle theater with such fury that we never get to the truth much less the reconciliation. Rather than our children (and us) learning about what Black Americans have experienced and are experiencing now, we gin up hysterics at local school board meetings, inflamed that our White children are being taught to hate themselves. Where is the similar report for the United States? Who has ever said to Black Americans, your painful history is not only acknowledged but a debt must be paid?

The case example of General Milley illustrates the security risks rigged advantage poses for our nation. His desire to understand what happened on January 6, 2021, signals that he comprehends that in the digital age,

- internal fault lines may be aggravated by external forces without having to fire a shot;
- there are security risks to the United States from within by those who have long equated the United States with rigged advantage. As the January 6, 2021, insurrection demonstrates, they are willing to attack the USA to sustain rigged advantage.

The case of Bishop Tutu illustrates what has never happened in the United States to mitigate fault lines that threaten our national security from both foreign and domestic enemies. Truth and reconciliation have yet to lance a festered wound that infects our present and compromises our future.

In Part II, let us consider not only issues related to national security, but global competitiveness.

What is the future competitiveness of rigged advantage in

1. global markets where capital is increasingly managed by people of color, and
2. global markets where trends and innovation are less concentrated among Western consumers conditioned to the rigged advantage of the United States?

Since Whiteness so far has coalesced sufficient numbers to sustain rigged advantage, demographic projections surely project a demise of the Whiteness coalition at some point in the future.

When will rigged advantage lose its value?

Since Whiteness *is privileged to be unaware of itself and therefore ill-equipped to project related impacts*, it is unlikely capable of answering such a futurist question before it is too late. Once, drinking worked for alcoholics. Still, rigged advantage works for an elite few. How much longer? I pray this book hastens the day.

Also, given the extraordinary talent in the diverse pipeline already, it may be "too late" already. From the vantage point of higher education today, I can say the future is very bright. Today's students hardly care for any of the baggage of rigged advantage. They exude a natural revulsion to marginalization. They readily construct diverse teams for problem solving. They value multiple perspectives since that makes them more competitive and productive. I cringe when pundits criticize them as snowflakes couched in safe spaces. Believe that stereotype at your peril. You may be best served to anticipate smart, fast, inclusive catalyzers who reach a goal together before the competition has a chance. They will be competitive in global markets when rigged advantage lingers as an albatross.

Capital, norms, skills, abilities, and networks honed out of rigged advantage will become increasingly obsolete as rigged advantage loses value. Since minority rule can sustain rigged advantage past its competitiveness, demographic changes will not be sufficient to extinguish the dinosaur, but minority rule cannot hold forever. The question becomes, "How long can Whiteness hold its value as a collusion to sustain rigged advantage?" How long? Not long!

CHAPTER 5

STEP 5
WE PRESENT THE PROBLEM

Step 5 Governs Step 11: We Choose Reverence

Key Words: **Findings, Confession, Expression, Relief**

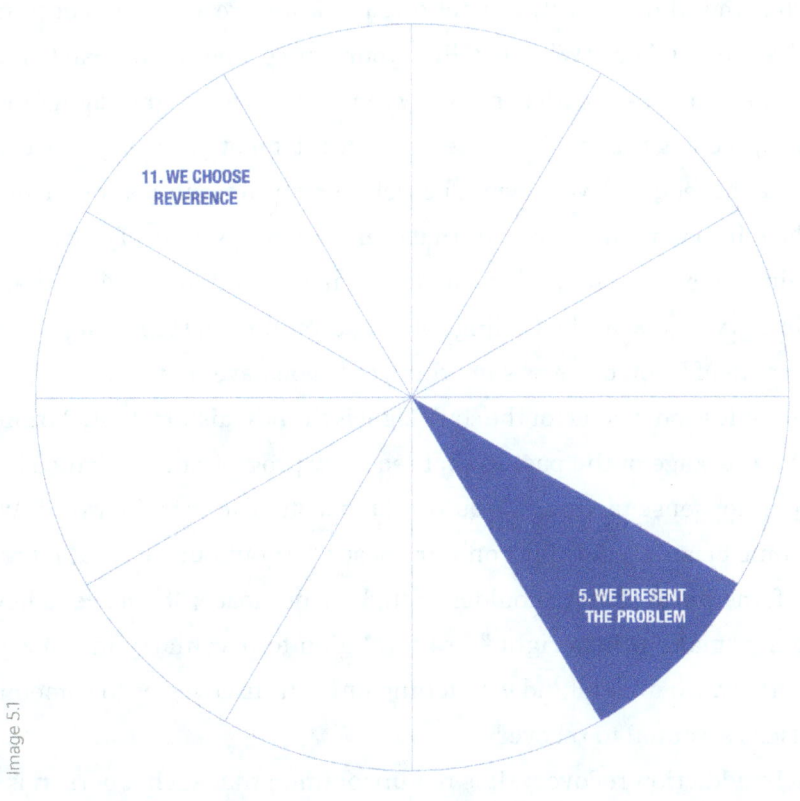

Image 5.1

What I Learned From Alcoholics About the Fifth Step of AA

> *"Admitted to God, to ourselves, and to another human being, the exact nature of our wrongs."*[1]

The AA Big Book describes the first five steps as building an arch through which "we shall walk a free man at last."[2] About step 5 itself, the AA *Twelve Steps and Twelve Traditions* says that scarcely any step is more necessary to longtime sobriety and peace of mind than this one. Step 5 actualizes a degree of humility that "amounts to a clear recognition of what and who we really are, followed by a sincere attempt to become what we could be."[3] Without telling your story to another human being, your self-assessed path to recovery remains largely your imagination. Also, keeping this inside enables you (the arbiter of the mess you are in) to be the feedback you keep. The well-known communication theory, the Johari window,[4] shows us that there are things none of us can see, things only I can see, things only you can see, and things we can see. Unless we present the findings of our account from step 4, step 4 will remain of limited use as something only you have seen.

Confession is good for the soul. Light is the best disinfectant. Purging the wreckage of the past so that recovery progress has a chance is a commonsense tactic and a cultural touchstone across the world. We "come clean"; "get things off our chest"; "air out our dirty laundry"; "lift the world off our shoulders"; "lighten our load"; "turn over a new leaf"; "make things right." From religion to psychiatry in the 21st century, we understand why telling our self-discoveries to someone else is essential to recovery.

In addiction recovery, it is not uncommon that such a person is a religious leader (pastor, priest, rabbi, imam) or a counselor. The ideal listener understands the process of a person admitting there is a problem, believing something can be done about that problem, wanting something to be done about that problem, and detailing in writing exactly what the problem is. The listener serves as a springboard who can ask questions that may help the person clarify content, validate when appropriate, or nudge for digging deeper when it may appear a person arrived premature from an inadequate effort to prepare for step 5.

The rigorous accounting of step 4 must be presented. What is the point of producing a report if findings are not disseminated? Discoveries cannot remain hidden. Steps 5, 6, and 7 include language at which some may balk. "Nature of our wrongs" and "defects of character" are ways of expressing that what is dysfunctional must be made functional or removed.

What of This May We Apply to Our Problem, Rigged Advantage?

Imagine if we took a personal inventory and took pains to perfect that accounting. For examples other than rigged advantage or alcoholism, imagine for any of the following:

- We caught a malignancy early, but did nothing else
- We identified foundation cracks, but did nothing else
- We observed a crop infestation, but did nothing else
- We exposed electrical fire hazards, but did nothing else
- We engaged an entire organization in robust strategic planning, documented some brilliant planning, but left the strategic plan on the shelf

This is the equivalent of completing the fourth step without a fifth step.

You have done the work of the fourth step. It is time that we take the fifth step. We do this individually and collectively. It is worth bearing in mind a process note for our progress.

The spiritual practice of zooming between levels of objective focus becomes increasingly vital in practicing these steps. It facilitates our ability to use the recovery model at both an individual and societal level. In addiction recovery, we experience mortally urgent motivation for our individual work. The serenity prayer reinforces discernment that most of what can be changed is within us. Yet, almost transcendentally, the recovery group's striving in common, itself, becomes a higher power where individual intent manifests exponentially across a social network. This becomes a strong example of why step 5 step governs complementary step 11. The work accomplished individually in step 5, enables the collective in AA's step 11 to pray only for God's will for us and for the power to accomplish that will.

As we continue now applying these recovery principles to a nation, remember that there is work I do and there is work we do. The recovery work I do, even when it is absolutely for me alone, ripples its effect. This is precisely the import of the saying; you must be the change you wish to see in the world. We plant seeds. We tend to germination. We reap a harvest seemingly more abundant than seed could have imagined. The work we do individually invests in our presence at the societal level. We will continue now to "farm" step 5.

Rigged advantage remains like a weed rooted in our garden of democracy. This is precisely why rigged advantage persists as a legacy of slavery to this day. Kudzu will teach us why we work both individually and collectively. Most Southerners can talk about kudzu, usually with wide-eyed animated wonder! Kudzu is the "vine that ate the South." This invasive species is a vine first brought to the United States from Japan and Southeast China in 1876 to be featured as an ornamental at the Philadelphia Centennial Exposition. The U.S. Soil Conservation Service used it in the 1930s–1950s for erosion control. The problem with kudzu is that it grows up to a foot per day to lengths up to 100 feet.[5] Kudzu vines will cover everything in its wake acres at a time, including buildings and forests.

Kudzu has a lot in common with rigged advantage.

Both are an import that first appealed as useful then outcompeted the ecology as an invasive, out-of-control chokehold cascading throughout the ecosystem.

James Miller from the U.S. Forest Service at Auburn, Alabama, says that "for eradication, every kudzu plant in and around a patch must be killed or the spread from any surviving plants can make all prior efforts and investments useless. This means that landowners sharing a patch must arrange to treat the whole patch simultaneously."[6]

As a nation, like landowners who share a patch of kudzu, we must collectively commit to ridding rigged advantage. This is the vision of *Twelve Steps for White America* to serve as a rigged advantage eradication framework, where we can reach across our divides to solve a common problem.

Remember, when alcoholics complete this step, it is often accomplished with a counselor or religious advisor in private who understands the context and purpose. While that applies to individuals, we must coalesce our individual work to ultimately do this work as a nation. The effectiveness with which we accomplish this step as a nation will be proportional to the work each of us accomplishes individually. This individual reporting of the accounting that has been accomplished in step 4 must compound to a tipping point sufficient to change the present course of this nation, where rigged advantage, like kudzu run amok, chokes out the hopes of our democratic future.

In step 5, we shift from stifling selfish egocentric entanglements to mastering rewarding and dynamic relationships. We extend ourselves into a larger community. We understand there is a cost to us personally when negative actions toward and about "others" compromise our own extension, our enlargement, our transcendence. We begin to shift the "miraculous" from something foreign to us to something that catalyzes within us. We choose reverence so reverence chooses us. This simultaneity becomes a "pearl of great price." What we may have sought to repair for others' sakes we come to realize we repair for our sakes. For those who believe it is going to take a miracle to achieve a United States of America, I agree! That miracle germinates within us. The greatness of our potentiated democracy germinates across the plantings of generations. Please hear a southern country redneck tell you some farmer's wisdom, "Don't curse your seed." There is a period between planting and sprouting where we must have faith in things unseen! Honor the investments of generations of ancestors with what you believe is possible, with what you are willing to do to clear out the wreckage of the past, and with what you offer to the story of being an American when hope called on you to do the right thing. Use step 5 to proclaim a righted course for our nation.

Learning Outcome

Recognize, describe, and present specific knowledge, skills, and abilities rooted in Whiteness-affiliated rigged advantage.

CHAPTER 6

STEP 6
WE RESOLVE TO CHANGE

Step 6 Governs Step 12: We Consecrate Liberty Free From Rigged Advantage

Key Words: **Resolution, Intentional, Unintentional, Merit-Rich**

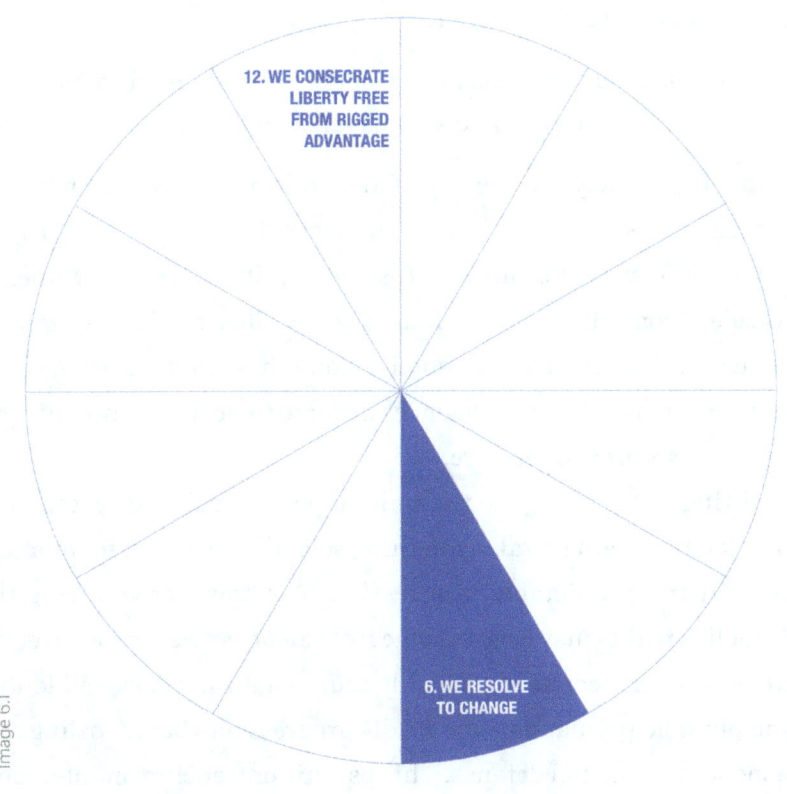

Image 6.1

What I Learned From Alcoholics About the Sixth Step of AA

"Were entirely ready to have God remove all these defects of character."[1]

We marvel at how the instinct for survival can carry the human spirit to seemingly miraculous feats of heroism.

> *She alone survived a plane crash while help arrived days later.*

> *He amputated his trapped arm.*

> *She lifted the wrecked car off her husband's body.*

> These stories of human survival amaze those who have not faced similar tragedy.

> Beneath our amazement we wonder if that same triggered survival instinct could save us if needed.

This is precisely the tragedy of alcoholism that unfolds, which is so hard to express. Objectively, alcoholics "should" be able to trigger that heroic instinct for survival. Instead, family and friends witness a cascade of contortions succumbing to an invisible murderer seemingly abetted by the victim. For alcoholics, something that is destroying us with repeated costly consequences becomes a normal way of life. No problem. Nothing to see here.

Hitting bottom may be the only hope to shock the system and override the death spiral. Something seismic must shift to intercept alcoholism's predictable progression. For however shocking the alcoholic's reality may have become from an objective perspective, the subjective perspective is a steadily sculpted masterpiece of identity (and physiology) adapting to a deadly progression's bamboozling that suspends instinctual defense. This psychic entrenchment intercepts the normal instinct to survive. It may be perhaps the greatest part of the tragedy of alcoholism: We are hostages, and it looks like we are just letting it happen.

Instinctually encoded survival is disrupted. Although we may even appear to be the same and continue to function in many areas, especially masquerading in our professional networks where people are kept at some distance, we are the walking dead. Without this hostage dynamic being intercepted, the progression will lead us to being "locked up" or "covered up." As a condition of operations, consequence after consequence is normalized, dismissed, rationalized, or blamed on others, who are fiercely resented. He, she, they, those, and them become important parts of the explanation of what is not working in the life of an alcoholic. We blame. We scapegoat. We manipulate. We outwit. We create alternative narratives to explain away incongruity. We go to any lengths to externalize what is happening to us. Ironically, it is intolerable even while tolerance to alcohol is in the etiology of our problem. Co-opting others whom we can manipulate to collude with us, we weave together a rationalized world that sufficiently coheres within our imaginations to enable our destruction to persist. Challenging this "world view" is verboten.

The condition of alcoholism is a house divided against itself. It takes over the life of a human being. Alcoholism will persist progressively until the host is dead.

What of This May We Apply to Our Problem, Rigged Advantage?

Rigged advantage will identify with America, sing about America, wave the flag of America, accuse others of anti-Americanism as long as America is synonymous with rigged advantage. If White Americans could not see it before January 6, 2021, it is abundantly clear forevermore that White supremacy can corrode this nation, not only from out of the past, but it is also deadly now. In the days following the attack on our nation's Capitol, the systems that count on White supremacy and anti-Blackness to ensure rigged advantage for White Americans through minority rule, stacked courts, and gerrymandering scrambled to rationalize home-grown terrorism. The living legacies of slavery commit sedition attacking one of the three branches of government. Later the very same day, elected officials, whom themselves were attacked, colluded to overturn the results of a free and fair election where Black and Brown voters wielded unprecedented influence. If you have ever personally known an alcoholic whom you had to watch die because of their illness, you have insight into what happened at our nation's Capitol that day.

A book by Doyle, *An American Insurrection, the Battle of Oxford Mississippi, 1962*[2] was published 20 years before the January 6, 2021, insurrection. The 1962 insurrection erupted over integrating the University of Mississippi.[3] James Meredith's attempt to enroll precipitated the intervention of the U.S. Supreme Court, the Kennedy administration, and a federalized National Guard presence for Meredith to enroll amid rioting.

Mississippi Governor Ross Barnett taunted Attorney General Robert Kennedy and President Kennedy, pontificating that this was "our greatest crisis since the war between the states."[4] The governor's greatest crisis was a Black man enrolling at Ole Miss, not the backlash riot. James Meredith's 1962 televised trail-blazing required a military-style occupation of the Ole Miss college town, Oxford, Mississippi. Rowan Oak, William Faulkner's home in Oxford, remains a literary tourist attraction. Faulkner's nephew, a captain in the federalized Mississippi National Guard, protected Meredith from the mob of violent White insurrectionists, defending their way of life from democracy's march forward.[5] The insurrection at Ole Miss and the insurrection at the U.S.

Capitol illustrate that there have been at least two insurrections in my lifetime. The insurrection on January 6, 2021, sprouted from the same roots as the insurrection in 1962.

Here is what the events share:

A state CEO manipulates racialized undercurrents to incite riot against "x" so that the status quo (sustained by White supremacy) benefits elite White Americans in power. Certifying Biden's win by over 7 million votes the day after a historical slave state elects two senators—one Jewish, one African American—is a templated replay of the "crisis" of James Meredith enrolling at Ole Miss. This templated repeat should not be a moment for seasoned journalists to exclaim "What's happening to our country?" Seasoned journalists should fulfill their reporting duty to compare the two insurrections and make clear the racialized through-lines common to each insurrection. It is a predictable playbook tactic that persists because the United States has never repented and atoned for slavery. We keep doing it. Slavery legacies are alive in the present.

My horror at seeing the 2021 insurrection unfold was only exacerbated when I listened to seasoned journalists wring their hands "How is this happening!" instead of tracing the historical lineage from the 1962 insurrection to the 2021 insurrection. The 12 steps proposed in this book show that telling the truth is only an initial step in a recovery from rigged advantage. Telling the truth is an uphill battle but it is necessary just to get started with problem-solving. How many presidential lies were the American people been subjected to before the media was even capable of using the word, lie? Journalism proved an insufficient fortification when democracy stumbled against an onslaught of emerging fascism. In journalism's bow to ratings to maximize shareholder value, we are relentlessly triggered by "both sides" theatrics that usurp the 4th estate's responsibility to inform democracy.

Our democracy is not sufficiently informed. Twenty-four-hour news cycles could inundate the American people with more information than a three-network television history ever could. But one could argue that information serving democracy was better delivered in 20 minutes per day in the Cronkite era than the 24-hour flailing of media echo chambers with he-said she-said and others-disagreed segments we are triggered with today. For information to have an impact on the active support of the American people to sustain democracy, accurate information will need to be presented, processed, and applied in venues of civic engagement. Media consolidations and social media that triggers base instincts for profitable clicks, along with addiction, and other diseases of social disorder exacerbated amid widening inequality are but a few of the tools that keep our consciousness sufficiently distracted, gnawing at each other's dignity to exhaustion. This is exhaustion by design. It enables status quo rigged advantage to persist while the rest of us are turned on each other. We are right to be outraged. But we only collude with oppression when we rage against each other. Later, in step 11, I present loving-kindness meditation. Far from being new-age daintiness subject to mockery, this training to resist the triggers to turn on each other is the practice of revolution sufficient to uproot rigged advantage.

Remember, rigged advantage depends on the frenzied distraction of exploited people exemplified in the 1962 and 2021 insurrections. If we cannot teach history, learn from history, and plumb history for the voices that did not control the narrative, we are not resolved to change. Step 6 is "We resolve to change." You may have read step 6 initially as being simple, but as I have now laid it out, I hope I have made the case for how daunting, even seemingly out of reach, step 6 is, given our present conditions.

The legacies of slavery (even when in remission in isolated cases) are intertwined in our habits, norms, identities, rituals, laws, precedent, policies, families, and communities. Clearer now for some than ever before, these deadly legacies collude as the enemies of change toward a more perfect union. Like alcoholism, these legacies in the form of rigged advantage will destroy their host (a United States of America) without sufficient intervention.

White Americans are responsible for dismantling the rigged advantage that flows to them to this day rooted in the legacies of slavery. The United States remains at risk on this fault line, compromised until a repair is complete. *Twelve Steps for White America* outlines the steps needed for the repair.

Even after the case I have just made, I am not dismayed. Not at all. I am clear-eyed. I would rather turn the light on to see where the snake is in the room, than worry in darkness. I know from my own claw back from the jaws of alcoholic death that what it takes to solve our current dive into the abyss is a set of problem-solving solutions we use every day. I have no doubt that the many Americans who have given their lives to uphold and defend, even with its imperfection, what this country can become, will prevail.

Learning Outcome

Contrast intentional versus unintentional beliefs and behaviors that reproduce rigged advantage, then dedicate self to a merit-rich democracy.

CHAPTER 7

STEP 7
WE HUMBLY TURN TOWARD CHANGE

Step 7 Complements Step 1: We Admitted Our Problem: Rigged Advantage

Key Words: **Humility**

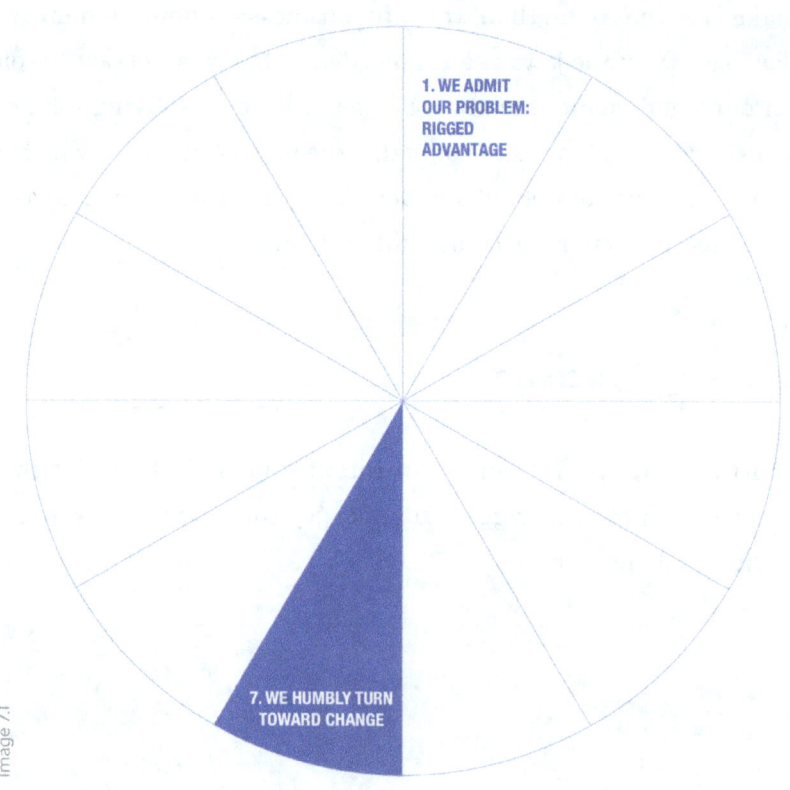

Image 7.1

What I Learned From Alcoholics About the Seventh Step of AA

"Humbly asked Him to remove our shortcomings."[1]

Quit doing what you are doing and do something else. Steps 1 through 6 have been prep work. Essential though they may be, not one of those steps has accomplished anything for someone other than the person doing the work (with the exception that knowledge that the work has begun, itself, may provide some relief to those who have been oppressed by it). Hopefully, our work accomplished in steps 1 through 6 have sufficiently enabled us to see both the unremittent suffering to date as well as the opportunities that lie ahead. White Americans en masse must be unrelenting about this step.

Alcoholics Anonymous lists a specific prayer to accomplish step 7. It is in the "twelve and twelve" book discussion on step 7 where a very memorable line occurs, which alcoholics can immediately identify. As a result of the work accomplished in steps 1 through 6, "we saw that we needn't always be bludgeoned and beaten into humility. It could come from our voluntary reaching for it as it could from unremitting suffering."[2]

There comes a point in recovery where we shift from relentless demoralization toward the hard work of recovery not just to avoid alcoholic consequences, but because we begin to realize, and see examples all around us, where working the steps leads to a better life. It is something so desirable that we are compelled to accomplish the difficult steps ahead. This shift from pain toward freedom is the humility which this step is all about.

What of This May We Apply to Our Problem, Rigged Advantage?

This is a pivotal step that is governed by step 1: We admit our problem: rigged advantage.

Turn from the entrenchment of entitlement that comes from generations of living in a country where your identity affords you privilege off the backs of marginalized others. Only then will the American experiment with democracy be fully realized.

I was raised in a political family—political to the extent that my civil rights–working parents knew at least two things: who gets elected matters and ensuring that Black Americans are registered to vote matters. My mother and father were respected among the local Black community. When my mother and father put their names on the ballot for local elections, they knew they had no chance of winning. But they also knew that the campaigns would rally voter registration in the Black community, and it would bring more Black people to the polls to vote, many for the first time and under threat for their (and our) lives. Sometimes you win when you lose.

As I got older, my mother and father worked to reunite the Democratic Party in Mississippi. Earlier, the racist Democratic party in Mississippi, known as the Dixiecrats, were challenged by a growing movement for inclusion. Fannie Lou Hamer, a leader of the Mississippi Freedom Democratic Party, encouraged by Student Non-Violent Coordinating Committee (SNCC) member Bob Moses, emerged onto the national stage at the 1964 Democratic National Convention as a powerful and brave voice for justice. At that time, the Dixiecrats were denying Black Mississippians the opportunity to serve as delegates. The Mississippi Freedom Democratic Party challenged the seating of the Dixiecrat delegates. What happened at the 1964 Democratic National Convention is historical and riveting. It is spellbinding to watch television footage of Fannie Lou Hamer addressing the convention. With unquestionable authenticity and courage of convictions, Mrs. Hamer rocked the boat of status quo politics, sick and tired of being sick and tired.

Any season of political campaigning brought a near festive atmosphere to our home. I thought everyone was as riveted and engaged as we were, but I would learn otherwise. After years of political enthusiasm in retrospect, two historical political events stand out to me: Regan in Philadelphia, Mississippi, at the Neshoba County Fair and Trump in Alabama. My assessment of these two stand-out events in the timeline of southern political history was validated when Republican operative Stuart Stevens, writing in his book, *It Was All a Lie*, showcased these exact two events.[3]

My selective rose-colored nostalgia can remember the many good times I had at the Neshoba County Fair, an annual rite for Mississippians held in the county just next door to Scott County, where I grew up. "Mississippi's Giant House Party" had a character all its own—especially since die-hard fans of the fair own cabins at the site of the annual fair so they can vacation there the entire week of the fair. One year, my uncle Joe, who had been a studio musician in Nashville, made sure we stopped by to see Chet Atkins perform. Even visibly drunk, Chet Atkins was a great guitarist worth seeing. I always remember the smells of Pronto Pups and fresh saw dust spread over the ground to help with the red clay mud if it rained hot and humid during Mississippi's relentless August.

As usual in the South, things are more than one thing at the same time. Neshoba County was also where Chaney, Goodman, and Schwerner had been murdered by the KKK colluding with law enforcement. These three Freedom Summer workers were reported missing earlier in the summer of 1964. Their disappearance was a national news event that ultimately fueled support for the passage of the 1964 Civil

Rights Act. Their bodies had recently been unearthed near the Neshoba County Fairgrounds when *The New York Times* ran a story on August 8, 1964, about the fair with these first two sentences:

> The white people of Neshoba County put aside today talk of the murder of three civil rights workers and flocked to their fairgrounds for a week of reunion, fun and politics. But the "nigra issue" was present, nevertheless, just as it has been since the turn of the century when James K. Vardaman, as Governor and Senator, rocked the pavilion with his anti-Negro thunder.[4]

This historical site, replete with the history of anti-Negro thunder and murdered civil rights workers buried nearby, is where Ronald Reagan launched his campaign for president against Jimmy Carter, August 3, 1980, 16 years after Freedom Summer. For perspective with the math, the book you are reading is published in 2022. Sixteen years ago, was 2006. That is how fresh civil rights wounds were when Reagan launched his campaign declaring his support for the South's rallying cry of White supremacy, "states rights."[5]

Thirty-six years later, when I saw news footage of the first senator to endorse Donald Trump, Senator Jeff Sessions, presenting candidate Donald Trump to a wildly supportive stadium full of Alabamians, I was taken aback.[6] In an earlier era, a wealthy northerner "carpet bagger" could not get a vote. It took a minute for the visual to sink in even for me. What would have formerly represented a Southern antithesis had now become its racialized hope, cloaked within the sustaining exploitation of rigged advantage. There it was. And it was difficult to process since it needed a southern-programming reboot. Even inherited wealth northerner narcissistic carpet-bagging Biblical illiterates with contempt for rednecks can be heralded if they are perceived to deliver on the promise of "our way of life" and "states rights" re-branded as "make America great again." The masquerade of southern heritage was laid bare. What I had to process was eye-opening; Southern heritage only matters to the extent that it sustains rigged advantage, which relies on White supremacy and anti-Blackness. That is the part that matters. Stuart Stevens nails it. The rest is all a lie—a means to the end of sustaining rigged advantage.

Most Southerners know that when Mama says, "You can do that if you want to" it is not permission. It is a warning intended to intercept idiocy. Its aftermath companion is "How'd that work out for you." Jefferson Beauregard Sessions, III "did that because he wanted to." The tell all book surely to come could reveal to us how that worked out for him. Whether he levels with us about the impact or not, we have a record of catastrophic humiliation that is not unlike the demoralization every alcoholic knows all too well.

I wrote earlier in the book that part of the insidiousness of alcoholism, especially to the observer, is that our natural instincts to survive appear to be hi-jacked. The inevitable end is a progression toward incarceration or death. The southerner in Jeff Sessions would have instinctually known that his mutated support for a previous era's political anathema, could not end well. But, in the way alcoholism hijacks instinctual survival, Session's collusion with strange bedfellows to sustain rigged advantage hijacked the good sense a Southern mama "wouldda gave him."

However folksy this analysis may be, understand that our nation is now at risk because functional democratic sensibilities have been hijacked by a system rigged to sustain its advantage for a few, who, like alcoholics, can no longer trust themselves by themselves to survive. They are demonstrably capable of burning down our house. These are the people who now pose the greatest threat to a United States of America. While prosecution may be due, it bears repeating that prosecution is not the point of this book. In the same way I do not condemn an alcoholic, but I may condemn drunk driving, I do not condemn those who are hijacked. I offer here a treatment plan for a beloved nation, so loved that I will not function as a co-dependent colluder at odds with the constitution of the United States, which I have several times over the course of my life pledged an oath to defend.

Rigged advantage in my lifetime has been a two-steps-forward, one-step-back dance between an advance of civil rights and its relentless sabotage to sustain the status quo for those benefitting from it. Trumpism is the inheritance potentiated by Ronald Reagan (and Goldwater before him) who himself was backlash for landmark civil rights progress under Kennedy and especially Johnson, fueled by the great civil rights movement leaders we say we revere. Reagan's Morning in America ads and his race-baiting of welfare queens, and his taunting fears over "I'm from the government and I'm here to help" are the gauntlets thrown down to launch an era fully realized by the Trump presidency, not an aberration, a fulfillment.

This era is ultimately the fight of rigged advantage to sustain itself through failed trickle-down economics, minority rule, gerrymandered districting, consolidation of media exacerbated in commodified social media echo chambers, tax policy to redistribute wealth to the richest while shrinking the middle class and squandering American democracy if it no longer purveys rigged advantage. An increasingly frenzied race against demographic inevitability, the January 6, 2021, insurrection, a repeating template of the 1962 riot at Ole Miss, protesting the admission of African American James Meredith, heralds a new era, which at this very writing witnesses Putin's invasion of Ukraine characterized by Trump as smart, genius, and savvy while his political lackeys toe the line. For even Reagan, this must be a line too far even for rigged advantage. But responsibility remains.

Enslavement activates within us when based on race alone we presume the entitlement to question the whereabouts of Black Americans, question competence, harangue a leader, filter an applicant pool, eliminate candidates for organizational fit, support minority rule. We have not turned from slavery. We have at times trimmed the weeds, but the future of the garden of democracy depends on pulling these weeds out by the roots. Step 7 is the turning point where that can happen.

To turn from rigged advantage requires a daily personal program of change by a sufficient tipping point of White Americans if there is hope for the American experiment with democracy. That is precisely what this 12-step program is intended to accomplish. If you have a better program or don't need a program, move on. On its face, the evidence indicates that some program is desperately needed by millions of White Americans for the nation to endure.

Learning Outcome

Relinquish White-affiliated rigged advantage to habituate justice then liberty for all.

CHAPTER 8

STEP 8
WE IDENTIFY THE HARM

Step 8 Complements Step 2: We Believe Something Can Be Done

Key Words: **Disparities, Socio-Economic Outcomes**

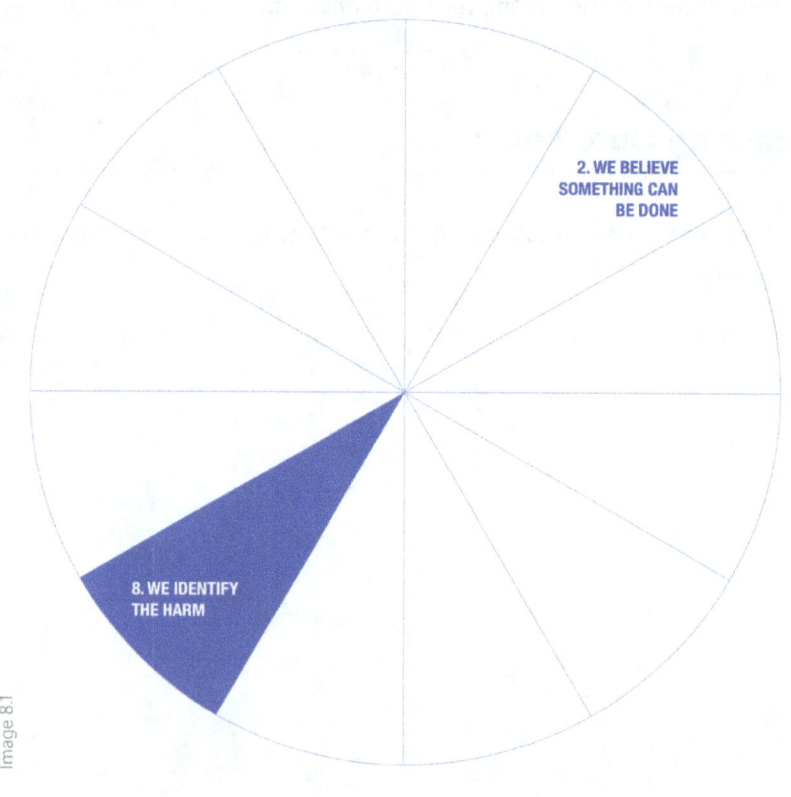

Image 8.1

What I Learned From Alcoholics About the Eighth Step of AA

> *"Made a list of all persons we had harmed and became willing to make amends to them all."*[1]

The Big Book of Alcoholics Anonymous compares early recovery to a family of tornado victims who have been crouched in a storm cellar. Emerging after the annihilating storm, the alcoholic family, devastated and demoralized, sees a swath of destruction. The alcoholic says, "Ain't it grand the wind stopped blowin'?"[2]

Learning to see ourselves is a lifelong lesson under the best of circumstances. How well we have been seen matters. While childhood does not have to determine the rest of your life, it can surely inform your lens onto the world. Children have an insatiable appetite for being seen. "Look what I can do!" shrieks out from every playground. Many other parental shortcomings may be excused if the child hears, "Look at you!" "I see you!" Some children grow up to grasp the vastness of the universe and shudder, "I'm so small, meaningless, and insignificant." Some children grow up to grasp the vastness of the universe and swell with marvelous pride, "I am that! What a wonderful world."

Beholding is a complex ability. For children who are seen and validated by significant others, beholding emerges as a lifelong gift. They behold their own life. They behold other lives. They behold their worlds. They are curious about others. They can behold their circumstances with their identity intact and resilient, even when circumstances are challenging. "Beholder" parents can rest assured that who they are matters more than particular mistakes. "Beholder" parents make way for a child to grasp the vastness of the universe and swell with marvelous pride: "I am that! What a wonderful world." Some children just seem to come into this world with this ability and sustain it even when few beholders are present.

There are spiritual light years between "that is vast, but I am small" versus "that is vast; I am that." "I am that" arguably reverberates through time in the Genesis creation story when God rested after creation. The "rest" of God, a pause to survey what has been created, is taught to us, enshrined as wisdom in one of the earlier narratives in literature. This principle appears as one of the great sayings from the Upanishads that God (Brahma, universal consciousness) and Atman (self, soul, individual consciousness) are not separate but one.[3]

Both "smallness" children and "vastness" children can grow up and become ensnared by alcoholism. Alcohol works for smallness beholders because it can quell anxiety about one's place in a big world. Alcohol works for vastness beholders because it can medicate the chasm between a potentially glorious existence with the cruel reality that alcoholism increasingly squanders any hope for it. In the snares of alcoholism, smallness beholders are right to perceive that what is happening to them is annihilating, while vastness beholders are right to perceive a wasteland of what could have been—for smallness beholders, incapacitating fear; for vastness beholders, gasping grief.

Alcoholism is an erosion and erasing of the soul that mirrors degradation in the brain. Whether one tends to behold small or vast, fear and grief becomes all-consuming. Fear and grief grow larger as the soul and brain recede. Beholding tendencies shaped in childhood become diseased. They fester where beholding the other diminishes while beholding a diseased and festering self becomes a nightmare of daily living. Others become reduced to projected personifications of fear and grief, objectified, and resented for the loss they represent.

For alcoholics in recovery, it can be so satisfying to be among others in similar circumstances. Since our "beholderometer" has been so broken, a meeting where every other person is a mirror of likeness, becomes an awakening opportunity. Hearing from others what happened to them comes like news from home for a person exiled from any contact long ago. In my own recovery, hearing my story come from the mouths of others was, at first, water for thirst and then medicine for transformative healing. During my very first meeting, at St. John's Lutheran church across from the sweet-smelling Shipley Do-Nuts, a man in a mechanic's jumpsuit with the embroidered-name Sammy saw me sitting on my tremor hands, still shaky after waking up from a nightmare pool of sweat the night before. Looking past my 1980s mousse-spiked hair and my new credit-card sweater, Sammy came up to me afterward with an unreserved bearhug and said, "Don't worry, little buddy; we're gonna love you 'til you can love yourself."

For months, I had been clenching and clinging to the side of a cliff. With little strength left, Sammy, and everyone at that first meeting, made me feel that finally letting go might be ok. I really had no choice. Night sweats. Nightmares. Stumbling to the car the next morning after drinking, praying that the grill was not damaged. Rage and tears. It becomes so bad. For some, the elevator down to hell may not go all the way. They can get off the elevator early before the last floor. For them, that is their bottoming out. For many observers, it may come as a surprise that their colleague even had a problem since so much in their life signaled high performance. For me, I could show you international travel for anthropology study, college graduation, my first "real" job, a new car. You may not see me stashing hidden alcohol at work and in the car. Waking up at night to drink. Hands trembling. Unpunished infractions. Chaos. Loss of control. Blackouts. Demoralization. Suicidal ideation.

Managing impressions becomes paramount. What only I see. What I let you see. What I cannot see. What you try to show me. The presentation becomes an exhausting masquerade. The justification of surviving means that I need you at arms length so you cannot get a good look. You will see what I show you. You will believe what I tell you. I am smarter than you. I have a better life than you. I am happier than you. Who are you to tell me anything? Why do I care what you think? I hope you like me. I don't want you here. You are out of bounds. Get in your lane. There is nothing to see here.

How well we see or do not see can reverberate across history. You may think of narcissism as someone only seeing themselves; but, in fact, the narcissist has a damaged lens problem. The alcoholic has a broken beholderometer. For the alcoholic, if they were not already predisposed to narcissistic personality disorder, the condition evolves to mimic narcissism because the beholderometer becomes increasingly distorted. The exhausting masquerade needed to protect and defend alcohol's power hold, misshapes the lens out onto the world. What we see, what we have to see, what we cannot see, what you must not see—believe my concocted replacement narrative—it all becomes twisted into something that looks inexplicably dysfunctional to an outsider who can see it.

Remember that this step, step 8, is governed by step 2, "We believe that something can be done." Step 2 is a determination that it is not futile to take the next steps toward solving a given problem because it can be fixed. Step 8 simply says that, in light of step 2, where we believe that something can be done about a problem that can be fixed, we determine who has been impacted by the problem? There is nothing complicated about this at all. Problems do not exist in a vacuum. Alcoholism is a personal problem but it impacts others. Answering the question "Who is impacted by the problem?" is not possible if in step 2 you did not believe something could be done about the problem.

While this is absolutely not complicated, remember we are asking this of someone whose "beholderometer" is damaged. Does it not make more sense to sequence the remedy like this?

1. Fix the beholderometer *before* trying to behold that there is a problem (step 2).
2. Then, once the beholderometer is fixed, determine who has been impacted by the problem (step 8).

Of course, the idea of using an unbroken tool to fix something has an almost irrefutable logic to it: Something that is not broken would work better to solve a problem than something that is broken.

However, that is not always how a repair works!

Consider a sports injury, a sprained ankle. There is an acute intervention where at first you may not walk on your foot because it is so painful. But to get better, you do not wait until your ankle is totally healed to walk again. You begin to gingerly walk on the foot to aid in healing. You start healing while still injured because that helps the process of healing.

The implications of this are huge if you are paying attention. As it turns out, the repair we fashion for others becomes the very and only remedy we have for returning our beholderometer to operation. Earlier in the book, I offered a nuanced take on "it is more blessed to give than receive." I offered you an assurance that this book is written with good intentions for you because I cannot have what I do not give. Here is another window into that teaching.

> You have to try to walk on an injured foot to return that foot to functioning. You must give to get. If you believe something can be done about a problem, you must identify who has been harmed by the problem and repair the harm not for their sake but for your sake, that you may be healed.

What of This May We Apply to Our Problem, Rigged Advantage?

Like the dysfunction of alcoholism, rigged advantage is a dysfunction happening to some while impacting others. Rigged advantage is a racialized economic objective embedded in colonial plantation economies, which have historically benefitted an elite group of White men and by extension those White men's families. While not all White men shared equally in rigged advantage bounty, the consent and collusion of most Whites to a system of rigged advantage was required to sustain it for the few Whites who benefitted the most. Derivative benefits of Whiteness (such as White supremacy), like crumbs from the table, bribe the collusion of these exploited Whites to sustain egregious inequality for an elite group of power Whites despite inhumane impact on others.

> In the way that the dysfunction of alcoholism happens to the alcoholic but impacts others, rigged advantage is a dysfunction happening to White Americans, with horrific impacts on Black Americans (and, by extension, impacts on others who are Othered as not White). Like alcoholics in recovery, White Americans must practice first things first if we are going to recover from generations of rigged advantage. We set out to remedy the problem of rigged advantage in order to heal ourselves. First things first means that the sequence of problem solving matters. To heal any dysfunction, the host of the dysfunction must start the healing process by admitting there is a problem, and the problem is ours.

The problem may be so entrenched over so many generations that you struggle to believe something can be done about the problem. That is the case of rigged advantage in America. Consider this: This book is one of boundless optimism and hope. This book presumes that problem-solving principles are universal across the human condition. These are the problem-solving principles that have enabled humanity to progress. This book shows that these problem-solving principles are used every day, from solving the problem of dirty dishes to solving the problem of alcoholism, to solving the problem of rigged advantage, which is still entrenched within the American experiment with democracy.

Despite the pervasiveness and the depth of degradation rigged advantage has wrought among the American people, I am showing you that the problem can be solved. As one who has knocked on death's door with alcoholism only to now thrive for over 35 years sober, it may be easier for me to believe than it is for you to believe that we can emerge from our dark night. But believe it. Let me believe it for you until you can believe it for yourself. It is not optional. This is the second step you must take: "We believe something can be done." This second step governs step 8. You cannot identify the harm if you do not believe something can be done about the harm.

Recalling that "first things first" means that the problem-solving sequence matters, consider this: *If we begin* this part of the 12-step sequence thinking that White Americans need to provide a remedy to Black Americans for generations of exclusion from social and economic participation and systematic denial of equal protection, *we are out of sequence.*

There is a problem, and *we* have it (step 1).

We believe something can be done about the problem (step 2).

We want something to be done about the problem, so we make a decision to that end (step 3).

We detail the problem (step 4).

We present the problem (step 5; by the end of step 5 you should already be clear who has the problem with rigged advantage).

Being clear about the problem, we resolve that a change is going to come (step 6).

Resolved, we turn toward change (step 7).

If we have been rigorously honest and taken each previous step with determination, we arrive at step 8 with the clarity and capacity to identify who has been harmed.

Although a litany of documentation could be provided to illuminate who has been harmed, we examine one graphic on the next page. As we explore the implications, let us suspend righteous indignation regarding how racist we are not. Let us suspend how we in the present are not responsible for ancestral slavery. Let us suspend how much any individual White person has struggled since there is a difference between you and your group. What is true for you does not have to be true for your group. I am the grandson of sharecroppers who used an outhouse. My father never finished high school. My "inheritance" was a surprise derivative of bureaucracy that netted less than $4,000. My dirt-road poverty-limited opportunities, psychiatric hospitalization, emergency room overdose, suicidal ideation, alcoholism, socially outcast gay stigmatized in rural Mississippi, threatened by White supremacist terrorists, none of my struggles has anything to do with how my group, White America, has benefitted from rigged advantage.

Stop. Turn.

Repentance is not optional. White America must acquire the very basic skill that differentiates me and we. The category "we" has characteristics. The category "me" has characteristics. When we talk about rigged advantage, you, like me, may think you have had a difficult life history. I have compassion for you as an individual, and I hope you have compassion for me. I greatly appreciate when someone is able to acknowledge that while I am so blessed now, how far I came to be here is remarkable, defying the odds. How difficult "me" has had it has absolutely nothing to do with irrefutable evidence that rigged advantage has disproportionately favored the category "White Americans."

Look at the two graphics that follow to understand that this reality cannot possibly be acceptable as the American dream. This cannot possibly be the best you believe the United States of America can be.

> If nothing else resonates in this entire book, look at this graphic and make a commitment that this must change for a United States of America.

Step 8: We Identify the Harm | 115

THE U.S. HAS NOT RECOVERED FROM PLANTATION SLAVERY
INSUFFICIENT BLACK AMERICAN "PROGRESS" FROM BEING PROPERTY TO HAVING PROPERTY COMPROMISES THE INTEGRITY & FUTURE OF THE USA

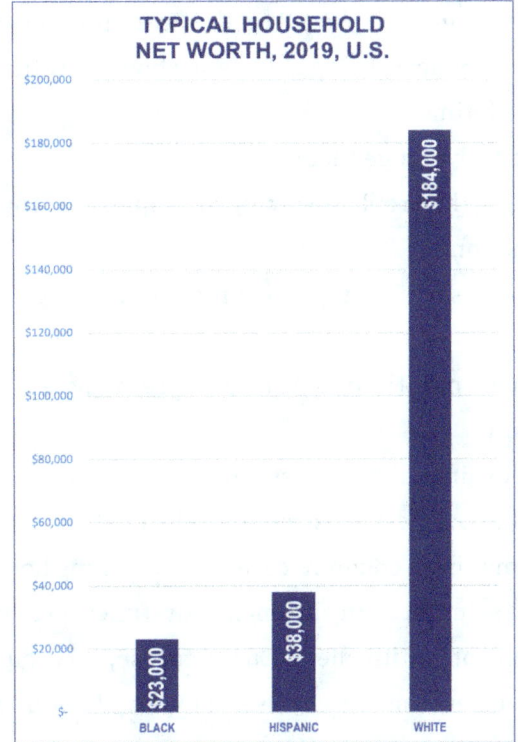

"Income disparities are as big as in the pre-civil rights era.

In 1950, the income of the median white household was about twice as high as the income of the median black household.

In 2016, black household income is still only half of the income of white households.

The racial wealth gap is even wider and remains as large as it was in the 1950s & 1960s.

The median black household persistently has less than 15% of the wealth of the median white household.

The financial crisis hit black households particularly hard and has undone the little progress that had been made in reducing the racial wealth gap during the 2000s.*

Over seven decades, little progress has been made in closing the black-white income gap.

The racial wealth gap is equally persistent and a stark fact of postwar American history.

The typical black household remains poorer than 80% of white households."

FEDERAL RESERVE BANK OF MINNEAPOLIS

Kuhn, Schularick, Steins (2020). Income & Wealth Inequality in America, 1949-2016 *Journal of Political Economy*, vol 128 #9

Image 8.2
Has Wealth Inequality in America Changed over Time? Here Are Key Statistics
December 02, 2020, Ana Hernandez Kent, Lowell Ricketts. Federal Reserve Bank, St. Louis
Retrieved 1-14-2022 From: https://www.stlouisfed.org/open-vault/2020/december/has-wealth-inequality-changed-over-time-key-statistics

*Wolff, E. N. (2017). Household Wealth Trends in the U. S., 1962 to 2016: Has Middle Class Wealth Recovered?, Working Paper 24085, *National Bureau of Economic Research*.

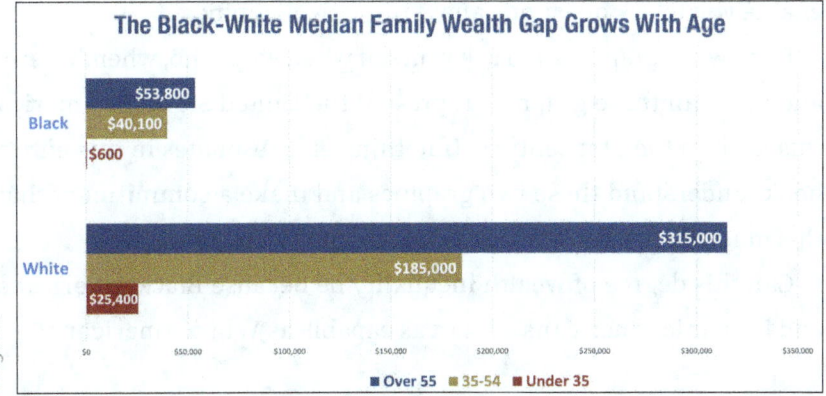

Image 8.3

The first snapshot illustrates the importance of disaggregating data to understand the variance among groups by looking at subgroups at a point in time. The second graphic, based on the Federal Reserve Bank Survey of Consumer Finances, using 2019 data, shows how that variance plays out over a lifetime.

Disagree with my rigged advantage theory.

Fault my logic for applying the problem-solving principles of recovery to our nation's dysfunction.

Resist the notion of legacies of slavery, which may sound inapplicable in a modern world.

Be offended by me even mentioning White supremacy, anti-Blackness, and exploitation.

Find my presentation of spirituality distasteful.

Balk at my assurance that our best days could be ahead of us.

Of course, I think I am making a coherent case for explicating both a problem and a realizable solution to an entrenched dysfunction that threatens our security and competitiveness. But of course, it is your prerogative to use anything here that may be useful to you. If nothing else, you are experiencing a case example of how a recovering alcoholic applies recovery principles in all his affairs.

It is absolutely a recovery tradition to *take what you need and leave the rest.* In that spirit, this book may do nothing else for you than to enable you to ask questions about these two graphics.

Review the graphics and ask yourself what, why, who, when, where, and how can these graphics represent the United States of America this far into the 21st century. If nothing else resonates in this entire book, understand these two graphics and make a commitment that this must change for the sake of United States of America.

Can this degree of wealth inequality be because Black Americans and Hispanic Americans are not as capable as White Americans?

Are we sufficiently structured as a nation to believe that all is well and that, over time, Black Americans and Hispanics are on track to catch up?

Even if you believe catching up is on the horizon, how long is too long?

Is it because White Americans are just better at being American citizens that Black households have less than 15% of the wealth of White households? (Remember that the Supreme Court once ruled that Dred Scott was not a citizen.)

Understand that as you look at the graphic, these are median numbers (not averages, because exorbitant wealth for a few would skew the representation).

How do we hold these two things at the same time?

1. In a capitalist meritocracy, we want to reward hard work, innovation, and competition.
2. Can this degree of wealth inequality be explained by merit alone?

The problem of rigged advantage has surely harmed us and compromised our national security and economic competitiveness across the globe. It has also impacted others; but be clear "they" are not the problem. "They" are horrifically impacted by the problem, but the problem of rigged advantage is happening to us whether you are an elite power White absconding wealth from a system rigged on your behalf or you are a struggling White American whose Whiteness is exploited to sustain a version of a romanticized America for some, but a yet unrealized America for far too many White Americans and others. Therefore, we must admit it and get to work on each of the next steps, knowing that if we do, all of us can achieve the United States that results from a more perfect union. Our best days are ahead of us.

Since you are White you are part of a group of White Americans. Membership has many privileges, but it also has responsibilities. Specifying the centuries of harm from slavery, post reconstruction,

Jim Crow, civil rights–era violence, the new Jim Crow, corporate underwriting of a racialized agenda since the 1960s, and minority rule/Trumpism may seem overwhelming. Since accountability for individuals varies, what then is the accountability for any given White American?

> Of course, what American living today was responsible for slavery? None. Does what happened then still reverberate across conditions and outcomes today? Yes. You need to be able to answer yes and want to fix it because that persistence is incompatible with justice then liberty for all. It threatens national security and compromises global competitiveness.

Are you accountable for knowing what has happened?

Do you know some of the key turning points in legislative and judicial history?

For example, who is Dred Scott?

Do you know the reference if someone refers to

- Colfax
- Coushatta
- Thibodaux
- Tulsa
- Wilmington
- Harperville?

What is the history of lynching as entertainment for White Americans?

Our laws are rooted in property rights. How does our nation having considered enslaved people as property linger today?

Is race still a predictor of social and economic outcomes today?

How has the generational ability/inability to accumulate wealth impacted economic mobility in the present?

Do you know what the disparity is for household wealth in the United States today?

What about educational outcomes when disaggregated by race? Is a given higher education institution capable of delivering its promises regardless of the race and socio-economic status of the students it serves? How do local property taxes determine educational opportunity early in a child's life?

You make decisions about this every time you vote or neglect to vote. Are you sufficiently informed? What about more local instances of interaction? Do you know what happens/happened where you live?

It may prove helpful to you to see examples of research and remedies, which have been compiled by organizations with significant knowledge and capacity for addressing remedies. The following is only a small sample of resources and organizations that prove helpful to my ongoing study. You must do your own work.

The Othering and Belonging Institute at the University of California, Berkeley, is led by Director john a. powell, who holds the Robert D. Haas chancellor's chair in equity and inclusion and is a professor of law, African American studies, and ethnic studies. Searching publications at belonging.berkeley.edu will lead you to a repository of structural racism remedies.[4] Whether you support or oppose any given remedy, you will nonetheless be exposed to a categorization of remedies formulated across a breadth of policy areas.

You could enrich your work on steps 8 and 9 with a McKinsey and Company report on the state of the economy for Black America. McKinsey's 2022 report, "The Economic State of Black America: What It Is and What It Could Be,"[5] offers a digestible and revealing look at a wide range of data already conveniently compiled to inform your ability to formulate remedies that eliminate disparities on socioeconomic outcomes.

Opportunity Insights features "The Opportunity Atlas: Mapping the Childhood Roots of Social Mobility" (Raj Chetty and others).[6]

The National Equity Atlas is an illuminating resource available at nationalequityatlas.org. The atlas is produced by PolicyLink and the USC Equity Research Institute (ERI).[7]

PolicyLink also provides an exemplary equity blueprint, "For Love of Country: A Path for the Federal Government to Advance Racial Equity."[8]

Prosperity Now (formerly the Corporation for Enterprise Development) provides data and policy for what it will take to build a fair and just economy for all.[9]

The W. K. Kellogg Foundation invests in racial equity.[10]

The MacArthur Foundation's "The Just Imperative" is committed to centering conditions in which justice can thrive.[11]

The Zinn Education Project is a one-stop for history that has not been whitewashed.[12]

Learning Outcome

For peace and prosperity, formulate remedies that eliminate disparities in socioeconomic outcomes.

PART III
03

RENEWAL

12 STEPS for WHITE AMERICA IN A NUTSHELL

PART ONE STEPS 1-4	PART TWO STEPS 5-8	PART THREE STEPS 9-12
TRUTH	**RECONCILIATION**	**RENEWAL**
REPENTENCE	ATONEMENT	REDEMPTION
Stop, turn.	*Make things right.*	*Live democracy's promise.*
Unshackle the past.	Strengthen U.S. security & global competitiveness.	Make way for all so our best days are ahead of us.

image III.1

JUSTICE then LIBERTY

Make Way for All so Our Best Days Are Yet to Come

In Part I of the book, we learned the simplicity of Steps 1 through 4.

Step 1. We admit our problem: Rigged advantage.

>Learning outcome: Identify the gap between presented and realized democracy in the United States.

Step 2. We believe something can be done.

>Learning outcome: Recognize potential for personally impacting democracy's promise.

Step 3. We decide to act.

>Learning outcome: Commit to a personal program of liberation for the common good.

Step 4. We Detail the problem.

>Learning outcome: Identify, analyze, and categorize specific knowledge, skills, and abilities rooted in Whiteness-affiliated rigged advantage.

Part I demonstrated that we already know *how* to do what needs to be done for a United States of America. Not only do we know how, but we also actually already know a great deal of *what* needs to be done. Because freedom is not free, each of us has a part to play to ensure the promises of our great democratic republic. In each of us, part of the problem and part of the solution manifests, whether we intend it or not, whether we have given it a second thought, or whether it concerns us at all. Ideally, we are free *in* a democracy, not free *from* it. If everyone were a "free-rider" there would be nothing to ride.

Problem solving is universal across human cultures or we would not have made it this far. For solving problems in any language across the spectrum of humanity, we start by telling the truth. Then, we stop and turn from (known since ancient history as repentance) what does not work toward what works. We cut ties to what does not work to utilize what works and manage the risk of unnecessary relearning, which threatens evolving progress. For the problem of cutting ties to rigged advantage in a divided United States, I used the potent and painful language that we must unshackle the past.

This is very simple:

Truth (be honest).

Stop, turn (quit doing it).

Unshackle the past (move on).

Simple but not **easy**, is it?

While it may not be easy, it truly *is not complicated.*

If it is simple, not complicated, and we solve problems every day, *what about this problem proves resistant*? It became evident in steps 1 through 4 that we are taking on a very big problem by dividing it into pieces, taking this one step at a time. While the ingredients of this problem-solving process are nothing new, the recipe's directions in this book outline a very important problem-solving process as practiced by recovering alcoholics, human beings whose lives have been trapped, hijacked onto a trajectory of being locked up (prison) or covered up (grave).

PART I, Steps 1–4

Everyday Problem-Solving Process	Application to Rigged Advantage
There is a problem.	1. We admit our problem: rigged advantage.
Something can be done about the problem.	2. We believe something can be done.
I want something to be done about the problem.	3. We decide to act.
What exactly is the problem?	4. We detail the problem.

Part I is primarily an *inward process of discovery*.

Part II prepares your discovery to *venture outward*.

PART II, Steps 5–8

Everyday Problem-Solving Process	Application to Rigged Advantage
Okay. Got it. This is a problem.	5. We present the problem.
Now that I get it, I choose to change it.	6. We resolve to change.
I want to replace the old behavior with the new.	7. We humbly turn toward change.
Others have been impacted.	8. We identify the harm.

Steps 5 through 8 built on the inward discovery and established a pathway outward toward the "Other": what we perceived to be separate from "us" both as individuals and the group with which we identify.

Step 5 can be thought of as a confessional, coming clean, getting honest, a rehearsal of what you discovered, clarifying or refining ideas by hearing them out loud. The expression "Music to our ears" is a saying we use not only because of the pleasantness of an idea we more fully learn and understand something when what we have learned is not just an idea; it is something heard and presented back to us. By this extension, it becomes authenticated, validated, and reinforced. We have many expressions related to this phenomenon. We come clean. We get it off our chest. We unburden ourselves. A weight is lifted off our shoulders. Confession is good for the soul.

Step 6 is a resolution about what you do now that you have come this far in the process. As we all know from our years of "New Year resolutions," a resolution represents an intention—something necessary but insufficient. An intention does not achieve the outcome of the resolve, but there is no result without it.

Step 7 is a getting-started step. Step 7 is the first step toward a future now made possible by your progress in summary: (a) truth, (b) belief,

(c) will, (d) inventory, (e) expression, (f) resolution, (g) start, and now, (h) account.

Step 8 is where some sobriety arrives and begins for the storm-shelter family we mentioned earlier. Instead of the alcoholic emerging from the storm cellar after a tornado and surveying the damage with the proclamation "Ain't it grand the wind stopped blowing," the alcoholic has worked the steps sufficiently to now ask the question, "Who has been impacted by the wreckage of my stormy life, and how?"

Astute readers will notice that we are already over half-way through the steps, and we are still only preparing to do something: to work toward a solution for the problem of rigged advantage.

Step 5. We present the problem.

> Learning outcome: Recognize, describe, and present specific knowledge, skills, and abilities rooted in Whiteness-affiliated rigged advantage.

Step 6. We resolve to change.

> Learning outcome: Contrast intentional versus unintentional beliefs and behaviors that reproduce rigged advantage, then dedicate self to a merit-rich democracy.

Step 7. We humbly turn toward change.

> Learning outcome: Relinquish Whiteness-affiliated rigged advantage to habituate justice then liberty for all.

Step 8. We identify the harm.

> Learning outcome: For peace and prosperity, formulate remedies that eliminate disparities in socioeconomic outcomes.

> **AN IMPORTANT NOTE: USE THE #12SWA WORKBOOK**
>
> You may feel that you need additional study to have accomplished the learning outcomes for steps 1–8. This is to be expected. The book is written with the intention that you will be working in the workbook that accompanies the text. Both the book and the workbook scaffold learning from one step to the next, but they also scaffold learning between the book and the workbook. If you are reading this book without the benefit of the workbook, you may sense that something is missing. You would be right. Take advantage of the workbook to strengthen your learning.

Revisit Governing and Complementary Steps to Strengthen Learning

Steps 1–6 each govern complementary steps 7–12. Each complementary step is enabled or limited by the proficiency of its governing step. Remember that taking the first step to solve any problem enables the sequence toward solutions. Recovering alcoholics can tell you that the rigor which with you are able to grapple with the first step will set the parameters for all that is to follow. Some alcoholics talk about "hitting bottom." The idea is that unless you have become thoroughly convinced there is a problem, you are not ready to undertake the (possibly) harrowing rigor required to work the steps and achieve recovery.

Look at the following graphic and ask yourself, "In what way does the complementary step rely on its governing step?"

Begin With One Seven

In the abstract, it is common sense that few turn toward change without perceiving a need for change. This tandem relationship becomes a more complex dynamic to master in practice. If resistance rears its

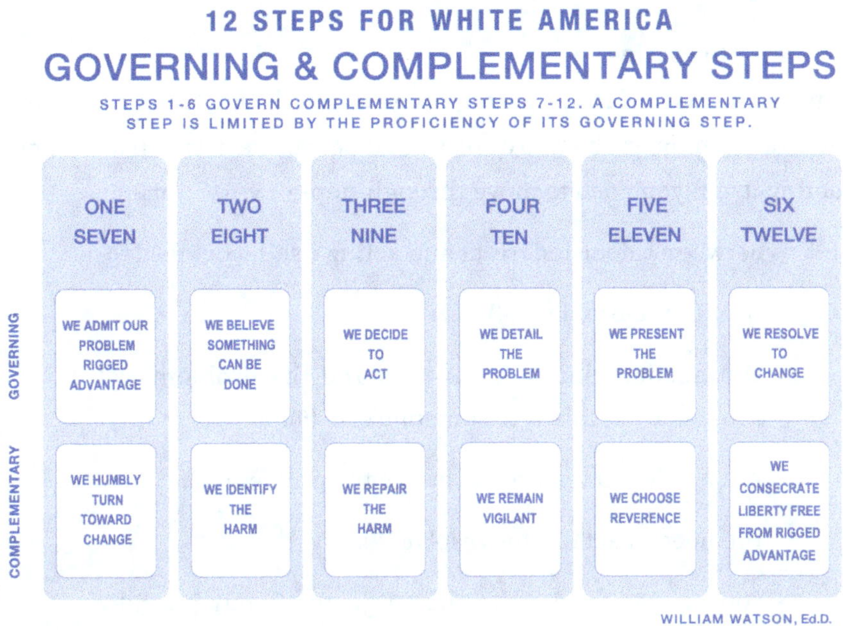

12 STEPS FOR WHITE AMERICA
GOVERNING & COMPLEMENTARY STEPS

STEPS 1-6 GOVERN COMPLEMENTARY STEPS 7-12. A COMPLEMENTARY STEP IS LIMITED BY THE PROFICIENCY OF ITS GOVERNING STEP.

	ONE / SEVEN	TWO / EIGHT	THREE / NINE	FOUR / TEN	FIVE / ELEVEN	SIX / TWELVE
GOVERNING	WE ADMIT OUR PROBLEM RIGGED ADVANTAGE	WE BELIEVE SOMETHING CAN BE DONE	WE DECIDE TO ACT	WE DETAIL THE PROBLEM	WE PRESENT THE PROBLEM	WE RESOLVE TO CHANGE
COMPLEMENTARY	WE HUMBLY TURN TOWARD CHANGE	WE IDENTIFY THE HARM	WE REPAIR THE HARM	WE REMAIN VIGILANT	WE CHOOSE REVERENCE	WE CONSECRATE LIBERTY FREE FROM RIGGED ADVANTAGE

WILLIAM WATSON, Ed.D.

Image III.2

ugly head, step mastery means that you go back and discern where your progress faltered. Deepen your understanding of the problem. Resist bamboozlers who profit from your distraction. Clear attachments that hinder change.

Review Two Eight

How will you ever identify the harm if you do not truly believe something can be done about the problem? Perhaps you have not truly admitted that a problem even exists. Have you underestimated the magnitude of the problem? Do you continue to displace blame for the problem onto "Others"? Maybe you have sufficiently dealt with these issues in step 1, but in an equally dysfunctional swing of the pendulum, you now fret that the problem is so entrenched and overwhelming you shut down. You do not believe this can change. If you cannot practice step 2, you will not identify the harm. From the outside, you may appear insensitive to the need for repair, but inwardly, you need help, encouragement, a rationale for how to envision something better.

Review Three Nine

This is an easy relationship to perceive. You decide to act, then you act. Take a moment here to observe that between a decision to act and acting itself, you need to move through steps 4, 5, 6, 7, and 8.

> Between a decision to act and acting itself, you need to specify the problem (4).
>
> You needed clarity, to understand the problem well enough to explain it to someone else (5).
>
> You needed to resolve to change the problem (6).
>
> You needed act on this resolve (7).
>
> You needed to identify the subjects of your intended actions (8)
>
> and only then, can you act (9).

You may know the drill of deciding to act and then acting so well you no longer notice the increments involved. If you struggle with repairing harm, Three Nine is worth revisiting.

Review Four Ten

This is perhaps the easiest governing-complementary relationship to perceive. For recovering alcoholics, clearing out the wreckage of the past is not a one-and-done deal. To prevent relapse, we account for as much as we can when we can in step 4, but we can only do so much at that stage of our progress. Time and practice enable us to improve our inventory. For recovering alcoholics, step 10 says, "Continue to take personal inventory and when we are wrong, promptly admit it." This recognizes that step 4 is never finished. A final note about Four Ten is that while we want to mitigate wrong to others, the reason we promptly admit it is for our sake, that we sustain recovery. As a nation, our best days could truly be ahead of us if we clear out the wreckage of our past and remain vigilant to keep our eyes on the prize!

Review Five Eleven

There is something transformative about understanding a problem well enough to express it to another human being. Confession is good for the soul. When we "get things off our chest" we "lighten our load." We develop. We unfold. We become. We actualize. These are components of spiritual transcendence. Recovering alcoholics practice this step as "Sought through prayer and meditation to improve our conscious contact with God as we understood him, praying only for knowledge of his will for us and the power to carry that out." We shift from stifling in selfish egocentric entanglements to mastering rewarding and dynamic relationships. We extend ourselves into a larger community. We understand there is a cost to us where negative actions toward and about "Others" compromise our own extension, our enlargement, our transcendence. An old hymn talks about this as a foretaste of glory divine. This foretaste begins to shift the miraculous from something foreign to something that catalyzes within our spirituality. We choose reverence even while reverence chooses us. This simultaneity becomes a "pearl of great price." What we may have sought to repair for others' sakes we come to realize we repair for our sakes. For those who believe it is going to take a miracle for a United States of America, I agree! That miracle is already within us.

Review Six Twelve

Our resolve is manifest. Change means that instead of hoarding the promises of democracy in a tainted system of rigged advantage, where liberty only for some is exalted, we hold it sacrosanct that liberty by definition is only realized absent of rigged advantage. We cannot say we are one thing while practicing another thing. Integration, integrity means that we are what we purport to be. A house divided against itself will not stand. We cannot exalt liberty in the face of the injustice of rigged advantage. We must practice justice then liberty for all to realize our greatest potential.

Here is an additional exercise for studying the relationships between governing and complementary steps.

Imagine that the Mandala represents a 12-sided pavilion in a park. Walk up the steps into the pavilion and stand in the first of the 12 sides and recite governing step 1. While reciting governing step 1, look across the pavilion and recite complementary step 7. Repeat this process for each governing and complementary pair until you have stood in each of the 12 sides and recited each step.

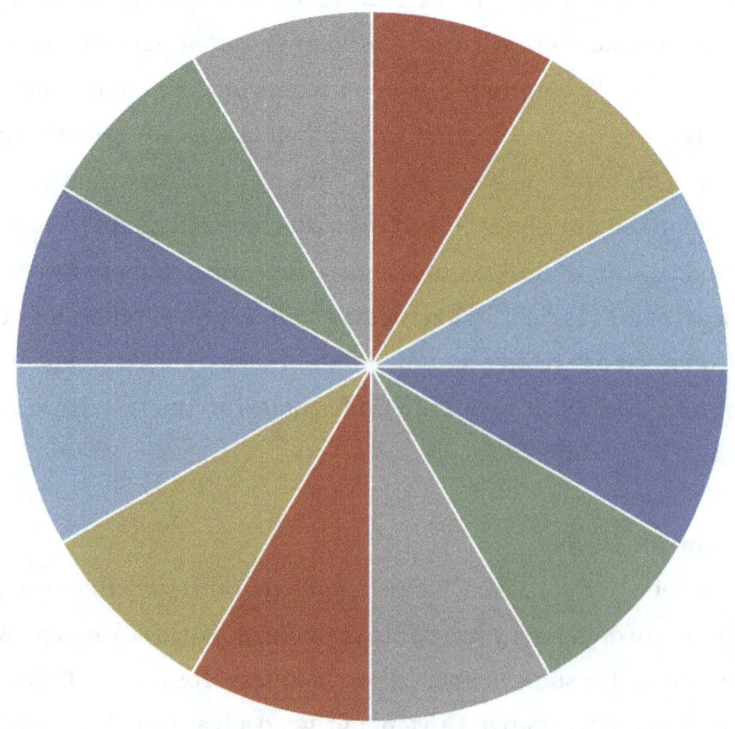

Image III.3

PART III Steps 9–12

Everyday Problem-Solving Process	Application to Rigged Advantage
Here's how I will fix it.	9. We repair the harm.
Don't slip back into old ways.	10. We remain vigilant.
I'm grateful for this change.	11. We choose reverence.
I can change other things and help anyone else if needed!	12. We consecrate liberty free from rigged advantage.

Step 9. We repair the harm.

Learning outcome: For peace and prosperity, implement remedies that eliminate disparities in socioeconomic outcomes.

Step 10. We remain vigilant.

Learning outcome: Habituate rigorous self-assessment to sustain justice then liberty, replacing periodic remission of rigged advantage with its eradication.

Step 11. We choose reverence.

Learning outcome: Synthesize personal spiritual discipline as the pathway to relinquish rigged advantage for the common good.

Step 12. We consecrate liberty free from rigged advantage.

Learning outcome: Dismantle rigged advantage for an integral democracy where competition thrives from race-neutral merit.

White Americans are increasingly aware that not only Black, Indigenous, and other People of Color pay the price for rigged advantage (which relies on White supremacy and anti-Blackness). Too many White

Americans, just trying to make ends meet, trust power White elites who scapegoat "Others" as the real problem. Exploited and bamboozled, that trust is killing us, "deaths of despair" at alarming rates.[1] The work of #12SWA is not something we need to do for "others." We need to save "us" so that a United States of America—for all—can thrive in a secure and competitive future. Burning down our house does not work.

Tipping Point of Resolve

Now that our national dysfunction is "overwhelmingly in our (meaning White America's) face" there is an increasing urgency that something must be done about it. We then realize that "it" has been overwhelmingly in the face of Black America all along. We can only get through it if there is a tipping point to understand the problem and resolve to change it. As the middle class continues to shrink and the next generation's promise is compromised, more White Americans realize that the membership they pay for Whiteness is too great. Rigged advantage for some = bad for all. It is not just bad for "others."

CHAPTER 9

STEP 9

WE REPAIR THE HARM

Step 9 Complements Step 3: We Decide to Act

Key Words: **Atone, Atonement, Repair, Rectify, Remedy**

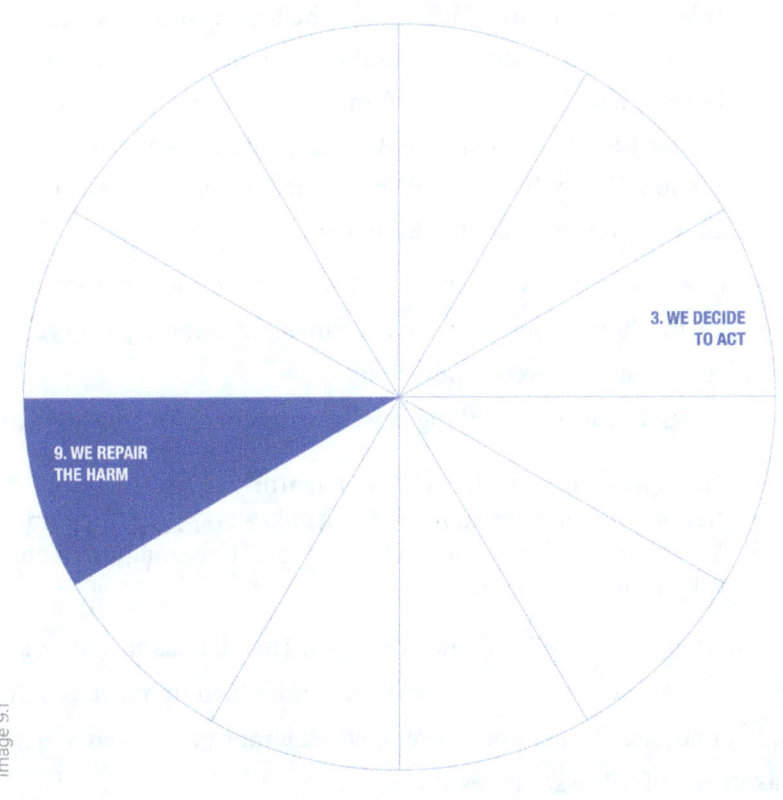

Image 9.1

What I Learned From Alcoholics About the Ninth Step of AA

> *"Made direct amends to such people wherever possible, except when to do so would injure them or others."*[1]

Alcoholics Anonymous cofounder Bill W. wrote,

> Learning how to live in the greatest peace, partnership and brotherhood with all men and women, of whatever description, is a moving and fascinating adventure. But, every A.A. has found that he can make little headway in this new adventure of living until he first backtracks and really makes an accurate and unsparing survey of the human wreckage he has left in his wake. The readiness to take the full consequences of our past acts, and to take responsibility for the well-being of others at the same time, is the very spirit of Step Nine.[2]

We now review what we have learned about how alcoholism works since the method of operation (the storm) signals the types of casualties targeted in our rescue operations.

In our early history of drinking, our learning concluded the following:

- "That worked so well, I will do it again."
- "It not only works great for X, but it also works great for Y and Z."
- "X, Y, and Z no longer need me to adapt; I have magic in a bottle. Why reinvent the wheel?"

What worked so well became preferred. Then it became habituated. Over the course of the habit becoming embedded in our psychology and our physiology, our body developed a tolerance where more alcohol was needed for the same result.

Once we have learned to tolerate it and we need more to produce the same result, we find we become predictably patterned into losing control over how much we drink. Consequences begin to mount. Psychologically, we are trapped. Physiologically, we are trapped. For whatever games we may play with ourselves and others, we know we are no longer are the authority over our lives. Spiritually, we shrink in shame. Thirty-five years sober, one of the richest blessings of my life is that I can count on myself to reach the goals I set for my life. I will never forget what it is like to no longer trust myself with myself. That is a demoralization that is hard to explain to someone who has never experienced it.

Of course, "Bartender, I'll have a shot of demoralization" is not how it starts. No drinker ever drank the first drink with the following toast:

May this drink, like the drink of so many around me, start as a predictably rewarding elixir but spiral downward to become for me:

- a wretched decline of my hopes and dreams;
- an exploitation of those around me to compensate for my decline;
- a living-dead decay of internal suffering blamed on anything else while I march toward prison and/or death.

Variables include genetic predisposition (how dry is your kindling), social norms, the human spirit (the transcendental unknowns that conspire to save us from ourselves).

While the variables fashion an individual tale, the common themes are predictable.

The trap takes on a life of its own and sadistically ensnares you to become its chief defender.

> *I don't have a problem. You are the problem. This world is a mess. Who wouldn't drink? I'm sick of you telling me what to do. Walk in my shoes before you judge me. I can handle this. I can quit anytime I want to. I just need to get focused. All these consequences are the problem. I just need to learn to control it. I'm so sick of people who don't do right. These parasites are living off me. The world's caving in on me. I'm not gonna take it. If they think they are coming for me, think again. I had it so*

> *good and now look at what others are doing to me. Give me a break. Who are you to judge me? Get off my back. What do you want from me? Why are you failing me? Good luck with that.*

Not only are we duped, the very nature of the problem for so many of us is that we lose the ability for accountability. We become incapacitated, incapable. Our ability to respond deteriorates. What we do not use, you lose. Our skills atrophy. Over reliance on alcohol means that a diversity of responses becomes limited.

For the outsider to protest how someone's alcoholism impacts them while demanding responsibility may let off steam, it will produce little outcome in the alcoholic because, by definition, the ability to respond is compromised. If an organism loses its ability to respond and adapt, it is not going to survive. If we cannot learn from our mistakes and use that learning to inform future choices and behaviors, we become vulnerable. Consequences lose their informative strength because we can no longer process the information. Pair this psychological decline with a physiological trap that only gets worse over time, and you have what an outsider sees as inexplicable self-destruction.

What of This May We Apply to Our Problem, Rigged Advantage?

Repentance and atonement are two sides of the same coin. When one determines the need to quit doing something to someone, a realization is embedded that a wrong needs to be made right. The social contract tends to recognize a wrong and then provide a remedy. In this section, which builds on each previous step, we will finally reach action that directly impacts others. Without the previous steps, it is virtually impossible for this step's potential to be fully realized. Indeed, what must happen may be mind-boggling. Make no mistake, the urgency of now demands that nothing less than epic atonement will preserve the future of our nation's experiment with democracy.

If you are White and the only America to which you will remain an ally is one sustained by the strategies of White supremacy and anti-Blackness, then you must come to terms with the fact that the end of your intention is insurrection and sedition. If the greatness of America means devotion to an America that sustains its advantage for White Americans while others are denied justice and liberty, then you do not love the United States of America. You are not a patriot. What you love are the legacies of slavery—a memory of the plantation, minority rule, exploitation of others, rigged advantage, the disproportionate use of force to dominate, the dysphoria of freedom proclaimed by slave holders, enclaves of Whiteness for Whiteness all the while knowing that minority rule can only hold for a while longer. It must feel like desperation, like an alcoholic who knows that this is unsustainable. You will be left in a minority that is positioned to reap the harvest sown.

If you are still struggling at step 9, you need to back up and rework your previous steps. Each step paves the way for the next. The successful completion of each step enables the realization of what is to come. Step 9 may be triggering and seem overwhelming. But before you abandon this step, let us stay a while longer and zoom in on a specific example.

If a bully on the playground is harassing your child, the behavior absolutely must stop. Is the bully held accountable in a way that counts against his record of achievement? What if the bully is never held accountable but the behavior stops? The two children, the bully and the bullied, will still attend school in the same class. Is an apology necessary? Does the apology embody an acknowledgement of the wrong and intent to make it right? What if the bullied child was scared to go on a field trip to a museum about which an essay could have earned extra credits? What if a third child (a friend of the bullied child) developed a resentment toward the bully and fought him? Out of context, was the fight perceived to be unprovoked? If so, that fight resulted in suspension because he attacked the bully seemingly out of nowhere. This third child missed some important material and got behind while suspended. Grades suffered.

Given that the entire class is competing for a placement in an elite middle school from which a trajectory toward a selective prestigious university admission is common, consider the following: The bully's behavior was not recorded or held against him in any way that could harm chances for placement in that school. The bullied child shows absenteeism and poorer grades. The friend has a record of aggressive behavior. One of these three children is on a more lucrative and competitive trajectory than the other two. Add to this some rationalizations about the children along the way. The bully knows how to game the system to avoid getting caught. Even when he is caught, his excuses are considered trustworthy since he has been at the school since 1st grade and his wonderful family are such great supporters/contributors to the school.

The bullied child had been transferred into this great elementary school from an "inner city" school with a bad reputation. Assumptions are made that the child is not yet prepared to keep up after all, apparently not the fit that was envisioned when the largess of admission was trialed. Later, counselors will encourage him to apply to schools and then colleges that are more matched to his academic level. The friend of the bullied child already had an altercation on his record since he got in a fight over a girl being called a racist slur, but that reason was never identified at the time. Feeling obliged to fulfill this role, his behavior is repeated with increasing consequences, and he eventually becomes involved in the juvenile justice system. In 6 short years one of these children sailed into Stanford on scholarship where he graduated without debt. His wonderful family had established a trust for him. Believing he could go anywhere and do anything, after Stanford, he studied as a Rhodes Scholar at Oxford.

Use your critical thinking skills to identify this scenario as within one generation at one school where each child had what appeared to be an equal opportunity for advancement. The story here occurs over a relatively short period of time—within a 10-year time frame. Telescope out to imagine the compounding impact over generations if one of these children started as the brutalized property of the other. How many compounding effects cascade across the generations?

My 20-year practice in higher education was a constant study in removing barriers for students. The tip of the education iceberg, the much exalted "teaching and learning" enterprise within education that drives much of the funding model, may be what you may imagine education is all about. Even in your own memory, you may think of classes and teachers, courses and professors, studying and testing to be education. These are considered core functions. All that other activity, such as matriculation, counseling and advising, student activities, administration, facilities, security, specific service programs (which evolved by advocacy since institutions themselves could not build adequate service infrastructure for someone not already fitted to the mold's efficiencies), were not considered core, they were ancillary.

During the recession of the 2000's, I was honored to be part of a college that met the challenge of our time. As an institution, we asked and answered a question. Some of us were inspired by MacArthur Fellow, Lisa Delpit, who wrote *Other People's Children*.[3] We answered this question about the community we served, "Are 'they' other people?" or, "Are 'they' our people?" The answer matters because you will do for your own, what you will not do for "others." With college leadership and community partners, I created and led teams built for proficiency in mitigating socioeconomic conditions that could derail a student's progress toward goal attainment.[4] We long abandoned any notion that some utopian state of meritocracy existed where students arrived "equally" challenged by life's circumstances. We started from a premise that success was inherent. Success could be developed (unfolded) if barriers were removed. For most students, the teaching and learning part of the educational enterprise was not the problem—especially when culturally responsive teaching and learning was an institutional priority. The problem was primarily the multitude of socioeconomic barriers that derailed the teaching and learning enterprise.

I envisioned our work as mimicking the privileges of the middle class. Since our program design and its interventions had to be reverse engineered to the problem to mitigate that problem's impact on student persistence, we became intimately aware of the lives of our students. They were hungry. We ensured access to food. They did not come from a long line of cultural capital where money management was necessarily a generational inheritance. We provided financial coaching. Students needed transportation. We created multiple supports for transportation. On any given day, I could manage a food truck delivery to stock an on-site food pantry and manage wealthy donors and leading policy makers who were never hungry while trying to make it in life.

One foundation sought us out because their scholarship investments had a less than 50% persistence rate (completing a semester and enrolling in the next semester). Partnering with our program of socioeconomic supports in the context of financial coaching, their scholarship recipients would receive their money contingent upon maximizing the use of those funds in a partnership with a personalized financial coach. We replicated the safety net that middle class status takes for granted when achieving their educational goals. After the 1st year of the foundation investing their scholarship funding with our students in financial coaching, their 50% persistence rate was transformed to a 97% persistence rate. This rate far exceeded the general population for the college despite multiple barriers these students faced.

Step 9: We Repair the Harm | 141

Students applied for the funding after receiving group-level orientation to the scholarship and then received individual support to complete the application. Rather than a cruel survival of the fittest gauntlet designed to eliminate those with an incorrect comma, the fully supported exercise was designed to mimic applying for a job to support career building. Everyone who tried would grow and develop from this process. They received ongoing financial coaching, even if they were not selected for this scholarship.

Unforgettable, my heart reels still as I recall one student's need statement. It read,

> I support the four generations who live in my 2-bedroom apartment. I will be 20 years old in 2 months. I work full time. I go to school full time. I keep a straight A average. If I get the scholarship, I will ask if I can get an air mattress since the sofa I sleep on hurts my back. That's not good for my multiple sclerosis.

The Silicon Valley icon, a *Time* magazine "Man" of the Year, whose family foundation funded these scholarships, invited my team to present our program results to the foundation. He was sitting at the modest conference table. As a lifelong musician, I can read the room to see if I have it! He was off my radar. He was a bit gruff, seemingly inattentive, busy on his iPhone. His sweatsuit had seen newer days, and I irreverently caught myself thinking, "This guy would go undetected on the San Francisco Muni (the bus system I was on when a driver told an elderly woman she could not stay on the bus with a live chicken, so she snapped its neck on the spot)." Knowing his stature among the icons of not only Silicon Valley, but among all business giants of all time in global enterprise, I challenge any of you to have sat there unconcerned with his impressions of a project that cost him less than $200,000 per year. It may sound like a lot of money in other contexts, but proportionately to what else received his attention, sitting for this hardly seemed an effective use of his time. It made more sense if you knew he immigrated to this country with nearly no money. He had not forgotten what it was to start with little. As iconic as he was, he remembered being where most of my students were, heroically trying to make ends meet with a vision for a better life.

He did not look up from his phone the whole time I was trotting through some outcomes that usually got oohs and ahhs at national education conferences. At the end, he finally looked up, asked one needle-in-a-haystack question while everyone perched a bit edgier in their seats. No one would have ever prepared to answer that question, nor did I, but for unrelated reasons, I knew the answer. As he looked back to his phone, he quickly glanced up and said, "Thank you for your good work." All exhaled gladness and pretended like gauntlets did not exist!

Not long after that, he passed away. His wife and daughter wanted to visit our financial capability center that housed the scholarship program in their name. We had financial coaching, an English language institute (in one of the most linguistically diverse counties in America), an employment center with the state system colocated on site, a program colocated with us that led medical professionals with "foreign-earned" credentials to recredentialling in the United States to mitigate workforce pipeline shortages, and a food pantry open to not only students, but anyone in the community who needed something to eat.

When the scholarship program started, I began a practice of taking a proud headshot of everyone who received a scholarship. I placed the 4 x 6 picture in a standard 5 x 7 in frame with a white mat and hung them along the walls of the center. As the semesters went by, the photos expanded into something of an art installation of beautiful, proud dignity on the way to a better future. By the time the icon's wife and daughter came to visit the program after hearing reports only, the walls were covered. It had become common to see families wander the halls to see a loved one's photo as a point of pride. Especially on graduation days, the halls were busier than the usual flow. But today, a regular day of me managing both billionaires and the broccoli delivery—as one does with a social justice doctorate—the only visitors were Mrs. Icon and her adult daughter.

Before sitting down for something of a program review, they walked the halls marveling at the photos like so many before them. Since the "art installation" did not identify itself but for one small plaque you could miss, they asked me, "Please tell us more about all of these people." When I said, "Everyone of these people received a scholarship in your name and 97% of them used the scholarship to successfully persist toward their credential." They teared up. "I wish he could have seen this" they said.

I've thought about that moment so often. It was such a humanizing moment. I had never realized that I had been serving anyone but students who met unimaginable challenges to succeed with their educational and economic goals. Without realizing it, I had also served the legacy of an iconic Silicon Valley billionaire. Something so human and accessible about their yearning that their patriarch could have seen such beauty had a visceral impact moved me. For them, the actual financial cost was a drop in the bucket. But how it mattered—to them, to his memory, to their encounter with beauty and dignity from a very different caste, to my ability to behold both their beholding and behold my own poverty experiences as one who identified with all of those on the walls, leading in the present and catalytic. In that visit, I had a profound almost "end-of-life" review of what matters.

Education can mean so much to so many, but as a transformer of conditions set by race, class, and caste, it has no equal. What it actually takes to transform our nation into a trajectory of greatness free from rigged advantage is full of common sense, compassion, beauty, and dignity. Resentment, culture wars, antagonism, and exploitation can help signal to us, like symptoms presenting disease, diagnose the problem, but beyond that, they cannot approximate how transcendent it is to see moments of a United States of America when it has a meritorious chance. I love those moments. Those moments where hope is the velocity of democracy.

My career in higher education was about fabricating middle class–like containments. These containments mitigated cascades that would have derailed economic and educational goal attainment among a diverse group of students, which our nation's rigged advantage marginalizes. We squander this talent at our peril. Without it we cannot compete in global markets where advantage rigged in Whiteness is already obsolete. Because of the persistence of rigged advantage, we have been behind for a long time. When you have consistently underinvested in the future "majority" of your nation, your nation's future includes decline. The decline will not be because the so-called supreme Whites are no longer the majority. Unless we change, it will be because of underinvestment, what Gloria Ladson-Billings calls educational debt.[5]

In higher education, I was constantly discounted for producing "boutique" demonstration programs that countered rigged advantage in an extraordinary crucible of circumstances—unnatural and unscalable. I agree, if we accept the premise, that extraordinary workarounds must counter rigged advantage. It is way past time for workarounds that tolerate rigged advantage. My educational practice to demonstrate effective workarounds to rigged advantage in some ways enables rigged advantage to persist—a sort of "We can make this mess work out if we do all of this!"

I grew weary of tinkering at the margins of the legacies of slavery. This book is a prescription for eliminating rigged advantage altogether. It should provide a clarion call that it is way past time for the United States of America to finally be what it presents, a competitive meritocracy where *democratic* entitlements guarantee a proliferation of talent where we are well, potentiated, and emergent.

Step 9: We Repair the Harm | 145

> At this juncture in American history, we place our bets. Will rigged advantage parasitically persist to extinguish its U.S. host, or will our cherished democratic entitlements, a level playing field of opportunity not rigged for some while exploiting others, extinguish rigged advantage and catapult a secure and competitive United States into its fullest potential in the 21st century?

Step 9, we repair the harm, will of course require you to zoom back and forth between that which is in your direct control and that which is not. Steps 1 through 8 will have led you through a scaffolded process of becoming clearer regarding the difference between the two. Step 9 requires you to educate yourself about both harm and repair and to determine the steps you will take individually and determine the steps you will support as a nation for the repair needed for our security and competitiveness. If it feels daunting to educate yourself specifically about harm and repair, an intermediate step could be reading a primer on social action by Rebecca Toporek and Muninder Kaur Ahluwalia, *Taking Action: Creating Social Change Through Strength, Solidarity, Strategy and Sustainability*.[6]

The brilliant work of so many individuals and organizations not only in the United States but across the globe contribute more than "typical news outlets" may present. This underrepresentation could lead you to conclude falsely about the potential of our future. Not only am I undaunted, I am excited to anticipate the seeds of a great harvest where the future of a United States of America holds our best days ahead.

The work to repair the harm is already being brilliantly documented and presented by so many. This is work for you to discover. A sample introductory list for your review cannot adequately illustrate the extent of high-quality resources that could inform you regarding repairing the harm. Knowing already that I am leaving out so many, I will provide you with a "getting started" list of resources I find reliable and informative. This list may lead you to the many more resources available to prepare your step 9 progress.

I recommend that you start by searching for each of these online. At first, just glance at each for an introductory impression and then return to those that match your interests for further exploration. Remember that these comprise a minute portion of my list. They are not your list. You will build your own list. You must do your own work.

- Equal Justice Initiative
- PolicyLink (A Blueprint for Racial Equity)
- FSG
- Prosperity Now
- William A. Darity, Jr. and Kirsten Mullen (*From Here to Equality: Reparations for Black Americans in the Twenty-First Century*)
- UC Berkeley, Othering and Belonging Institute (targeted universalism)
- USC Race and Equity Center
- Center for Law and Social Policy
- Stanford Center on Poverty and Inequality
- OXFAM, Inequality Kills Report
- The McKinsey Institute for Black Economic Mobility
- The Federal Reserve Banks (economic disparities)
- Center for Humane Technology
- National African American Reparations Commission (NAARC)
- U.S. Congress H.R. 40, Commission to Study and Develop Reparation Proposals for African Americans Act
- Institute for Justice and Reconciliation (Patron Desmond Tutu)
- Western States Center
- Southern Poverty Law Center

Learning Outcome

For peace and prosperity, implement remedies that eliminate disparities in socioeconomic outcomes.

CHAPTER 10

STEP 10
WE REMAIN VIGILANT

Step 10 Complements Step 4: We Detail the Problem

Key Words: **Remission, Eradication, Junkyard dogs**

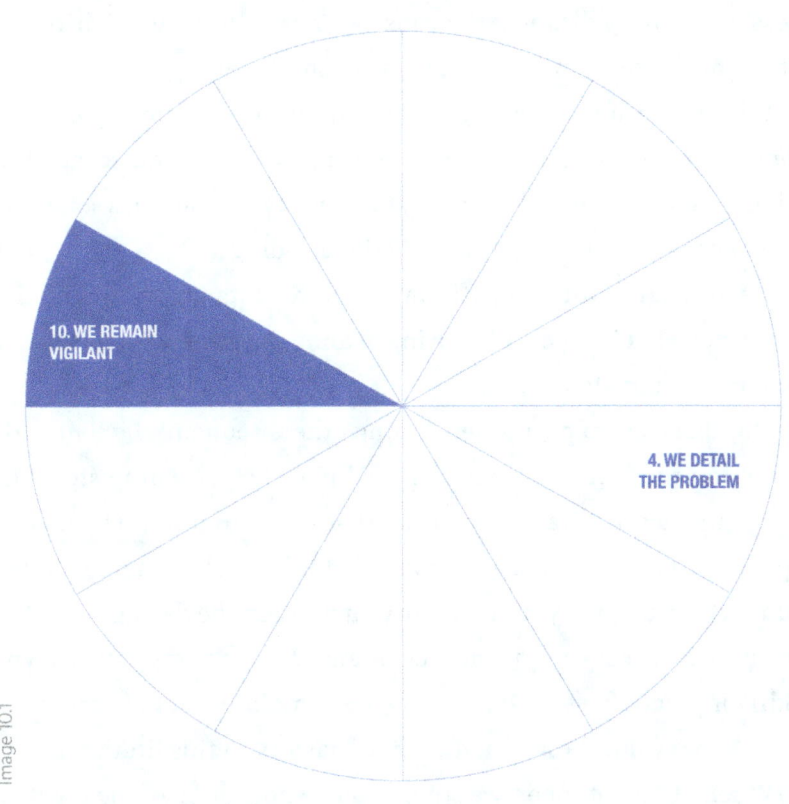

Image 10.1

What I Learned From Alcoholics About the Tenth Step of AA

"Continued to take personal inventory and when we were wrong promptly admitted it."[1]

The governing and complementary nature of steps 4 and 10 are self-evident. We keep our inventory current. Keep doing what you learned and began to practice in step 4. Clearing out the wreckage of the past is never a one-and-done experience. The imprints of survival, which are hardened against deadly alcoholism and buried in our consciousness, will hardly disappear because we have attempted an inventory of wrongs, shortcomings, or defects of character.

What we become in the face of horrific dysfunction may possibly be forgiven, reconciled, transformed, repaired, and even transcended, but a hole is left bored into a boundary of integrity that now has something of a bandage where triage stopped the bleeding.

Healing takes time, repetition, truth, repentance, reconciliation, and renewal. It is especially during healing time that we habituate the progress of our steps so far.

Step 10 is a step positioned among others sequentially, but it also draws on the work of other steps. Obviously, governing step 4 has direct impact. But have a heads up that work from step 11 (personal spirituality) and step 12 (applied spirituality) will provide ongoing support for keeping your inventory current. In the daily grind where it is easy to forget everything, acceptance becomes my go-to survival skill for practicing step 10. Acceptance remains one of my great challenges in my quest for a modicum of mastery in this lifetime!

When I first got sober, we studied the third edition of the Big Book, where one could reference page 449. You can see in the following photo that my beloved Big Book is a bit worse for wear: it's splotchy, the cover is missing, and the spine is a bit stressed (how like real life!).

Step 10: We Remain Vigilant | 149

I was tickled when I moved to San Francisco to find a meeting group called the 449ers down the block on Potrero Hill (get it? San Francisco Forty Niners? It always reminded me of years earlier when my clinical supervisor in Hattiesburg compared me to Joe Montana, but I didn't know who that was). Page 449 is part of the third-edition story "Doctor, Alcoholic, Addict." This Big Book story is one of the most trusted and revered stories in Alcoholics Anonymous. Page 449 is about acceptance. I am *immensely grateful* for this story's role in keeping me sober. (The story is written by Dr. Paul O. who later wrote a book called *There's More to Quitting Drinking Than Quitting Drinking*.)[2]

> And acceptance is the answer to all my problems today. When I am disturbed, it is because I find some person, place, thing or situation—some fact of my life— unacceptable to me, and I can find no serenity until I accept that person, place, thing, or situation as being exactly the way it is supposed to be at this moment. Nothing, absolutely nothing happens in God's world by mistake. Until I accept my alcoholism, I could not stay sober; unless I accept life completely on life's terms, I cannot be happy. I need to concentrate not so much on what needs to be changed in the world, as what need to be changed in me and in my attitudes.[3]

Through the years, it helped me when I understood acceptance not as approval or sanction, but more as a simple but profound acknowledgement that something is what it is. My prosecutorial mind wants to jump to the wrongness of something before I even acknowledge the reality of something. Jumping to *wrongness* first limits what I can understand about it. A breakthrough came for me when I understood that by acknowledging the reality of something, I can better understand what is wrong with it. Once I adequately understand it, then I can better check it off my list of prosecutorial duties and be free to stay sober for another day.

You may find that acceptance helps you with your continuing inventory. Also, continue to work on your contextualized family history with help from your *Twelve Steps for White America* workbook. As you do, I recommend that you relish in this discovery of others by watching a PBS series featuring Harvard Professor Henry Louis Gates, Jr., called *Finding Your Roots*. Each program features at least a couple of people who are famous enough to catch your celebrity interest. The series features Gates revealing their genealogical discoveries, which expert teams have compiled and presented page by page.

The guests are profoundly impacted. In their discovery, I sense how profound and immediate the past (ironically not as past anymore) must be for each of us. We come to see in each other the stories that enter the room when we enter. We appreciate and honor that we are the ones who made it, who survived to discover, tell, and contribute. With that appreciation, we become more than each other's triggers in our subjective exploitation. We behold our humanity, literally encoded in our DNA, which transcends what we call the present.

While each person's discovery is riveting for me, I cannot unsee one of the most poignant and beautiful expressions of how the past can touch the present. Actress Maya Rudolph, mother to children whom she adores, sat across from the table from Gates as he turned the pages of her personal ancestry. One of those turned pages revealed to her for the first time an encounter with an ancestor. Without him, she would not exist today as a celebrated contributor to American culture and a mother to her beloved children.

Gates introduced her to her ancestor as a 5-year-old boy who was enslaved. When she met him on the page, her present reality, imagining her own children at age 5, and comparing them to her 5-year-old ancestor living under the brutality of plantation slavery, transferred her mothering and adoration back in time to him. As the veil of unknowing lifted and the cruelest reality set it, her realization was excruciating for all to see. It meant that his mother could at any moment watch him being snatched away from her, sold right out from under her care. He could be beaten into submission. As a possession, if his whereabouts got out of the enslaver's control, state-sanctioned practices such as fugitive slave patrols could terrorize his escape and hunt him down like no more than a wild animal. To have humanity slaughtered out of the soul is an unforgettable amputation. All of that horror became real to Maya Rudolph as her mothering yearned to reach back in time and save him.

If you are a White American and you believe that slavery is a thing of the past, it likely means that you have never had a moment where Maya Rudolph, nor any other Black American's pain, transferred back in time to save an enslaved ancestor, is made real to you.

As I try to write the next sentence,

I must say that it is difficult.

I want to try to say something to you, in compassion, that helps you realize the condition of your soul.

How do I tell you what you cannot see?

How do I describe for you something so profoundly sad as the conditioning of this depravity, this twisted entitled oblivion to the pain of others in your community?

My grandfather grew up in a home (where I played as a child) where his living elders fought for Maya Rudolph's 5-year-old ancestor to be enslaved, with no future, no hope, totally vulnerable to brutality.

I gasp.

I cannot breathe.

That is not a relic of the past. Legacies of slavery permeate the present. Maya Rudolph is present. I am present. We are here, now, with this, in this wrenching pain.

How can I rest without repentance, atonement/reconciliation, and renewal? How can you dare scoff at repentance and atonement. God have mercy on your soul.

If you have never arrived at a point where this crushing reality suffocates you with horror, then the spirituality that keeps me sober enables my heart to break for your soul. How in your condition can you mock the outcry for your redemption as "woke" culture out to get you? This is a soul-sickness wreaking atrocity for others, while it amputates your own salvation.

I must straddle my commitment to you and stay firmly yoked in my intention to behold you with compassion and respect, knowing that if I condemn you, I lose the privilege and power to impact you. The truth of your soul's condition is the greatest compassion and respect I can deliver to you.

For *your* sake, do not let one more day of your life pass without an urgency to know exactly how your past lives on in the present.

> As a White American,
>
> it may be that,
>
> here,
>
> now,
>
> reading this,

you realize for the first time,

the work ahead.

Imagine this. Look Maya Rudolph in the eye and let her look back into yours to see a fierce resolve; you cannot change the past, but never more will your callous ignorance perpetuate the past in rigged advantage, created then, still operating today. For your sake, do not argue. Do not dismiss. Do not project and displace. Heal yourself to let healing begin (we have hardly started) in our nation.

If you are arriving at this for the first time, it helps me hold onto my compassion for you to think of a junkyard dog—an animal that has been brutalized to its *ugliest instinctual aggressions*, just to protect the junkyard owner's junk. Exploited Whites guard the junk of a small elite group of power Whites who trickle down some scrappy benefits of membership in the "White club." Like a junkyard dog, you get to guard, you get to run to the end of your chain with a foaming aggression, you may even get to bite under the right conditions (insurrection, for example), and for that service, you may get something to eat, and you can rest assured that you are not those others, you are with the junkman. White, like the junkman.

It is pathetic. (You are not pathetic.)

It is tragic. (It does not have to be this way.)

Just like an alcoholic's existence could be more than a death spiral of addiction, your existence can be more than the guardian of junk.

No wonder that you are enraged.

No wonder that you feel somebody needs to pay.

No wonder that you want some restoration.

But be clear. Make sure you understand who is yanking your chain. Black Americans getting some relief from you is not the point. This book is for you that you may break that chain that binds you. This treatment plan is for you that you may consecrate true liberty free from the trickle-down junk of rigged advantage.

This is how rigged advantage operates a Whiteness collusion using White supremacy and anti-Blackness to sustain itself. Exploited White Americans protect someone else's junk. Step 10 continues the work of step 4 since rigged advantage patterns are difficult to eradicate. Exploited Whites' duties condition you into (sometimes metaphorically and sometimes actually) the *ugliest instinctual aggressions.*

It is true (step 1) that slavery legacies, which persist in the present, are surely horrific for Black Americans and other People of Color who are also Othered in the process. But this book is written for you. How much longer can you tolerate it that any White Americans are commodified as junkyard dogs to guard the junk of a few elite power Whites? How long? Not long.

What of This May We Apply to Our Problem, Rigged Advantage?

How do we rid ourselves of something we cannot see? How do we remain vigilant to guard against something we have never been trained to understand in the first place? Culture significantly informs how we label and interpret circumstances, issues, and ideology. I once sat at a table with four aspiring African American college presidents and one White aspiring college president. Having been supervised by African Americans for the vast majority of my time in higher education and by African American women mostly, I recounted several instances when the college president, my boss, and I would enter a professional room where I would be the one assumed to have the highest rank. I have seen my African American boss in a room of colleagues at times when a facilitator could not even notice her hand in the air. It became ridiculous how often I would have to redirect to my boss, the CEO of an institution with a multi-million dollar budget serving several thousand college students.

The African Americans at the table then took the conversation further by talking about the many considerations they account for when entering a room and engaging that room as a leader. What cannot be said. What must be said. What is somewhat provocative. What would convey gravitas. What is needed to manage the presumption of incompetence that too many unfortunately are looking to confirm. Are these the right clothes? What about my hair? At what point in the engagement will I have earned a pass to do what is needed for the engagement to have been a success?

I know that as a White man, in those same rooms, I am automatically seen, acknowledged, and presumed competent. In California, all I need to manage is what people think of a Southern accent (apparently all diversity is not a good thing!), but that is about the extent of what I ever concern myself with regarding presentation. As a quick example, a Silicon Valley leader approached me after a meeting to "compliment me" on how especially articulate he found me to be! (I was a C-suite higher ed administrator with a doctorate. What could have warranted such a surprised assessment?) He had no idea how much he had just disclosed to me. I digress.

Incessant attention to impressions management burdens leadership for African Americans. Back at the table's conversation engaging with everyone, I asked the other White man at the table if he was aware that his African American colleagues went through all that every day. His response, apparently entirely oblivious to their plight, was, "I don't have time to do all that. I'd never get anything done!" The pathos that swirled around that table was palpable, but he could not see himself, that table, that moment, nor his colleagues. All I could think is "My God, we have so far to go." Whiteness requires no self-reflection.

With this background, let us consider experience that is common among many White Americans compared to experience that is common among many Black Americans. Many (if not most) White Americans regularly walk into the "rooms" of life (work, school, worship, shops, courts, weddings, reunions, townhall, clubs, concerts) and never stop to account for the Whiteness in those rooms. In other words, it is "normal" for the world of many White Americans to be so "White" that the Whiteness operates invisibly—so normalized that it is not even noticed. For example, White Americans generally do not walk into a room thinking "Everyone in this room is White." Since it would be an exception for that normalcy to get any notice, that exception ("Whiteness interruptus") would usually mean that something *disordered* the Whiteness order.

Conversely, many Americans who are People of Color, and Black Americans specifically, walk into the rooms of life where they may be the only Black American in the room. Historically, as a survival mechanism among White domination, most Black Americans performed a calculation in relation to Whiteness that

- determined how many Black Americans are in the room (if any others are present);
- estimated the status of any other Black Americans in the room or nearby;
- accounted for how their individual presence may trigger "Whiteness interruptus";
- adopted a socialized performance deemed most acceptable to mitigate consequences for "Whiteness interruptus"—as *Whistling Vivaldi*[4] illustrates;
- calculated a return on investment for how either their contribution or silence will be rewarded or punished (now or later); and
- managed elaborate code switching to ensure that White Americans were as comfortable as possible.

While this list is presented in the past tense (the most comfortable setting for White American readers who want to believe this is a thing of the past), this is an ever clear and present danger where any misstep by any Black American of any age or class could have deadly consequences.

- A child might be playing with a toy gun in a park (Tamir Rice, murdered).
- A teenager might be walking home in a hoodie after buying Skittles at the convenience store (Trayvon Martin, murdered).
- A father driving with his girlfriend pulled over with his child in the back seat (Philando Castile, murdered).
- A jogger in the neighborhood stalked by White men and a pickup truck (Ahmaud Arbery, murdered).
- A young EMT recently graduated sitting in the private sanctity of home, invaded (Breonna Taylor, murdered.)
- A man just outside a convenience store thrown to the ground (George Floyd, murdered—state-sanctioned execution without due process recorded in the light of day while a traumatized world of witnesses gasped). The initial report cites no problems with police actions.

This litany of 21st-century lynching is a present tyranny incompatible with the ideal of the American story. Horrifically, this list could go on for pages. This is the *modern-day United States of America for Black Americans*, a legacy of racialized violence present on this soil seeded more than a century before the tyranny of King George III became a catalyst triggering colonial resistance. This is not debatable history simply because it may be uncomfortable or incompatible with an idealized image of American potential. Such hypocrisy mocks the very name of a United States of America. It is a quicksand that bogs our future security and competitiveness. Triggering this original sin, our enemies war against us without firing a shot. Precisely because I love my country, I lament that these conditions persist to poison American potential.

White Americans can enter the room on a regular basis and never consider their Whiteness because it is rarely a life-and-death matter.

If such abandon (otherwise known as justice, liberty, peace, and the pursuit of happiness) is ever possible for Black Americans, it is with the survival knowledge that at any minute calculating their relationship to Whiteness is an ever-present necessity for themselves and their children. It is not the daily lived experience of most White Americans to fear for their safety, worried that a misstep could mean their beloved children could be murdered for triggering Whiteness interruptus. It is present reality for Black Americans.

A beacon of justice and liberty for peace and prosperity shines a light on threats both foreign and domestic. White Americans must do the work necessary to eliminate rigged advantage and the horrific racialized violence upon which it depends.

> "I didn't know" is no excuse.
>
> "I didn't create it" is no excuse.
>
> "I did not intend ..." is no excuse.

Exploiting individually troubled circumstances and/or history to claim an exemption from the benefits of rigged advantage to White Americans at large is no excuse.

None of these excuses produces the work required of citizenship.

We must urgently do everything possible to excise this malignant tumor from our body politic. This is the work, but the headwinds are strong. Even though it is a condition of Whiteness to displace the burden of work onto the backs of marginalized others (a legacy of slavery that persists into the present), this work is not optional. American democracy is unsustainable without this work. Make no mistake, if you let "others" do this work, you should expect to reap what you sow. I'm afraid that is where we are. As of January 6, 2021, it must be plain for all the world to see. As long as Black Americans bore the brunt of America's fault lines, Whiteness enabled White Americans to live in a rigged-advantage fairy tale bamboozled, exploited, and placated by privileges of membership—enough crumbs to sustain the status quo.

Are those crumbs enough?

How long will you watch an ever-widening gap of inequality hoard unimaginable wealth for so few when so many, including you, despair and die?

How long? Not long!

As a country southerner from a farming tradition, the biblical parables about seed and harvest always resonated for me. I recognized from experience the potency of the seeding and harvest metaphors. Today, when I see spiritual mastery in others who are working for a United States of America, I see demonstrated a certain wisdom, which my experience frames as a

triumvirate of discipline required for social justice mastery:

1. "Don't curse your seed."
2. "Count your many blessings."
3. "Reap when the harvest comes."

Triumvirate mastery means that when we put in the work

1. we accept it and let it come to fruition;
2. we acknowledge exactly what our assets are and what they are becoming; and
3. we claim it and use our known capital strategically for what's to come.

Insidiously, the hegemony of rigged advantage persists when, after we've done the work and the results are in, we are still too triggered and immobilized by immediate fodder to relish and capitalize on hard-won progress.

It is sadly like someone, who always dreamed of being rich, letting a poverty mind rule them amid the blessings of realized abundance. I am so proud when I see in others the ability to accept fruition, acknowledge its value, and remember it as capital for the hard work ahead. Live your blessings well! This mastery exemplifies how we move into our abundance! When I see it in others, I am immensely satisfied because it shows me how to see myself with clarity. Reflecting on it is like sitting in a calm and medicinal meditation on what the yoga philosophers call *Aham Brahmasmi*: "I" am "that."

Exploited Whites may experience conditioning to interpret *Twelve Steps for White America* as a plan of social welfare to benefit underprivileged Blacks who are in need of White generosity. That is wrong. Those eyes cannot see; those ears cannot hear. These 12 steps will have an ultimate impact on others, but, like an alcoholic in recovery, these steps chart your liberty. These steps chart a pathway for White America's spiritual truth, repentance, atonement, and liberation (freedom).

Princeton Professor Eddie Glaude, Jr. teaches us in his excellent book, *Democracy in Black: How Race Still Enslaves the American Soul*,[5] that we experience a "value gap" (the belief that White people are valued more than others) and "racial habits" (the things we do, without thinking, that sustain the value gap), which undergird racial inequality. Like kudzu, the vine that ate the South, racial habits not only do not die hard, but they also seem to grow at an alarming rate.

Step 10 is our practice to ensure that we continue to account for the pervasiveness of our racial habits and position us for a more secure and more competitive global future.

Learning Outcome

Habituate rigorous self-assessment to sustain justice, then liberty, replacing periodic remission of rigged advantage with its eradication.

CHAPTER 11

STEP 11
WE CHOOSE REVERENCE

Step 11 Complements Step 5: We Present the Problem

Key Words: **Readiness, Acceptance, Discipline, Devotion**

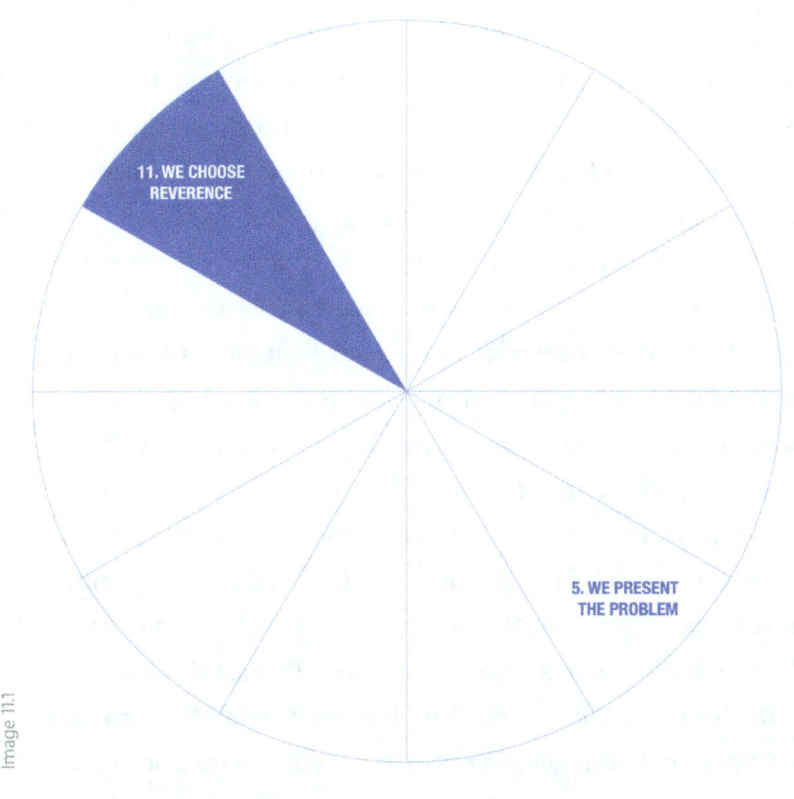

Image 11.1

What I Learned From Alcoholics About the Eleventh Step of AA

> *"Sought through prayer and meditation to improve our conscious contact with God as we understood Him, praying only for knowledge of His will for us and the power to carry that out."*[1]

Alcoholism steadily progresses to overtake body, mind, and soul. Wreckage, consequences, and codependents prove their reach beyond the host, but, fundamentally, alcoholism is a self-spiraling phenomenon. Alcohol operates first as behavioral reinforcement for a desirable effect: a solution. It becomes a nightmare from which periodic awakenings only reveal the horror that the nightmare mercifully masks. If sleep is the protector of dreams,[2] a nightmare may, at times, be more relief than the lived reality for an alcoholic. Normally, the terror of the night resolves in the morning. Waking reality for the alcoholic may be more grim since there is no waking up from its fate.

The terror of alcoholism is a trajectory of despair, a hopelessly worsening condition hurtling toward incarceration, secondary disease, and death by homicide or suicide. An alcoholic's nightmare may mercifully sort and process the day's torment, but the natural equilibrium of the new day never comes. The ancient hope "weeping may endure for a night, but joy cometh in the morning"[3] never comes. Before alcoholism, cycles of trial and error were Earth school's humane instruction for growth and development. Now, the slings and arrows of outrageous fortune[4] only accelerate the slide to hell lurking lurid among the living. Without learning, life becomes increasingly meaningless.

During the last days of my drinking, the people who remained in my dysfunctional orbit who were paying attention could see hell lurking lurid in my life. They would have seen my death as inevitable instead of a shock. Casual acquaintances, kept at a distance, may have sensed that something was off. These last days of my drinking hell lived alongside the final days of earning my bachelor's degree. That meant that most of my world consisted of settings where I could skirt in and skirt out with an appearance of dignity and promise. To ensure the masquerade, people were distanced and reduced to no more than characters objectified in my waking nightmare. One character loomed large. My religion professor, Clayton Sullivan, passed me in the hall one day and yelled with his one volume booming voice as he kept walking by, "Watson, you have been here a long time. Do you even know how many credits you have?" I had no idea. But, any answer I could rattle was for me alone since he rounded the corner escaping any fallout from the grenade he just launched.

Sullivan was not my advisor officially. I took several of his courses—enough to be amused at the "Oh my God" expression of new students on the first day of class. One of the upper-level electives was offered at night, "The Life of Jesus." In retrospect it should have been titled the "Life of the Maccabees" because it took a while for the course to get to the Jesus part of it. The course attracted some of the townies, who were mostly fundamentalists looking for an advanced Sunday School lesson. With no concern for ruffling pious feathers, he huffed on the first night, "If you think we are going to roll a spinet in here and belt out a round of 'Stand Up Stand Up for Jesus,' you better leave now. You are in for a world of hurt!"

The only person who could care any less what church folk thought was my father. Frenzied after a hellfire and brimstone sermon, my 12-year-old little legs ran home to "witness" to Daddy "lest his soul be lost forever in a pit of hellfire." Normally a stasis of equipoise and congeniality, his temper exploded, and he yelled at me, "You can go to church with them racist sombitches if you want to, but I'd rather go to hell." I could see that my father and Clayton Sullivan had a lot in common, which belied the chasm between a lack of a high school diploma and a doctorate in theology.

It did not surprise me that Sullivan later wrote a book titled, *Rescuing Jesus From the Christians*.[5] After taking several of his courses, I was used to the intellectual tug of war Sullivan relished. His lectures would devolve from a legible chalk board frenzy into indecipherable hieroglyphics as his monologue freight train sped up. I would jab into his rhythm with some counterpoint just to break it up. It was always exactly what he wanted so his "reduce-you-to-rubble-dance" could begin. "Watson! Good God. ... All the mental jackrabbits you chase."

He loved it. I was awake and brave! Few others wanted to poke a snake, but I enjoyed it. Sullivan and I were equally shocked to run into each other at a Sunday morning service of the local Unitarian Universalist Church where he was the guest speaker. I had never actually pictured him as the minister he had trained to be! I could not hear what he was saying over all the mental contortions I was working through to behold it all.

About a week after the "how many credits" grenade, he saw me again as he perched over the ledge of a railing on the second floor of the undergraduate library. I walked into the atrium entrance through the ground floor. The first thing you could see was this massive plant that was cared for by one of the librarians. I later saw him working at some "N'Awlins" (we hate it, but you buy it, we sell it) kitsch store in the French Quarter. The library was a hushed setting so the decorum shock of a professor yelling down at me turned almost every novitiate head toward me—not the librarians, just some side-eye from them. Experience taught them that a return to quiet would be quicker without confronting him. Sullivan bellowed "Hey! Watson, you are smart enough to be a hospital administrator. What *are* you going to do with this philosophy and religion shit?"

Like those baseball legends in the movie *Field of Dreams* he turned and disappeared into the stacks before I could even utter "What the hell?!" Mortified, I remember in that intense moment of embarrassment hoping this could be my last round in the cycle of rebirth! Nostalgia now remembers the episode as my 20th-century version of an ancient Greece walk among the stoa with a philosopher-teacher![6] When he later published an irreverent book of fiction representing his experience of southern Mississippi, *Why Beulah Shot Her Pistol in the Baptist Church*,[7] I was amused but, again, not surprised.

He was right. I had no idea how many credits I had. Every semester, my actual advisor signed off on whatever I handed to him. Once, when sensing that I felt advisement should entail a bit more, he countered, "Watson, if you are smart enough to get A's in philosophy and linguistics, you can read a catalog. Have a great semester." My studies in philosophy, comparative religion, and cultural anthropology thrilled and comforted me at the same time. My mind and my soul stretched open with every class. I had not given a second thought to leaving.

The redneck iron curtain, which had staged my soul-crushing existence in the red clay hills of Mississippi, now opened onto decadent intellectual frontiers and exotic travel in Peru, Senegal, Mali, Côte d'Ivoire, and later Guatemala and Honduras. I ventured out of the provinciality of Mississippi poverty onto a globe of wonder and potential. Alcoholism threatened all of it. My emergent hopes were shunted by hell lurking lurid among the living. It seemed worse to have had a taste of another life. I could have decayed still trapped in a rural county strapped by poverty and a history of cotton plantation slavery, lynchings, a race war, and a burial plot for the notorious five-term U.S. Senator James O. Eastland, once described as "a symbol of racism in America."[8]

In these final days of both the bachelor's degree and a drinking nightmare, I was unintentionally taunted by a petite woman whose integrity and actualization were potent. The antithesis of what I had become, her example became an oasis in my desiccation. At the end of drinking for me, the long road to recovery was triggered not out of being beaten and bludgeoned by alcoholism, but something more powerful—a vision of what I was losing. As I squandered the hope created by educational opportunity, I felt like the rich man damned in hell looking up to Abraham in heaven, with the beggar Lazarus in his bosom. She embodied what I could have been. In the end, this became the final straw that broke an alcoholic camel's back, that my chance for a better life was slipping away.

Officially, she was the Methodist minister for the campus (director of the Wesley Foundation),[9] but she was beyond any stereotype I could muster for a minister. Her authenticity was electric. Mickey, the minister who came to see me in the psychiatric hospital interrupting my suicidal ideation, was the first herald in my alcoholism. Now her. I thought it avant-garde that a Methodist minister was married to a man who was Jewish. Their baby took her last name with his last name being hyphenated to it.

At a student gathering in her home, she served me my first vegetarian chili. This is a minor detail except that soon after that I became a lifelong vegetarian. I imagined her rationale beyond the trendiness of it. Would *I* kill the cow to eat it? It was not complicated. Months afterward, I was getting ready for an anthropology trip. My lent-like fasting intended to ready me for an ultimately unrealized visit to monks in Nepal. I had been told that it would be offensive for them to smell a meat eater. The preparation instilled a lifelong practice of seeing the completeness of a thing, what Yogacharya Ellen Grace O'Brian would later teach as drawing the circle.[10] Where do I enter a cycle of action, and what is the result of my engagement with that activity?

The Methodist campus minister (one of the early women so ordained in Mississippi) was a political activist who supported a movement protesting U.S. involvement in Central America. The slaughter of U.S. nuns in El Salvador was a recent outrage.[11] The atrocity of the slaying of Archbishop Óscar Romero of San Salvador (canonized by Pope Francis in 2018) felt like an evil in which the United States was colluding.

Formed in 1983, Witness for Peace[12] opposed U.S. funding of the Contras and sent thousands of U.S. citizen "witnesses" to Nicaragua to see and then tell the story of what was happening there. This Methodist minister was organizing a contingency for Witness for Peace. I yearned to go. I could apply what I was learning in classes about the history of the Jesuits in Latin America[13] and key theorists and intellectuals such as Paulo Freire,[14] Gustavo Gutiérrez,[15] and Leonardo Boff.[16]

Coming of age and learning in this dynamic of activism was everything I had hoped for when imagining if I would ever escape the red clay hills of Mississippi. Yet, here I was, an alcoholic in circumstances as rich as ever, but trapped in hell, looking heavenward toward Lazarus in Abraham's bosom. The psychic and soul pain I felt surely sensed that a blessed future was in forfeiture. Not only was the past painful, but the present was also mortally degrading, and the future seemed squandered out of reach. I did not think I would be alive past 30.

How could I realize that in those final moments of despair a seismic shift potentiated a great future? Like a phoenix rising, my decline was not the end. The benefit of hindsight teaches me some deep spiritual truth. While what I could see was death and despair, my trajectory to greater fulfillment than I could have ever imagined was already underway. There, in what I perceived to be catastrophic loss from which I would not recover, the solution was seeded. Hope was germinating. I was already on the path to recovery and a transforming transcendence of power, mastery, and abundance. Recovery begins even before it looks like recovery.

What of This May We Apply to Our Problem, Rigged Advantage?

You have learned so far that your personal practice working the *Twelve Steps for White America* benefits you foremost. You work these steps so that you may live free from rigged advantage wrought off the backs of marginalized others. These principles teach you that while it is essential to make things right with others, the reason we work the steps is for our own freedom. Applied here, we work the steps that we may be free of the debt incurred by rigged advantage. This shift from wronged others to liberating ourselves is a pathway of choosing reverence by practicing acceptance, discipline, and devotion to better days ahead for all.

To practice step 11, it is very important that your work on steps 1–10 has been rigorous. Keep in mind that step 11 is a complementary step. Step 11 is governed by step 5, "We present the problem." Step 5 required you to present the results of steps 1–4 to another human being.

If you have not understood steps 1–4 well enough to effectively present the problem to another human being, you do not have a sufficient foundation to follow the spiritually/ethically rooted concepts introduced in step 11.

It may be that as you read through step 11 you want to fight it. Fight it if you need to. Fight hard. Struggle with it. Let yourself welcome that. It may mean that it is presenting itself in a way that requires something of you. Choosing reverence requires willingness, discipline, and some mastery. Be sure that the fight is about step 11 and not governing step 5. If steps 1–5 were not thorough, you are not going to have a successful experience with step 11.

By the time you are at step 11, it is something like sitting in a plane on the tarmac waiting for the rush toward lift off. You already decided to travel. You purchased a ticket. You arrived at the airport early, got through security, found the gate, boarded, and settled in hoping that person next to you is not going to be problematic. To practice step 11 without having taken all the previous steps with rigor, you are not cleared for takeoff. If you have taken the previous steps seriously with rigor, you can fly now. In other words, you are sufficiently prepared for the rigors of spiritual discipline that recovering alcoholics generally understand as "sought through prayer and meditation to improve our conscious contact with God as we understood Him, praying only for knowledge of His will for us and the power to carry that out."

Since step 11 is about choosing reverence, the following practices are provided as examples:

- Telescoping
- We versus me
- Ahimsa and Asteya
- Drawing the circle
- Crucible of loving kindness

These are examples of practices that have not only kept me sober but inform my practice regarding race in America. These are not meant to be exhaustive. I provide them to illustrate how one person makes sense of step 11. *You must find your own way.*

Telescoping

Choosing reverence is necessarily transcendent. It is in the choosing that we extend the reach of our self. We extend (telescope) beyond the immediacy of our individual reflection (self) to a larger panorama of humanity, a collective of selves comprising a whole greater than the sum of its parts. One could argue that this telescoping between individual and collective is an ethical (spiritual for some) practice that enables individual selves to experience the larger Self from which we no longer feel separate but recognize as one and the same. Some describe it as spiritual growth, feeling connected, plugged in, awakened, rededicated.

We practiced this telescoping skill earlier in the book when we examined perspective. To recap, from the perspective of me sitting at a computer keyboard typing for an hour, I haven't moved. However, since Earth continued its 365-day trek around the sun, the Earth moved

60,000-plus miles in the hour that I could assert I had not moved. Since I am on the Earth which moved, I moved while not moving!

>Telescope setting on (s)elf = I did *not* move.

>Telescope setting on (S)elf = I *did* move; I moved a lot!

>Imagine I am on the witness stand pressured by an aggressive prosecutor,

>"Your honor, I ask that the court declare Dr. Watson a hostile witness. Dr. Watson, can you please just answer the question. Did you or did you not move?"

>"I cannot tell a lie, your honor. I did move and I did not move."

>The judge declares,

>"Dr. Watson, this court finds you in contempt."

We try to understand the world in discrete black-and-white simplicities. We seek an amount of predictable certainty to get through the day. Sometimes our drive for simplicity twists the truth to a breaking point. But we do it every day. Race is an example. Race in the United States is so very complicated. One of the requirements of step 11 is a commitment to shift from a habit of twisting simplicity with blunt instruments to a practice of truth using a more sophisticated set of refined tools that equip us for effective citizenship in a complex democracy.

Telescoping from self to Self differs from the pessimist or optimist glass half full or half empty—that is a conclusion about the same fact. For example, 4 ounces of water in an 8-ounce glass, is perceived differently. Four ounces of water is the same regardless of your framework.

Telescoping is one's ability to transverse seemingly *different facts* held to be true at the same time.

I moved.

I didn't move.

And no, so-called alternative facts are not different facts held to be true at the same time since one is actually a fact and another is a politically expedient contortion more akin to our long tradition of bamboozling in America.

We Versus Me: What Is True for Us May Not Be True for Me. Something Not True About Me Can Still Be True About Us

A specific example would be the following: What is true for White American households may not be true for my individual White American household.

If in your imagination you could line up all the households in the United States, median refers to the number in the middle of the line. Half have more wealth and half have less wealth.

Regarding median wealth in America:

> White American households have eight times the household wealth that Black American households have.[17]
>
> However, I, an individual White American household, may be struggling financially to make ends meet, and in fact, I am worse off than my parents were.
>
> Things are getting worse for me even while median household wealth for all White Americans is eight times greater the Black American households. Both these things can be true at the same time.
>
> Finally, what **is true for median black Households may be true for my White household even though it is not true for the median White households.**

Next, for deeper exploration, let us look at some ancient spiritual principles that appear in some form in most major religions. Since Martin Luther King's nonviolence is a legacy of Gandhi, we will look at that concept, and we will look at an additional concept from a common source that has significantly influenced our lives.

Ahimsa (Nonviolence) and Asteya (Nonstealing)

Most would agree that the Reverend Martin Luther King, Jr. is one of the most influential figures of 20th-century American life. History has a way of washing the past in the present to remember however it suits us today.

To illustrate, let's recall the famous "I Have a Dream" speech and take a pop quiz:

> **True or false:**
>
> 1. MLK envisioned a future where people would be judged not by the color of their skin but the content of their character.
>   _____ True
>   _____ False
> 2. MLK described the reason for the March on Washington in part by saying "We have come to our nation's capital to cash a check."
>   _____ True
>   _____ False

My guess is that nearly everyone can immediately answer the first question, True. That is part of the sound bite history we are fed. Regarding the second question, fewer may be so sure. The sound bite is rarely "came to cash a check." I do remember "mole hills in Mississippi," of course! But admit it. Too many Americans have never actually listened to the whole speech. Even less have read it.

The MLK remembered is an American icon of Ahimsa, nonviolence, a visionary of a future where desegregation and the American dream of a meritocracy is realized. However, especially toward the end of his life, he increasingly addressed economic issues. King went to Memphis, where he was assassinated to advocate for better wages for sanitation workers. The policy context for that time was the Vietnam War. He protested war spending when our own people languished in poverty.

King lost favor in the civil rights movement and died with a 75% disapproval rating.[18] That low favorability rating, 25 points more unfavorable than in 1963, was shared by a growing contingent of activists who embraced change by any means necessary. His adherence to nonviolence in the face of White supremacists' anti-Blackness was perceived insufficient to impact the drastic change that was needed. He is esteemed now—especially as the sanitized nonviolent statesman—but by the end, it was clear that his message of economic justice was even more controversial than his dream of civil rights. His message of nonviolence (*ahimsa*) was more palatable than a message of nonstealing (*asteya*), then and now. But the message of economic justice was there all along. In the March on Washington, the part about cashing a check was true.

King's nonviolence was modeled on an earlier democratic revolution that he hoped to actuate in the United States. Mohandas K. Gandhi, the London trained lawyer in a suit and tie, returned to his homeland, India, the jewel of the British Crown, after practicing law in South Africa. For what he accomplished sans suit to free India from British rule, he became known as the beloved Mahatma (Great Soul) Gandhi. He did not invent new methods out of whole cloth. He was making applications from the Hindu tradition, *Sanatana* dharma.

Yoga philosophy is a practice of *Sanatana* dharma. As explained in *The Yoga Sutra* by Pantanjali,[19] the practice of yoga builds on 10 universal principles of dharma: five *yamas* (practices to avoid) and five *niyamas* (practices to do.) *Ahimsa* and *asteya* are among the five practices to avoid:

Five Yamas (Self-Restraint):

- *Ahimsa*: Nonharming
- *Asteya*: Nonstealing
- *Satya*: Truthfulness
- *Brahmacharya*: Right use of vital force
- *Aparigraha*: Nonattachment

It may be that the most famous of these *yamas* in the USA is *ahimsa*: nonviolence. Because of MLK, Americans generally know the practice of *ahimsa* whether they can say it or not, or even if they are unfamiliar with how the dharma came to the West.[20] In the early 20th century, India's great master Vivekananda paved the way in the United States for another great Indian Yogi, Paramahansa Yogananda, to come later. Yogananda's mass appeal taught these tenets of yoga across the nation. Even after his death (*mahasamadhi*) he has sold more than 4 million copies of his *Autobiography of a Yogi*.[21] His legacy of kriya yoga is practiced widely in the West, and he has appeared in pop-culture references. Steve Jobs read the autobiography every year. Copies were given away at his funeral.[22] Yogananda and his guru lineage was included in the album art for The Beatles' *Sergeant Pepper's Lonely Hearts Club Band*.

While some Americans may know *ahimsa*, fewer have ever heard of *asteya*, nonstealing. These principles appear in the Old Testament in the commandments as thou shall not kill and steal. However you may understand these tenets, step 11 may require you to practice telescoping with these tenets beyond your perceived capacity. That may require some strength training to practice muscles not commonly used. Here is another instance where recovering alcoholics can lead; you may conclude that you do not have the capacity, but here is a nugget of transformative truth: "Act yourself into the right way of thinking."

Regardless of how you feel, regardless of how you now think, you can still make a choice to act. Even if that choice to act feels forced or disingenuous, or inadequate, act nonetheless. Act. Act the same way again until you habituate a new practice that replaces the old one. Just do the next right thing and repeat. If this sounds ridiculous or impossible, just know that recovering alcoholics do it every day for all the days they remain sober. Here maybe more than anywhere in this book, the model of the dysfunction of alcoholism compared to the dysfunction of a nation's rigged advantage align.

Recovering alcoholics must learn to turn their will over. Some of us turn our will over to the care of God as we understand him/her. Others learn to turn our will off instead of over. Then, we ultimately recognize something of the divine for such a miracle to happen.

Whatever it takes, just get here any way you can. Remember, "We want something to be done." That was the third step. Did you mean it then, but you struggle with it now?

Act anyway. It made be hard, but it is so very simple.

If you are in this moment of step 11 and you are struggling, the struggle may not be just in the governing and complementary dynamic of steps 5 and 11; you may not have sufficiently practiced step 3: *We want something to be done*. In the middle of your resistance to step 11, you can always choose, even knowing yourself well enough to know you do not mean it. Choose anyway.

Repeatedly choose reverence and reverence will eventually choose you. You just need to do your part until that happens.

A seeming contradiction, we must work hard for the gift.

> Choose reverence until reverence comes for you. When that happens, your spirituality will come to **abhor** living deluded off the backs of marginalized others, not as much for their sake as for your own liberation. Your spiritual tastes will change. Rigged advantage will become something you cannot stomach. Only then will it truly matter to others where you stand on rigged advantage in America. When we know better, we do better. It is the **doing** that transforms our lives. The doing is the means to the end that we unshackle the past for our soul's sake.

Especially if you are newly awakening to the degree of bamboozling that power Whites exert over exploited Whites, a discussion about violence and stealing in the context of spiritual discipline may be difficult initially. But, if you are sufficiently settled in your seat on the plane, this is where you will come to know flying in a most liberating way! Still, you are heading into new territory where culture may be unfamiliar. Even the language may seem familiar, but the words are used in specifically applied ways that you will need to learn. Allow your grappling with this chapter to model for you the grappling it will take to not only choose reverence but to practice all of the steps.

Hopefully, I have contextualized the concepts of *ahimsa* and *asteya* sufficiently for you to make further applications of the two concepts. I apply these two spiritual principles to race and class in America. In the following table I present race and class as two sides of the same coin. The intention of the table is to visually compare how these principles have developed (or not) in our nation.

RACE AND CLASS: **Two Sides of the Same Coin**

RACE: *Brown v. Board* (Yes)	**CLASS:** *San Antonio v. Rodriguez* (No)
Opposes racial segregation historically enforced with violence	Does not oppose class marginalization and its de facto racial segregation
Ahimsa: Nonviolence	*Asteya:* Nonstealing
Focus of early MLK activism	More pronounced focus of later MLK activism
We **cannot violate children** using the same segregation tactics that controlled the enslaved on plantations.	We **can steal meritocracy from children** in the name of "freedom" regarding our property taxes.

In the history of the United States, the *presumption of whereabouts authority* by White Americans over Black Americans is a legacy of slavery. On the plantation, minority rule by the owner over possessions asserted absolute authority over where an enslaved person could be located. Violence was an essential enforcement strategy that brutalized Black bodies when necessary to achieve absolute control over their location. Post reconstruction, Jim Crow segregation was an extension of this presumption of whereabouts authority.

When *Brown v. Board* overturned *Plessy v. Ferguson* to say that segregation was unconstitutional, it inferred that strategies to enforce segregation, such as brutality, were to be extinguished along with segregation. When White Americans, who believe slavery is a thing of the past but still presume whereabouts authority over Black Americans, they re-enact a legacy of slavery where White people were entitled to control the location of "their property." Years after slavery was supposedly ended, Plessy said the presumption of whereabouts authority over Black bodies was legal as long as the separation was equal.

Of course, it was never equal, since the slavery template was enabled to continue. It is this *culturally embedded entitlement* in the United States of America that triggers a particular dynamic in politics and policy. White entitlement to whereabouts control is so sacrosanct it functions as an uber entitlement. When any other entitlement accrues to anyone other than power White elites, those so-called entitlements are demonized because they threaten the entitlement, the presumption of whereabouts authority to keep "others" in their place. "Others" is a category comprised of Black people and other people of color by extension. But to White Elites "Others" actually include all the exploited White Americans whose collusion is essential to sustain power White elitism. This is why so many White Americans are perceived to "cut their nose off to spite their face" regarding policy allegiances. From the time when a so-called "White" race was constructed, it had this specific intent: Fracture the national "interests" alliance between the enslaved and the indentured and co-opt the so-called "Whites" coalition to do the bidding of power White elites. The resulting coalition would have enough votes even in a so-called democracy.

Remember, Rigged Advantage Theory illustrates that exploited Whites displace their subjective experience of exploitation onto others through two primary strategies: White supremacy (a noun, an identity of membership with perceived benefits) and anti-Blackness (a verb, the activity of behavioral conditioning that trains control). By extension, this uber entitlement to rigged advantage reaches some bizarre conclusions: If Black bodies can swim in the city pool, fill it in—nobody swims; if Black bodies can have health care, fight health care for everyone; if Black bodies have the right to vote, fight democracy for everyone. This last horrific logical extension is exactly what is happening in our nation today.

> If democracy means that Black people and other People of Color actually share power in a meritocracy (meaning advantage is no longer rigged) we pull the fire alarm to install authoritarians to sustain rigged advantage; democracy be damned. All that patriotism and flag waving was a pretentious, posturing lie.

For those who succumbed to this lie, it is the most natural thing to yearn for a return to this stasis because for them it is synonymous with the nation itself. However normal though it may seem, nostalgic even, this yearning is an embedded conditioning rooted in the presumption of whereabouts authority by White Americans over Black Americans. This position by definition functions as a domestic enemy of the U.S. constitution. Our foreign enemies need only to trigger our fault lines. Social media fires this kindling with the ease of a touchscreen—arguably the most deadly and insidious weapon that has ever threatened our nation. If you actually love the United States of America (and not its exploitation for rigged advantage), then choosing reverence means that you are working toward a more perfect union. You are answering the call of duty and honor to a nation where justice, then liberty, is consecrated free from rigged advantage.

Brown and *Rodriguez* (*ahimsa* and *asteya*) inform how we got to this tipping point crisis. Spiritually, *Brown* references *ahimsa*, nonviolence. It is not surprising that a civil rights movement rooted in nonviolence would follow *Brown*. *Brown* addressed equal protection based on race. Segregation, which relied on violent enforcement—the same violent enforcement that earlier authorized fugitive slave patrols—was no longer considered constitutional based on race. Another case would come along to enable the court to address equal protection based on wealth/class, *San Antonio v. Rodriguez*. In *Rodriguez*, one side of the coin, race, would meet the other side of the coin, class, to be addressed by the Supreme Court. Ultimately the Supreme Court under Earl Warren ruled in *Brown* for equal protection based on race: No more segregation, historically rooted in violence (*ahimsa*, nonviolence), forges our future. A subsequent Supreme Court (with Nixon appointees under Burger) *did not* rule for equal protection based on wealth/class: *Asteya*, nonstealing, does not forge our future. Since race and class are two sides of the same coin, *Rodriguez* has the effect of cancelling out *Brown* while leaving the pretense of *Brown* to opiate our sense of justice.

Jeffrey Sutton writes in the *Virginia Law Review*,

> In *Brown v. Board of Education,* the Supreme Court observed that "education is perhaps the most important function of state and local governments" and held that it was a public service that "must be made available to all on equal terms." While Brown removed one obvious barrier to equal educational opportunities, it left in place another: the obstacle faced by poor school districts that wish to provide an education to their students "on equal terms"

> relative to the education offered by wealthier school districts within a State.
>
> Nineteen years after *Brown,* the Court decided another equal-protection case, *San Antonio Independent School District v. Rodriguez,* which gave the Court an opportunity to remove, or at least ameliorate, wealth-based barriers to equal educational opportunities as well. But the Court rejected the plaintiffs' claims.[23]

When it comes to race in America, our courts have set a precedent that the race side of the coin will have equal protection. The other side of the coin, class, will have no such protection. Since race and class are two sides of the same coin, *Brown* without *Rodriguez* has diminished value. Rigged advantage wins on at least two accounts. *Brown* provides the pretense of justice and progress, while *Rodriguez* (virtually under the radar for most Americans) sustains and facilitates rigged advantage. Rodriguez says education is not a constitutional right.[24] An adequate education system for all of our children, essential to democracy, persists into the 21st century haphazardly funded. Conversely, our elite universities, for which the rigged advantage elite can compete are among the best in the world. Celebrating excellence at our outstanding universities celebrates one of the U.S.'s best contributions to the world. Celebrating its elitism, based on selectivity among rigged advantage, while stigmatizing universal access to higher education in community colleges is a repugnant collusion with rigged advantage.

For a specific example of the implications of *Rodriguez,* we may look to northern California. San Mateo County, which abuts San Francisco, comprises a large portion of a San Francisco area to San José area commute, which passes along the Santa Cruz mountains, the environs of approximately seventy billionaires. The address where a child happens to reside in San Mateo County could mean enormous disparities in education funding. A school district at one end of the county spends about $11,000 per pupil per year. A school district at the other end of the county spends about $32,000 per pupil per year. This is *not* comparing a public school to a private school. These extremes are both public funding examples within the same county. The variance in funding is based on property taxes and shows the extremes of real estate between some south county properties and some north county properties.

In the United States, we say we are pro family, and we advocate morally for the rights of children. We morally believe that since children cannot defend themselves, we defend them, protect them, and provide for their welfare. We do not perceive ourselves to be a nation that holds a child accountable for where that child is born. But who we say we are and who we actually are, at least when it comes to funding children's education, lacks integrity. Instead of ameliorating (attempts notwithstanding) this integrity problem, we languish in a distracting culture war in which Church and State collude to sustain rigged advantage.

We are a nation performing a culture war over how the state may control a woman's body in the name of protecting (unborn) children. That issue (truly principled for many) is exploited to sustain rigged advantage, which relies on marginalized educational opportunities for our children. Culture wars are perfectly invented for distraction and demonization so that we do not think things all the way through.

Like blood for sharks, any given culture war issue may for a few be principled, but even for those few, the culture war itself rages to distract the American people from the stranglehold rigged advantage uses to exploit us. In the way that the so-called White race was an invention to dismantle the natural alliance between the enslaved and indentured servants, culture wars split the voting block power of citizens who would be otherwise unified around issues they have in common such as adequately funding children's education.

Americans have historically held sacrosanct the separation of Church and State. The collusion of the Church with the State to control women's bodies rallies a political agenda that threatens democracy in the name of rigged advantage. Rigorous honesty demands of you to "draw the circle"[25] of an action's complete cycle. Draw the circle to chart how even a principled position against abortion is coopted by a collusion of Church and State to sustain rigged advantage, itself historically fueled by a Church and State collusion of contorted biblical justification for slavery. This does not mean you may not hold a principled position against abortion. It means that you are accountable for how you allow your principles to be manipulated and co-opted to sustain rigged advantage, which violates millions of children already born. This particular manipulation is a Church and State collusion seeding a political movement of reactivity whose context defines a trajectory of consequences we face today, the so-called southern strategy.

The southern strategy[26] is a cynical and exploitative racist agenda adopted by politicos in the Republican party. The strategy was conceived amid the Southern backlash that followed the passage of the Civil Rights Act, which LBJ knew would cost the Democrats the South "for a generation."[27] The southern strategy depends on a racist and religious fundamentalist coalition weighted with antiabortion activists to ally with elite Whites to sustain rigged advantage. The legacy of plantation slavery, *presumption of whereabouts authority over Black bodies*, along with the *presumption of State authority to control women's bodies*, are inconceivable values of a political party dedicated to limited government. These two inconceivable presumptions of authority are nonetheless adopted by the so-called political party of limited government as a means to the end of sustaining rigged advantage. The presented value of limited government once cloaked the actual value of rigged advantage. But now, as Republican political operative

Stuart Stevens makes explicit in his book, *It Was All a Lie*[28] the cloak of pretense is all but gone.

Today, we are still grappling with what *Brown v. Board* grappled with. As long as we struggle over this, our democracy teeters and the chokehold of rigged advantage compromises our national security. According to *Brown*, public schools cannot segregate. In a nation where White household wealth is eight times higher than Black household wealth and, since a significant source of education funding is property taxes, *Brown* may have said no to racial segregation, but segregation by wealth accomplishes a similar injustice. It means that Black children and White children have different opportunity based on the wealth of their parents despite what *Brown* intended to accomplish. Rigged advantage is baked in. In *Brown*, we thought we actualized *ahimsa*; the violence of segregation is unconstitutional. In *Rodriguez*, we failed to prevent the stealing of opportunity from our Black (and Brown) children who are disproportionately impacted. *Asteya*, nonstealing, is unrealized. As Schaull wrote in the preface to Freire's *Pedagogy of the Oppressed*,

> Education either functions as an instrument which is used to facilitate integration of the younger generation into the logic of the present system and bring about conformity to it, or it becomes the practice of freedom, the means by which men and women deal critically and creatively with reality and discover how to participate in the transformation of their world.[29]

A democracy where education is not a right and where existing education functions to de facto marginalize Black children (and other children of color) has consequences; namely, integrating the younger generation into the logic of the present system makes us vulnerable to authoritarian impulses, which rise as a last resort to sustain rigged advantage for those who already benefit from it. Since it operates already baked in, individual voices from even those benefitting from the status quo (e.g., philanthropy) will at some tipping point on the continuum of inevitability be too late to resist. The question for many is, Is it too late?

Brown and *Rodriguez* (race and class) inform us about where we are today with rigged advantage. In *Brown*, White Americans may not exercise their presumption of whereabouts authority over Black bodies, which is a legacy of slavery. *Brown* represents the embodiment of our nation grappling with resistance to the violence upon which segregation is based. Our nation had an opportunity to ensure *Brown*'s actualization when *San Antonio v. Rodriguez* (based on class) came before the Supreme Court. Race and class intersect. But the Court rejected the necessary complement to *Brown* and said no to *Rodriguez*.

Drawing the Circle

Throughout this book, I have made the case that working the *Twelve Steps for White America* is for the liberation of White America from the trap of sustaining rigged advantage. When talking about nonviolence and nonstealing, one could incorrectly presume that these principles are for the benefit of others. As Yogacharya Ellen Grace O'Brian, who teaches in the tradition of Paramahansa Yogananda, writes in *The Jewel of Abundance*: *Finding Prosperity Through the Ancient Wisdom of Yoga*,

> Non-stealing is rooted in Self-Sufficiency, which comes when we realize we are inseparable from the Source. We are one with it. Stealing, envy, neediness, sense of lack all come from a sense of insufficiency—a state which can only come from separateness from the Source.

Even if you argue that, unwittingly, as a result of being bamboozled by exploitation, you had no idea that educational funding for public education was dependent on property taxes, where White household wealth is eight times higher than Black households, *you now know*.

As a nation, we may not have sufficiently educated ourselves about any given issue. We may not have listened or understood when the information was presented to us. We may have operated under a paradigm of justification. Consider all of these as you are presented with the following statement:

> Stealing from our children in order to sustain rigged advantage has consequences. Brown without Rodriguez masquerades as opportunity but instead sustains rigged advantage. This has been happening whether you intended it or not. A secure and competitive nation is not built on "I just didn't know. ..."

Argue that you did not know. Argue that you would never intend to steal from children. Now, knowing about the educational funding disparities for school districts even in the same county, you are faced with a different level of accountability. Draw the circle.

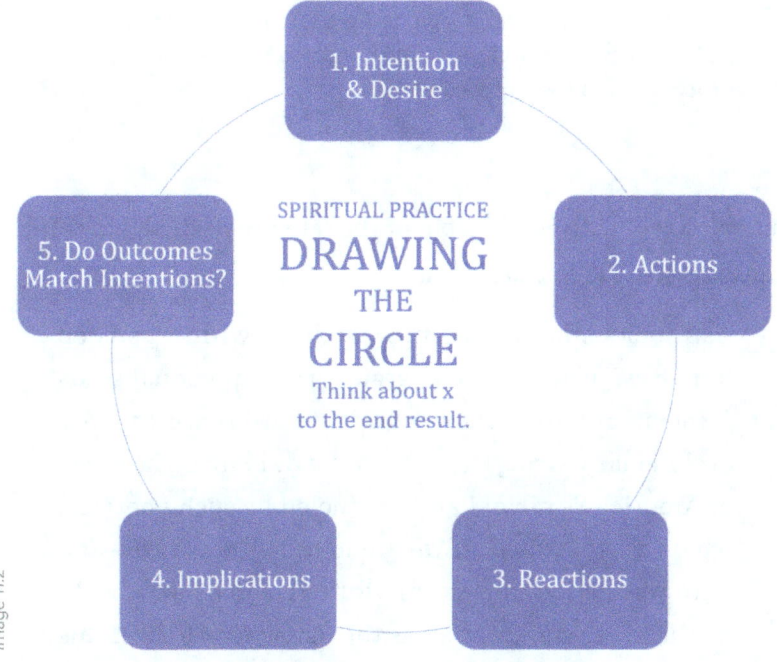

Image 11.2

Drawing the circle illustrates what you can do to actualize your accountability. To choose reverence is to *yoke yourself with the responsibility for your own freedom*. As long as your freedom depends on a rigged advantage system where others are marginalized, you practice neither nonviolence nor nonstealing. You violate. You steal. Draw the circle. After reading this, you may no longer passively "facilitate integration of the younger generation into the logic of the present system and bring about conformity to it." In step 11, *we choose reverence*, we use the key that unlocks the possibility of consecrating liberty free from rigged advantage. To choose reverence facilitates education essential to democracy. Reverence, itself, "becomes the practice of freedom, the means by which men and women deal critically and creatively with reality and discover how to participate in the transformation of their world."[30]

> To choose reverence, we synthesize personal spiritual discipline to re-align our integrity to not only nonviolence, but also, to nonstealing, since **the spiritual rot of rigged advantage is the stealing of a meritocracy from the American people**.

Larry Ward, a direct disciple of the late great Thich Nhat Hahn, writes in *America's Racial Karma*:

> As precious human beings, we have within us deep impulses, instincts and energies. These potential seeds of intention may be latent or hidden, and do not escape our evolutionary wiring and historic conditioning. The wheel of American's racial karma is fueled by such energies, which must be faced if we are to heal. Only if we—and here we are looking at our white friends—are able to do the inner work as well as the outer work to heal this

debilitating legacy of racialized suffering will we emerge from the current period.[31]

The Crucible of Loving Kindness Meditation

Finally, for those working toward mastery of the *Twelve Steps for White America*, the crucible of the loving kindness meditation supports the discipline necessary to counter the marginalization of others. (Hating haters is hateful: An eye for an eye makes the whole world blind!) The loving kindness meditation may sound quaint, something for a child trained in "Now I lay me down to sleep …" The willingness to begin the meditation is all that is necessary.

> *May I be filled with loving kindness.*
>
> *May I be well in body and mind.*
>
> *May I be safe from inner and outer dangers.*
>
> *May I be truly happy and free.*

You may customize the recitation to make it personal to you. I customize this meditation by adding a beginning personal to me, "May I be filled with gratitude for my wonderful life," and I end the meditation with "May I wish these things for all beings, in all places, at all times."[32]

Loving kindness meditation has become a discipline of my life—an elixir for my soul. The practice has broadened from one that is self-care-oriented (may I), to a practice that is other oriented (may you). In this Other-ly direction, I practice this meditation for those I love, then for acquaintances, and then others, even in the most stressful, unworthy, unforgiving settings. (It can be excruciating. It is called "practice" for a reason!)

I have learned through my practice that this Otherly direction is also self-care as I experience the gift/freedom of an open heart. I am not trapped in the cycle of hating hate. Always a work in progress, my

hopes for mastery express my soul's paradoxical desire to work hard for the gift of grace, paying the debts I owe to others.
In the practice of loving kindness, which I also hope for you,

> *I acknowledge a lifelong habit of negatively judging so-called difficult circumstances as unwelcome threats to be resisted.*
>
> *I intend to respond differently now. I welcome the gift of learning and liberation, which this difficult experience represents.*
>
> *I use acceptance and forgiveness to release resistance. I use gratitude to actualize the awakening this difficulty affords.*
>
> *I remember that I am not a separate self from what I perceive to be happening to me. Sometimes, I am actively engaging/producing this circumstance for my growth. The drama unfolding is soul's dream within dreams to return to the one, a return to love.*
>
> *Those whom I reflexively label as oppositional may be perfectly suited to teaching me during ideal times and conditions. I will not blame the participants in my dramas for God's casting choices. I will honor them for their service to my lessons in this school of life.*

Choosing reverence, I synthesize this spiritual discipline as my pathway to relinquish rigged advantage for the common good to achieve my own liberation.

Learning Outcome

Synthesize personal spiritual discipline as the pathway to relinquish rigged advantage for the common good.

CHAPTER 12

STEP 12

WE CONSECRATE LIBERTY FREE FROM RIGGED ADVANTAGE

Step 12 Complements Step 6: We Resolve to Change

Key Words: **Joy of living, Action, Humility**

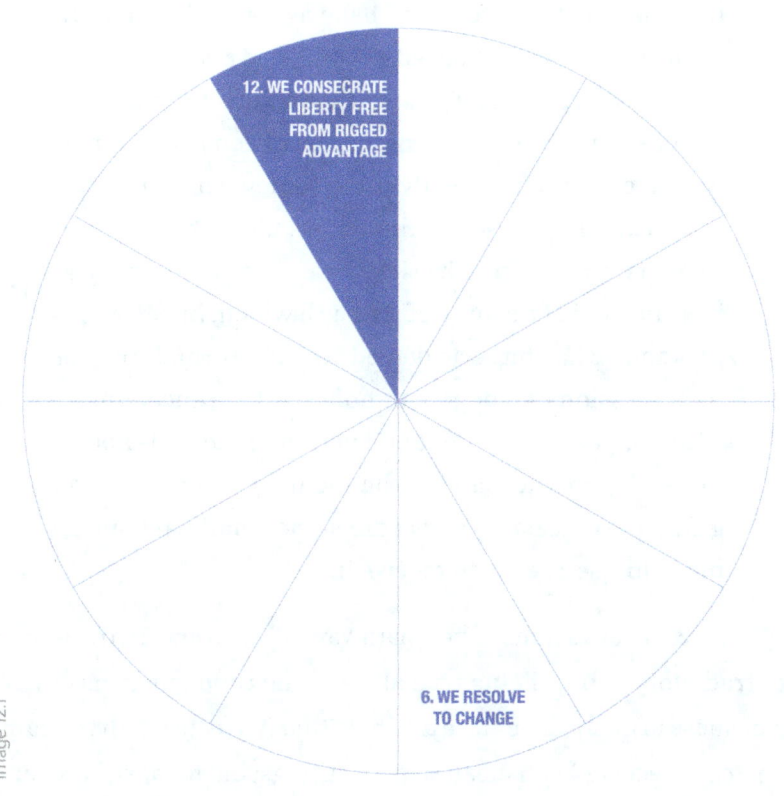

Image 12.1

What I Learned From Alcoholics About the Twelfth Step of AA

> *"Having had a spiritual awakening as the result of these steps, we tried to carry this message to alcoholics, and to practice these principles in all our affairs."*[1]

In AA there is the revered Big Book, but there is also the Twelve Steps and Twelve Traditions. As presented in the latter, the concept of spiritual awakening is as varied as the many who experience it, but it has common elements.

> The most important meaning of it is that he has now become able to do, feel, and believe that which he could not do before on his unaided strength and resources alone. He has been granted a gift which amounts to a new state of consciousness and being. He has been set on a path which tells him he is really going somewhere, that life is not a dead end, not something to be endured or mastered. In a very real sense he has been transformed, because he has laid hold of a source of strength which, in one way or another, he had hitherto denied himself. He finds himself in possession of a degree of honesty, tolerance, unselfishness, peace of mind, and love which he had thought himself quite incapable. What he has received is a free gift, and yet usually, at least in some small part, he has made himself ready to receive it.[2]

Paradox always seems to be a pathway to discovery. Two seemingly contradictory things being true at the same time quickens our consciousness to grasp or achieve a "whole that is greater than the sum of its parts." Recovery can mean so many things, but to most, recovery is

Step 12: We Consecrate Liberty Free From Rigged Advantage | 191

a process of working hard for a gift. The work of applying the simple steps in our lives can be so overwhelming that we exclaim, "What an order! I can't go through with it!"[3] The work is hard, an unimaginable boot camp transforming capability for a new life of promise. Few alcoholics in recovery could possibly claim that their hard work is the sole reason for their sobriety. Hard work is a necessary part of recovery, but the whole is greater than the sum of incremental steps, heroic though taking them may be. We work hard for the gift, which does not come without hard work. This is the paradox: Earning a gift. A gift is freely given without it costing something to the receiver. Hard work achieves specific and anticipated rewards—something earned. How, then, do alcoholics work hard for the gift of sobriety?

Perhaps our "philosophers' stone" (in a crucible something base becomes gold),[4] is humility.

You may recall that step 7 is where the essential role of humility was first introduced in our 12-step discovery. "We saw we needn't always be bludgeoned and beaten into humility. It could come quite as much from our voluntary reaching for it as it could from unremitting suffering. A great turning point came in our lives when we sought for humility as something we must have." As shown in my story in the previous section, the exemplar of the campus Methodist minister, a living embodiment of social justice saving the world became the most potent trigger for my turn toward getting sober. After all the beating I had taken from alcoholism, in the end, something attractive quickened my willingness to go to any lengths to get sober, to voluntarily reach for it.

The humility explicitly detailed in step 7 is considered fundamental to each step. We just reviewed the fundamental role of humility in the 12th step. However, since the 12th step is governed by step 6, let us explore the governing complementary relationship.

In the AA Big Book, step 6 is so monumental that it needs its own prayer:

> My Creator, I am now willing that you should have all of me, good and bad. I pray that you now remove from me every single defect of character which stands in the way of my usefulness to you and my fellows. Grant me strength, as I go out from here, to do your bidding. Amen.[5]

Recall that to get to step 6 where one is entirely ready to have God remove defects of character, one had to logically advance to that capability step by step:

1. There is a problem.
2. Something can be done about the problem.
3. I want something to be done about the problem.
4. What is the problem, specifically?
5. Here is the problem.
6. Now that I get it, I choose to change the problem. "Entirely ready" is the language of the step from AA.

- Step 6 governs step 12 (in AA).

   Having had a spiritual awakening as a result of these steps, we tried to carry this message to alcoholics and to practice these principles in all our affairs.

- Step 6 also governs step 12 (in #12SWA).

   We consecrate liberty free from rigged advantage.

In the AA tradition, it is abundantly clear that the alcoholic needs to clear out the wreckage of the past, retool the operating system's capacity, and, with resolve and humility, makes things as right as possible. Doing so strengthens the possibility of sustaining a program of recovery, which yields promises previously unimaginable, respects right relationships, and models universal principles for effectiveness across life's circumstances. Like anesthetic for pain, these promises include the following:

> We are going to know a new freedom and a new happiness.
>
> We will not regret the past nor wish to shut the door on it.
>
> We will comprehend the word *serenity*, and we will know peace.
>
> No matter how far down the scale we have gone, we will see how our experience can benefit others.
>
> That feeling of uselessness and self-pity will disappear.
>
> We will lose interest in selfish things and gain interest in our fellows.
>
> Self-seeking will slip away.
>
> Our whole attitude and outlook on life will change.
>
> Fear of people and of economic insecurity will leave us.
>
> We will intuitively know how to handle situations that used to baffle us.
>
> We will suddenly realize that God is doing for us what we could not do for ourselves.[6]

When these results are realized, there is a sense of gratitude that flows as a constant current through the most challenging days, through horrific disappointment, loss, and exuberance when dreams come true. None of these things, good or bad, were going to happen if alcoholism had its way. The bad and the good all arrive welcomed in this new phase of life, a phase which almost never happened. So happy to be alive, a chance to experience, experiment, learn, heal, and grow, our lives become the movie screen onto which we project the ongoing saga that is our existence. To transcend to this plane is to inch closer to the divinity that we already are, chipped away by every moment of life's lessons, until who we have become could never be traded for who we have been.

Would that not be powerful for a United States of America? What alcoholics could teach a nation is a lot! A nation practicing what alcoholics practice to recover could transcend a struggling United States from its fragile, teetering addiction to rigged advantage, to a plane where the promises of democracy, potentiated but yet to be fully realized, can actualize to a greatness we have yet to experience—a democratic republic where liberty is not consecrated for some by rigged advantage but where liberty is consecrated free from rigged advantage.

Sober,

spiritually awakened,

practicing these principles in all our affairs.

What of This May We Apply to Our Problem, Rigged Advantage?

The ideal of liberty tethered to the common good of social justice was expressed by Justice Brandeis at Faneuil Hall, Boston, in 1915:

> What are the American ideals? They are the development of the individual for his own and the common good; the development of the individual through liberty and the attainment of the common good through democracy and social justice.[7]

We cannot legitimately exalt liberty in the face of the injustice of rigged advantage. Our recovery from rigged advantage will practice known universal problem-solving principles in a scaffolded sequence to ensure the actualization of each step of progress we make.

First things first.

Rigorous honesty must become the water we drink to survive.

1. We have a problem. We must practice justice, then liberty for all to realize our greatest potential.
2. We must stop and turn (repentance) from our addiction to rigged advantage and believe that our national dysfunction can be uprooted to favor a competitive meritocracy.
3. We must want this; we must will this into being.
4. We must inventory the wreckage of this dysfunction.
5. We need to understand the problem and present the problem coherently to others.
6. With that coherence, we stand resolute to change ourselves in order to change our nation.
7. We adopt a yoke of humility that knows the degradation of dysfunction but yearns for the rewards of an American ideal.
8. We specify the wreckage of rigged advantage.
9. We repair the wreckage.
10. No longer content to trim the weeds of rigged advantage in our garden of democracy, we uproot rigged advantage and consign it to its rightful place as a historical artifact.
11. We revere the transcendence of what our great nation can truly actualize.
12. We consecrate, once and for all, liberty free from rigged advantage.

Hopefully, after 35 years of being sober, which is dependent daily upon my spiritual condition, I can acknowledge a certain form of spiritual *discipline*. After all this time having come so unbelievably far, I am more suited in the role of disciple who demonstrates some situational mastery under the right conditions. Mastery would seem to apply more generally regardless of favorable or unfavorable conditions. In 35 years, I have realized that a trajectory toward mastery can enrich the rest of my life. For the sake of this trajectory, I will be uncomfortable, take chances, explore my shortcomings, tolerate, endure, be still, claim victories, aspire, grieve, repair, restore, transmogrify bestial judgements and resentments, pray, meditate, yoke my anxieties, delay gratification when my eyes are on the prize, give to get, and release my self-appointed entitlement to prosecute you for what I have yet to repudiate in myself.

These are not imagined ideals; I work on all of this *to stay sober*. I work on all of this for my sake. Some of this improves what I can contribute to the common good. But the common good is only bettered when I am better equipped, better capitalized, to invest in the common good.

> Neither my sobriety nor my soul (which are now fused) can afford to live deluded by the privilege afforded to me off the backs of marginalized others.

So, I choose daily to adopt the yoke of spiritual discipline, for my liberty, my sobriety, my abundance. In this way, I am becoming the change I wish to see in the world. I cannot start with an externalized objective of making the world a better place or ridding the United States of rigged advantage, which is rooted in legacies of slavery. I start with the internalized objective of yoking myself for the best life I can live. I yoke for freedom. I consecrate liberty free from rigged advantage.

For a United States of America, we are pushing against some strong headwinds that appear to be overwhelming. Do not be overwhelmed. The appearance of "overwhelming" is not determinative, especially to a recovering alcoholic, but it is overwhelming nonetheless! To practice the 12 step principles applied to alcoholism or rigged advantage requires the rigorous honesty that 12-step practice is overwhelming. Both have deadly consequences if not realized. Both may be the demise of hopes and dreams. People recover from alcoholism, and a

United States of America can recover from rigged advantage rooted in legacies of slavery still present today.

Fundamental to understanding the headwinds we face is ideological rigidity. Before we delve into the content of ideological rigidity in the United States, let us delve into the process of ideological rigidity in the United States. Ideological rigidity in the United States has been calcified by at least two major developments:

- the ideological homogenization of gerrymandered districts whose elected officials are rewarded for resisting legislative compromise and
- the clustering of information delivery systems (for profit) into homogenous echo chambers where minimal permeability exists.

To analyze these two components, recall our ongoing comparison of the dysfunction of alcoholism to the dysfunction of rigged advantage.

Remember in our work on step 4, we described how alcoholism contorts natural instincts into mortal liabilities:

- A desire for love and connection may become a sex addiction.
- A desire for the pleasantries of social drinking becomes alcoholism.
- A desire for social cooperation becomes a bog of resentments and vendettas.
- A desire for spiritual fulfillment becomes fanaticism.
- A desire for mutual aid becomes calculated exploitation.

We could be here all day!

But, since we have differentiated the *process* of ideological rigidity from some specific *content* of ideological rigidity, we move on to discuss a very American "natural instinct," which has become contorted into a mortal liability. Let us here review the continuum of ideological permeability and then read the discussion before we continue with the rest of the chapter.

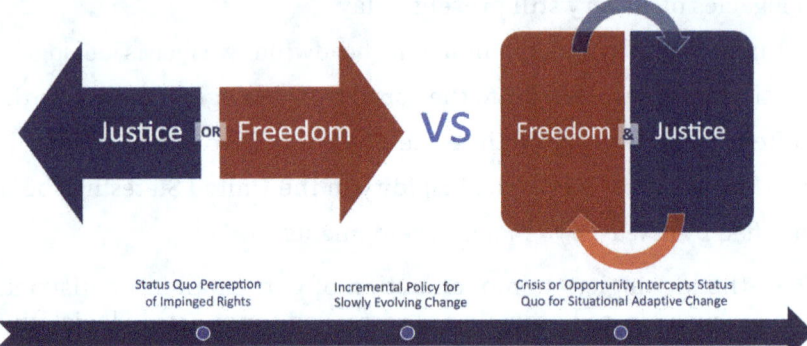

Image 12.2

DISCUSSION: CONTINUUM OF IDEOLOGICAL PERMEABILITY

Are Freedom and Justice a Zero-Sum Game?

In American democracy, given the balance of powers between the three branches of government (Legislative, Executive, Judiciary) and given the nature of the legislative process, deliberation and compromise are already baked in.

Compromise is conditioned within an ongoing balancing act where freedom (liberty) and justice are tandem works in progress. They are not fixed. They are aspirational ideals exercised in our body politic.

This exercise a natural American "instinct," where freedom and justice are ideals in progress.

Freedom and justice may appear to compete in what can be perceived to be a zero-sum game (i.e., Your freedom compromises my justice. My justice diminishes your freedom).

However, imagine a future where the greatest version of American democracy is not a "justice versus freedom zero-sum game" but is reimagined as "justice and freedom comprising an equation of multipliers." My justice multiplies your freedom. Your freedom magnifies my justice. That is where we could be. Where we have been is different. Even in my lifetime, when political jockeying presented as advocating

Step 12: We Consecrate Liberty Free From Rigged Advantage | 199

policy variance between the parties, interpreting the ideological roots of policy could be understood through a lens of *traditional* party ideology.

- Traditionally, Democrats venerate justice for all even when that may present to Republicans as curtailing freedom.
- Traditionally, Republicans venerate freedom even when that may present to Democrats as compromising justice.

Today, even the pretense of policy variance is discarded, the case made by former Republican operative, Stuart Stevens, in *It Was All a Lie*.[8] Rigged advantage no longer masquerades a policy tug of war between conservatives and liberals. The scales of that false equivalency have surely fallen from our eyes. The dysfunction of rigged advantage has contorted what may be considered a natural instinct. Political give and take, exercising the balance of freedom and justice, hijacks democracy into a zero-sum game where so-called freedom is the sheep's clothing on a wolf ravenous to huff and puff to blow the house down if justice curtails rigged advantage. The "house" is the United States of America, under siege by a coalition of Whiteness invented to sustain plantation slavery.

Enough. Being "White" cannot possibly mean this in a United States of America, where the best days for all are ahead of us.

Key Considerations
- The conditioning of ideological impermeability limits social adaptation, which depends on cooperation.
- Like an addiction that overtakes rational survival, ideological impermeability cuts its nose off to spite its face.
- Immediate triggers outweigh longer-term value.
- Situational permeability for adaptive purposes become tests of ideological purity.
- Variance or deviance is subject to excommunication (or what is increasingly known as cancel culture).
- Excommunication sustains purity but diminishes traits for adaptation, cooperation, and permeability across ideology—even situationally such as during times of crises or rare opportunity.

It serves a rigged advantage agenda for most of us to be triggered, attacked and attacking, and confused about false equivalents.

The wreckage of *my* past and the wreckage of *our* past overlap. I am triggered and reduced to incapacity so that my potential, my empowerment cannot pose a threat to the benefits enjoyed by beneficiaries of rigged advantage.

The key lever, which drives the actualization of liberty free from rigged advantage is a deliberate and informed resolve to change the problem. AA's version of this problem-solving principle acknowledges how essential it is for the tool to be sufficiently matched to the task ahead. If there are "defects" in the tool, "the task" will be more difficult to achieve. One of my favorites of the *7 Habits of Highly Effective People*[9] has always been *sharpen the saw*. All of the seven habits are worth another visit, but here is the other one I will reference:

> *Begin with the end in mind.*

For the alcoholic, beginning with the end in mind is a bit of a luxury since something as general as I do not want to die from this is about all that can be mustered. For the United States, when an individual realizes the following statement, the sadness may be overwhelming:

> In a nation at times frenzied about freedom from governmental overreach, it is perhaps the overreach of rigged advantage that strangles us the most. The American people long to be free in principle, but in practice, we struggle to be free when rigged advantage supplants meritocracy and sustains itself by distraction and demonizing dissent.

Our resolve is manifest. Change/recovery means that instead of hoarding the promises of democracy in a tainted system of rigged advantage, where liberty accrues for some, we hold it sacrosanct that liberty by definition is only realized absent of rigged advantage.

> We cannot say we are one thing,
>
> (America = liberty) *a presented ideal*

while practicing another thing,

(America ≠ justice) *an actualized reality.*

Since a house divided against itself cannot stand, our best days ahead depend on an integrated common good based not on a utopia of homogenized politics, but integrity, an integral alignment of the values we live by. When what we present becomes what we are, we achieve integrity. Our greatness in our future will manifest if we are practically and morally aligned between what we are and what we purport to be.

Such a house, united in purpose (liberty), for a united good, (democracy and social justice), is built on a rock-solid foundation.[10] If what we perceived to be a rock-solid foundation falters, we repair. We retrofit. We utilize modern engineering with our best tools and materials to strengthen what we have that it may grow. We utilize our innovation to our common advantage. Our financial, cultural, and social capital reward and reflect excellence in a competitive meritocracy. In rigged advantage, we hoard innovation and redecorate the living room while the kitchen is on fire.

I cannot despair for long. I will not give away my power to it. Like an alcoholic in the final days of drinking who looks back to see angels of mercy intervening for a mighty rescue, out of today's despair and anxiety we are already seeded for a future greater than present circumstances can imagine.

How can we imagine that our profound pain today already plants a harvest of future abundance?

How may we realize that in present moments of despair, a seismic shift potentiates a great future?

Like a phoenix rising, this may be a burning end of an era, but what burns is structural dysfunction for a renewed America that can rise. Recovering alcoholics can tell you that hindsight reveals deep spiritual truth. While what we may see today is despair, our trajectory toward greater fulfillment than we can imagine is already underway. In what we perceive to be catastrophic loss from which we cannot recover, the solution is seeded.

Hope is germinating.

We will be able to look back on this time as truth, reconciliation, and renewal already sprouting into power, mastery, and abundance consecrated free from rigged advantage.

Learning Outcome

Dismantle rigged advantage for an integral democracy where competition thrives from race-neutral merit.

NOTES

Statement on Alcoholics Anonymous and the Spiritual Foundation of Anonymity

1. A.A. World Services, Inc. (1989). *The twelve steps and twelve traditions: A co-founder of Alcoholics Anonymous tells how members recover and how the society functions.* Author. (Originally published in 1952)
2. A.A. World Services, Inc. (1989). *The twelve steps and twelve traditions: A co-founder of Alcoholics Anonymous tells how members recover and how the society functions.* Author. (Originally published in 1952). (p. 184)

Dedication in Memory

1. Beveridge, L. (2020, August 26). Civil rights activist Fannie Lou Hamer and opera singer Leontyne Price among inspiring women on Mississippi list. *USA Today.* https://www.usatoday.com/in-depth/life/women-of-the-century/2020/08/13/mississippi-woman-history-poet-author-activists-19th-amendment/5003960002/
2. Parry, M. (2019, November 8). The trouble with Ole Miss. *The Chronicle of Higher Education.* https://www.chronicle.com/article/the-trouble-with-ole-miss/
3. U.S. Department of Justice. (2021). *The U.S. Marshals and the integration of the University of Mississippi.* U.S. Marshal Service. https://www.usmarshals.gov/history/miss/02.htm
4. www.rowanoak.com
5. U.S. Department of Justice (2021). *The U.S. Marshals and the integration of the University of Mississippi.* U.S. Marshal Service. https://www.usmarshals.gov/history/miss/02.htm
6. Doyle's 2001 book (Doubleday) describing these events is titled *An American Insurrection, the Battle of Oxford Mississippi, 1962.* Interestingly, this is how the January 6, 2021, insurrection

is characterized. A state CEO manipulates racialized undercurrents to incite riot against "x" (backlash) so that the status quo (sustained by White supremacy) benefits elite White Americans in power. Certifying Biden's win by over 7 million votes the day after a historical slave state elects two senators—one Jewish, one African American—is a templated replay of the "crisis" of James Meredith enrolling at Ole Miss. This repeat is not a *"what's happening to our country"* moment. It is a predictable playbook tactic that persists because the United States has never repented and atoned for slavery. We keep doing it. Slavery legacies are alive in the present. White Americans are responsible for dismantling the rigged advantage the flows to them to this day from the legacies of slavery. The United States remains at risk on this fault line, compromised until a repair is complete. *Twelve Steps for White America* outlines the steps needed for the repair.

7. Stanford University Law School. (2021). *ABA women trailblazer's project*. Robert Crown Law Library. https://abawtp.law.stanford.edu/exhibits/show/constance-i-slaughter-harvey/biography?_ga=2.110698829.914675179.1597941222-1936040103.1597615574
8. Ibid.
9. U.S. Office of Energy Efficiency & Renewable Energy. (2016). *Fact #915: March 7, 2016 average historical annual gasoline pump price, 1929-2015*. https://www.energy.gov/eere/vehicles/fact-915-march-7-2016-average-historical-annual-gasoline-pump-price-1929-2015
10. Scott County Times Online. (2018). Slaughter Legacy honored: Forest Alderman W. L. and Mrs. Olivia Kelley Slaughter honored (posthumously) by Jackson Tougaloo Alumni Club. *Scott County Times*. https://www.sctonline.net/front-page-slideshow-features/slaughter-legacy-honored#sthash.74ptwXBg.dpbs
11. Ownby, T. (2017). *Mississippi Action for Progress (MAP)*. Center for Study of Southern Culture, Mississippi Encyclopedia. http://mississippiencyclopedia.org/entries/mississippi-action-for-progress/
12. FBI History. (1964). *Mississippi burning*. https://www.fbi.gov/history/famous-cases/mississippi-burning
13. McDavid, I. R., Jr., & McDavid, V. G. (1969). The late unpleasantness: Folk names for the Civil War. *The Southern Speech Journal, 34*(3), 194–204, https://doi.org/10.1080/10417946909372004

14. Sadoff, J. H., Sadoff, R. L., & Needleman, L. (2011). *Pieces from the past: Voices of heroic women in civil rights*. Tasora Books.
15. Clark, H., & Knowles, C. (2013). *Resolution in memory of Helga Burnham Watson*. Scott County Democratic Executive Committee.

How to Use This Book

1. A.A. World Services. (1989). *Twelve steps and twelve traditions*. Author. (p. 106).
2. Throwback. (2022, June 23). *Winston cigarettes commercial, 1955* [Video]. YouTube. https://www.youtube.com/watch?v=apD9_hLxqE0
3. FindLaw. (n.d.). *What does "caveat emptor" mean?* https://www.findlaw.com/consumer/consumer-transactions/what-does-caveat-emptor-mean-.html
4. John 1:12.
5. W, B., & Alcoholics Anonymous. (2019). *Alcoholics anonymous: The big book: The original 1939 edition*. Ixia. (p. 82)
6. Art Institute Chicago. (2009). *Nighthawks*. Edward Hopper. The Art Institute of Chicago. https://www.artic.edu/artworks/111628/nighthawks
7. Rowe, J., & Smith, H. E., (1912). *Love lifted me, 462*. Baptist Hymnal (1975 ed.). Convention Press. https://hymnary.org/hymn/BH1975/462
8. W, B., & Alcoholics Anonymous. (2019). *Alcoholics anonymous: The big book: The original 1939 edition*. Ixia. (p. 59)
9. W, B., & Alcoholics Anonymous. (2019). *Alcoholics anonymous: The big book: The original 1939 edition*. Ixia. (p. 60)
10. BBC News. (2013, July 29). *Pope Francis: Who am I to judge gay people?* https://www.bbc.com/news/world-europe-23489702
11. Center for Humane Technology. (n.d.). *Home page*. www.humanetech.com
12. Reich, R. B. (2021). *The system: Who rigged it, how we fix it*. Vintage.
13. Baldwin, J. (2021). *The fire next time*. Modern Library. (Original work published 1962). (p. 79)
14. King, M. L., Jr. (1967). *Beyond Vietnam: A time to break silence*. Common Dreams. https://www.commondreams.

org/views/2018/01/15/beyond-vietnam-time-break-silence; The Martin Luther King, Jr. Center for Non-Violent Change. (2022). *The beloved community: The fierce urgency of now* [Video]. https://www.youtube.com/watch?v=aujrJRFyI34

Part I

1. Janney, C. (n.d.). The lost cause. *Encyclopedia Virginia.* https://encyclopediavirginia.org/entries/lost-cause-the
2. The real story of Neil Young and Ronnie Van Zant from Lynyrd Skynyrd was more complex. But a "real story" can't match the power of coopted propaganda in the Southern culture war. See Greene, A., & Greene, A. (2015, January 20). Flashback: Neil Young covers "Sweet Home Alabama" in 1977. *Rolling Stone.* https://www.rollingstone.com/music/music-news/flashback-neil-young-covers-sweet-home-alabama-in-1977-186638/

Chapter 1

1. W., B., & Alcoholics Anonymous. (2019). *Alcoholics anonymous: The big book: The original 1939 edition.* Ixia. (p. 59).
2. A.A. World Services. (1989). *Twelve steps and twelve traditions.* Alcoholics Anonymous World Services. (p. 75).
3. *Wall Street Journal.* (2016, November 15). Henry Louis Gates discusses ideological divides among Black Americans. https://www.wsj.com/video/henry-louis-gates-discusses-ideological-divides-among-black-americans/77306EFF-CDD0-425A-B47A-E07737846D57.html
4. "Presumption of whereabouts authority" is a term conceptualized by the author to describe a legacy rooted in minority rule where exists a whiteness entitlement to authority over the physical location of Black Americans.
5. Glaude, E. S., Jr. (2017). *Democracy in Black: How race still enslaves the American soul.* Broadway Books.
6. powell, j. a. (2017, August 29). Othering and belonging: An embodied spiritual practice. *Deep Times: A Journal of Work That Reconnects.* https://journal.workthatreconnects.org/2017/08/29/othering-and-belonging-expanding-the-circle-of-human-concern/

7. Allen, T. (2012). *The invention of the White race: Racial oppression and social control* (Vols. 1 & 2). Verso.
8. Glaude, E. S., Jr. (2017). *Democracy in Black: How race still enslaves the American soul*. Broadway Books.
9. Harris, F., III, & Wood, J. L. (2021, February 12). Racelighting: A prevalent version of gaslighting facing People of Color. *Diverse: Issues in Higher Education*. https://www.diverseeducation.com/opinion/article/15108651/racelighting-a-prevalent-version-of-gaslighting-facing-people-of-color

Chapter 2

1. W, B., & Alcoholics Anonymous. (2019). *Alcoholics anonymous: The big book: The original 1939 edition*. Ixia. (p. 59).
2. A.A. World Services. (1967). *As Bill sees it*. Alcoholics Anonymous World Services.
3. Wakefield, J. C. (2015). DSM-5 substance use disorder: How conceptual missteps weakened the foundations of the addictive disorders field. *Acta Psychiatrica Scandinavica, 132*(5), 327–334. https://doi.org/10.1111/acps.12446
4. Park, S. C. (2018). The Goldwater rule from the perspective of phenomenological psychopathology. *Psychiatry Investigation, 15*(2), 102–103. https://doi.org/10.30773/pi.2018.01.25
5. American Psychiatric Association. (2010). *Home page*. psychiatry.org.
6. Tarasoff v. Regents of Univ. of Cal. 13 Cal. 3d 177, 118 Cal. Rptr. 129, 529 P.2d 553 (Cal. 1974).
7. Ghaemi, N. (2017, July 24). The ghost of Barry Goldwater and the censorship of American psychiatrists. *Washington Monthly*. https://washingtonmonthly.com/2017/07/24/the-ghost-of-barry-goldwater-and-the-censorship-of-american-psychiatrists//
8. Parmar, A., & Kaloiya, G. (2018). Comorbidity of personality disorder among substance use disorder patients: A narrative review. *Indian Journal of Psychological Medicine, 40*(6), 517–527. https://doi.org/10.4103/IJPSYM.IJPSYM_164_18
9. Case, A., & Deaton, A. (2020). *Deaths of despair and the future of capitalism*. Princeton University Press.
10. Sifton, E. (2003). *The serenity prayer: Faith and politics in times of peace and war*. Norton.

Chapter 3

1. W, B., & Alcoholics Anonymous. (2019). *Alcoholics anonymous: The big book: The original 1939 edition*. Ixia. (p. 59).
2. A.A. World Services. (1989). *Twelve steps and twelve traditions*. Alcoholics Anonymous World Services. (p. 34).
3. Zaragovia, V. (2014, October 1). *Cajuns are fiercely proud of their culture, but they're divided over the word "coonass."* The World. https://theworld.org/stories/2014-10-01/cajuns-are-fiercely-proud-their-culture-theyre-divided-over-word-coonass
4. powell, j. a. (2015). *Racing to justice: Transforming our conceptions of self and other to build an inclusive society*. Indiana University Press.
5. Glaude, E. S., Jr. (2017). *Democracy in Black: How race still enslaves the American soul*. Broadway Books.
6. Ibid.

Chapter 4

1. W, B., & Alcoholics Anonymous. (2019). *Alcoholics anonymous: The big book: The original 1939 edition*. Ixia. (p. 59).
2. Book of Daniel, chapter 3.
3. Billington, J. (2019). *Exploring the early Americas*. Library of Congress. https://www.loc.gov/exhibits/exploring-the-early-americas/columbus-and-the-taino.html
4. Satz, R. (1986). The Mississippi Choctaw: From the Removal Treaty to the federal agency. In S. J. Wells & R. Tubby (Eds.), *After removal, The Choctaw in Mississippi*. University Press of Mississippi. (p. 7).
5. Fishkin, J., & Forbath, W. E. (2022). *The anti-oligarchy constitution: Reconstructing the economic foundations of American democracy*. Harvard University Press.
6. Deranty, J. P. (2016). Exploited: Exploitation as a subjective category. *The Southern Journal of Philosophy, 54*(S1), 31–43. https://doi.org/10.1111/sjp.12185
7. Stoute, B. J. (2017). Race and racism in psychoanalytic thought: The ghosts in our nursery. *The American Psychoanalyst, 51*(1). https://apsa.org/apsaa-publications/vol51no1-TOC/html/vol51no1_08.xhtml
8. Sleeter, C. (n.d.). *Home page*. https://www.christinesleeter.org/critical-family-history

Part II

1. McGhee, H. C. (2021). *The sum of us: What racism costs everyone and how we can prosper together*. One World.
2. Phillips, A. (2022, June 27). The sex-trafficking investigation that's zeroing in on Matt Gaetz, explained. *The Washington Post*. https://www.washingtonpost.com/politics/2022/01/27/sex-trafficking-allegations-matt-gaetz/
3. Rev. (2021, June 23). *General Milley, Secretary Austin answer critical race theory questions from Matt Gaetz testimony: Transcript*. https://www.rev.com/blog/transcripts/general-milley-secretary-austin-answer-critical-race-theory-questions-from-matt-gaetz-testimony-transcript
4. Fortin, J. (2021, November 8). Critical race theory: A brief history. *The New York Times*. https://www.nytimes.com/article/what-is-critical-race-theory.html
5. Ankel, S. (2022, January 25). VA governor, who has banned CRT, launches tip line to report teachers. *Business Insider*. https://www.businessinsider.com/glenn-youngkin-launches-tipline-report-teachers-2022-1
6. Truth and Reconciliation Commission. (1998). *Final report*. https://www.justice.gov.za/trc/report/execsum.htm
7. Davis, F. (2019). *The little book of race and restorative justice: Black lives, healing, and US social transformation*. Good Books.
8. Zehr, H. (2016). *The little book of restorative justice*. Langara College.

Chapter 5

1. Alcoholics Anonymous. (1976). *Alcoholics Anonymous* (3rd ed.). A.A. World Services, Inc. (p. 59).
2. Alcoholics Anonymous. (1976). *Alcoholics Anonymous* (3rd ed.). A.A. World Services, Inc. (p. 75).
3. A.A. World Services. (1989). *Twelve steps and twelve traditions*. Alcoholics Anonymous World Services. (p. 58).
4. Communication Theory. (2014, July 10). *The Johari window model*. https://www.communicationtheory.org/the-johari-window-model/
5. The Nature Conservancy. (2019). *Journey with nature: Kudzu*. https://www.nature.org/en-us/about-us/where-we-work/united-states/indiana/stories-in-indiana/kudzu-invasive-species/

6. Miller, J. H. (1996). Kudzu eradication and management. In D. Hoots & J. Baldwin (Eds.), *Kudzu: The vine to love or hate* (pp. 137–149). Suntop Press.

Chapter 6

1. W, B., & Alcoholics Anonymous. (2019). *Alcoholics anonymous: The big book: The original 1939 edition.* Ixia. (p. 59).
2. Doyle, W. (2001). *An American insurrection: The battle of Oxford, Mississippi, 1962.* Doubleday.
3. Parry, M. (2019, November 8). The trouble with Ole Miss. *The Chronicle of Higher Education.* https://www.chronicle.com/article/the-trouble-with-ole-miss/
4. U.S. Department of Justice. (2021). *The U.S. Marshalls and the integration of the University of Mississippi.* U.S. Marshall Service. https://www.usmarshals.gov/history/miss/02.htm
5. U.S. Department of Justice (2021).

Chapter 7

1. W, B., & Alcoholics Anonymous. (2019). *Alcoholics anonymous: The big book: The original 1939 edition.* Ixia. (p. 59).
2. A.A. World Services. (1989). *Twelve steps and twelve traditions.* Author. (p. 75).
3. Stevens, S. (2020). *It was all a lie: How the Republican Party became Donald Trump.* Knopf.
4. Herbers, J. (1964, August 9). Neshoba County Fair unclouded by murder of rights workers. *The New York Times.* https://www.nytimes.com/1964/08/09/archives/neshoba-county-fair-unclouded-by-murder-of-rights-workers.html
5. Dearman, S. (2007, November 15). Ronald Reagan speech, Neshoba County Fair, 1980. *The Neshoba County Democrat.* https://neshobademocrat.com/stories/ronald-reagans-1980-neshoba-county-fair-speech,49123
6. Vitali, A. (2016, February 29). Alabama's Jeff Sessions becomes first senator to endorse Trump. *NBC News.* https://www.nbcnews.com/politics/2016-election/alabama-s-jeff-sessions-becomes-first-senator-endorse-trump-n527661

Chapter 8

1. Alcoholics Anonymous. (1976). *Alcoholics Anonymous* (3rd ed.). A.A. World Services, Inc. (p. 59).
2. Alcoholics Anonymous. (1976). *Alcoholics Anonymous* (3rd ed.). A.A. World Services, Inc. (p. 82).
3. Yogapedia.com. (n.d.). *What is Aham Brahmasmi?* https://www.yogapedia.com/definition/8231/aham-brahmasmi
4. Othering and Belonging Institute. (n.d.). *The structural racism remedies repository.* https://belonging.berkeley.edu/structural-racism-remedies-repository
5. Stewart, S., III, Chui, M., Manyika, J., Julien, J. P., Hunt, V., Sternfels, B., Woetzel, J., & Zhang, H. (2021). *The economic state of Black America: What is and what could be.* https://www.mckinsey.com/~/media/mckinsey/featured%20insights/diversity%20and%20inclusion/the%20economic%20state%20of%20black%20america%20what%20is%20and%20what%20could%20be/the-economic-state-of-black-america-what-is-and-what-could-be-f.pdf
6. The Opportunity Atlas: Mapping the Childhood Roots of Social Mobility. https://opportunityinsights.org/paper/the-opportunity-atlas/
7. The National Equity Atlas. https://nationalequityatlas.org
8. For Love of Country: A Path for the Federal Government to Advance Racial Equity. https://www.policylink.org/sites/default/files/pl_for-love-of-country_exec_sum_10.28.21a.pdf
9. Prosperity Now. https://prosperitynow.org
10. W. K. Kellogg Foundation. https://www.wkkf.org
11. The Just Imperative. https://www.macfound.org/about/how-we-work/just-imperative
12. The Zinn Education Project. https://www.zinnedproject.org/about/highlights/

Part III

1. Case, A., & Deaton, A. (2020). *Deaths of despair and the future of capitalism.* Princeton University Press.

Chapter 9

1. W, B., & Alcoholics Anonymous. (2019). *Alcoholics anonymous: The big book: The original 1939 edition*. Ixia. (p. 60).
2. A.A. World Services. (1967). *As Bill sees it*. Alcoholics Anonymous World Services.
3. Delpit, L. (2006). *Other people's children: Cultural conflict in the classroom*. New Press.
4. Graves, E. M., & Savage, S. A. (2015). *Promoting pathways to financial stability: A resource handbook on building financial capabilities of community college students*. The Federal Reserve Bank of Boston. https://www.bostonfed.org/publications/one-time-pubs/financial-capabilities-handbook.aspx
5. Ladson-Billings, G. (2006). From the achievement gap to the education debt: Understanding achievement in U.S. schools. *Educational Researcher, 35*(7), 3–12. https://doi.org/10.3102/0013189x035007003
6. Toporek, R. L., & Ahluwalia, M. K. (2021). *Taking action: Creating social change through strength, solidarity, strategy, and sustainability*. Cognella Press.

Chapter 10

1. W, B., & Alcoholics Anonymous. (2019). *Alcoholics anonymous: The big book: The original 1939 edition*. Ixia. (p. 60).
2. O., P. (1995). *There's more to quitting drinking than quitting drinking*. Sabrina Pub.
3. O., P. (1976). *Alcoholics Anonymous big book* (3rd ed.). Alcoholics Anonymous World Services, Inc. (p. 449).
4. Steele, C. (2010). *Whistling Vivaldi: And other clues to how stereotypes affect us*. Norton.
5. Glaude, E., Jr. (2017). *Democracy in Black: How race still enslaves the American soul*. Broadway Books.

Chapter 11

1. W, B., & Alcoholics Anonymous. (2019). *Alcoholics anonymous: The big book: The original 1939 edition*. Ixia. (p. 60).
2. Guénolé, F., Marcaggi, G., & Baleyte, J.-M. (2013). Do dreams really guard sleep? Evidence for and against Freud's theory

of the basic function of dreaming. *Frontiers in Psychology, 4*. https://doi.org/10.3389/fpsyg.2013.00017
3. Psalm 30:5, KJV.
4. Shakespeare, W. (1603). *Hamlet's to be or not to be soliloquy*. Leon Amiel.
5. Sullivan, C. (2002). *Rescuing Jesus from the Christians*. Trinity Press International.
6. Baltzly, D. (2019). Stoicism. *Stanford encyclopedia of philosophy*. https://plato.stanford.edu/archives/spr2019/entries/stoicism/
7. Sullivan, C. (2004). *Why Beulah shot her pistol inside the Baptist Church*. New South Books.
8. Asch, C. M. (2008). *The senator and the sharecropper: The freedom struggles of James O. Eastland and Fannie Lou Hamer*. The New Press; Zwiers, M. (2018, May 25). Eastland, James O. *Mississippi Encyclopedia*. https://mississippiencyclopedia.org/entries/james-oliver-eastland/
9. University of Southern Mississippi Wesley Foundation. (n.d.). *Our history*. https://www.usmwesley.org/our-history
10. O'Brian, E. G. (2018). *The jewel of abundance: Finding prosperity through the ancient wisdom of yoga*. New World Library.
11. Rohter, L. (1998, April 3). 4 Salvadorans say they killed U.S. nuns on orders of military. *The New York Times*. https://www.nytimes.com/1998/04/03/world/4-salvadorans-say-they-killed-us-nuns-on-orders-of-military.html
12. Witness for Peace. (n.d.). *Home page*. https://www.witnessforpeace.org
13. Martin, M. (1987). *The Jesuits: The society of Jesus and the betrayal of the Roman Catholic Church*. Linden Press.
14. Freire, P. (1970). *Pedagogy of the oppressed* (M. Bergman Ramos, Trans). Herder And Herder.
15. Gutiérrez, G. (1988). *A theology of liberation: History, politics, and salvation*. Orbis Books. (Original work published 1971)
16. Boff, L. (1988). *When theology listens to the poor*. Harper & Row.
17. Kuhn, M., Schularick, M., & Steins, U. I. (2020). Income and wealth inequality in America, 1949–2016. *Journal of Political Economy, 128*(9), 3469–3519. https://doi.org/10.1086/708815
18. Cobb, J., & Zocalo Public Square. (2018, April 4). Even though he is revered today, MLK was widely disliked by the American public when he was killed. *Smithsonian Magazine*. https://www.smithsonianmag.com/history/why-martin-luther-king-had-75-percent-disapproval-rating-year-he-died-180968664/

19. Feuerstein, G. (1989). *The Yoga-sutra of Patanjali: A new translation and commentary.* Inner Traditions.
20. Feuerstein, G. (1989). *The Yoga-sutra of Patanjali: A new translation and commentary.* Inner Traditions.
21. Yogananda, P. (2008). *Autobiography of a yogi.* Self-Realization Fellowship. (Original work published 1946)
22. Shontell, A. (2013, September 11). The last gift Steve Jobs gave to family and friends was a book about self realization. *Business Insider.* https://www.businessinsider.com/steve-jobs-gave-yoganandas-book-as-a-gift-at-his-memorial-2013-9
23. Sutton, J. (2008, November 11). *San Antonio Independent School District v. Rodriguez* and its aftermath. *Virginia Law Review.* https://www.virginialawreview.org/articles/san-antonio-independent-school-district-v-rodriguez-and-its-aftermath/
24. Sleeter, C. (2022). The practice of freedom: Social justice pedagogy in the United States. In T. K. Chapman & N. Hobbel (Eds.), *Social justice pedagogy across the curriculum: The practice of freedom* (2nd ed.). Routledge.
25. O'Brian, E. (2018). *The jewel of abundance: Finding prosperity through the ancient wisdom of yoga.* New World Press. (p. 140)
26. Chotiner, I. (2020, August 3). Why Stuart Stevens wants to defeat Donald Trump. *The New Yorker.* https://www.newyorker.com/news/q-and-a/why-stuart-stevens-wants-to-defeat-donald-trump
27. Nichols, J. (2010, November 11). The long goodbye. *The Economist.* https://www.economist.com/united-states/2010/11/11/the-long-goodbye.
28. Stevens, S. (2020). *It was all a lie: How the Republican Party became Donald Trump.* Knopf.
29. Shaull, R. (1970). Preface. In P. Freire, *Pedagogy of the oppressed.* Herder and Herder. (p. 15).
30. Shaull, R. (1970). Preface. In P. Freire, *Pedagogy of the oppressed.* Herder and Herder. (p. 15).
31. Ward, L. (2020). *America's racial karma: An invitation to heal.* Parallax Press. (p. 85).
32. Kornfield, J. (2008). *Guided meditation: Six essential practices to cultivate love, awareness, and wisdom* [Album]. Sounds True.

Chapter 12

1. Alcoholics Anonymous. (1976). *Alcoholics Anonymous* (3rd ed.). A.A. World Services, Inc. (p. 60).
2. Alcoholics Anonymous. (1989). *Twelve steps and twelve traditions.* A.A. World Services, Inc. (pp. 106–107).
3. W, B., & Alcoholics Anonymous. (2019). *Alcoholics anonymous: The big book: The original 1939 edition.* Ixia. (p. 60).
4. Editors of Encyclopedia Britannica. (n.d.). *Philosopher's stone.* https://www.britannica.com/topic/philosophers-stone
5. AA (1939), p. 88.
6. AA (1939), p. 96.
7. Brandeis, L. D. (1915). *True Americanism.* Louis D. Brandeis School of Law Library. https://louisville.edu/law/library/special-collections/the-louis-d.-brandeis-collection/business-a-profession-chapter-22
8. Stevens, S. (2020). *It was all a lie: How the Republican Party became Donald Trump.* Knopf.
9. Covey, S. R. (1989). *The seven habits of highly effective people: Restoring the character ethic.* Simon & Schuster.
10. Reich, R. (2019). *The common good.* Knopf.

BIBLIOGRAPHY

A.A. World Services. (1967). *As Bill sees it.* Alcoholics Anonymous World Services.

A.A. World Services. (1976). *Alcoholics Anonymous: The story of how many thousands of men and women have recovered from alcoholism.* Author.

A.A. World Services. (1989). *Twelve steps and twelve traditions.* Author.

Alcoholics Anonymous. (2011 reprint). *Alcoholics Anonymous.* Dover. (Original work published 1939)

Abend, G. (2008). The meaning of "theory." *Sociological Theory, 26*(2), 173–199. https://doi.org/10.1111/j.1467-9558.2008.00324.x

Alexander, M. (2010). *The new Jim Crow.* New Press.

Allen, T. (2012a). *The invention of the White race: Racial oppression and social control* (Vol. 1). Verso.

Allen, T. (2012b). *The invention of the White race: Racial oppression and social control* (Vol. 2). Verso.

American Psychiatric Association. (2010). *Home page.* psychiatry.org.

Ankel, S. (2022, January 25). VA governor, who has banned CRT, launches tip line to report teachers. *Business Insider.* https://www.businessinsider.com/glenn-youngkin-launches-tipline-report-teachers-2022-1

Anderson, C. (2017). *White rage: The unspoken truth of our racial divide.* Bloomsbury.

Asch, C. M. (2008). *The senator and the sharecropper: The freedom struggles of James O. Eastland and Fannie Lou Hamer.* The New Press.

Avelino, F. (2021). Theories of power and social change. Power contestations and their implications for research on social change and innovation. *Journal of Political Power, 14*(3), 425–448. https://doi.org/10.1080/2158379x.2021.1875307

Baldwin, J., & Schapiro, S. (2019). *The fire next time* (N. Weiner, Ed.). Taschen. (Original work published 1962)

Baldwin, J. (2021). *The fire next time*. Modern Library. (Original work published 1962)

Baltzly, D. (2019). Stoicism. *Stanford encyclopedia of philosophy*. https://plato.stanford.edu/archives/spr2019/entries/stoicism/

Baptist, E. E. (2014). *The half has never been told: Slavery and the making of American capitalism*. Basic Books.

Battalora, J. (2021). *Birth of a White nation: The invention of White people and its relevance today*. Routledge.

BBC News. (2013, July 29). *Pope Francis: Who am I to judge gay people?* https://www.bbc.com/news/world-europe-23489702

Beckert, S. (2015). *Empire of cotton*. Penguin.

Beveridge, L. (2020, August 26). Civil rights activist Fannie Lou Hamer and opera singer Leontyne Price among inspiring women on Mississippi list. *USA Today*. https://www.usatoday.com/in-depth/life/women-of-the-century/2020/08/13/mississippi-woman-history-poet-author-activists-19th-amendment/5003960002/

Billington, J. (2019). *Exploring the Early Americas*. Library of Congress. https://www.loc.gov/exhibits/exploring-the-early-americas/columbus-and-the-taino.html

Boff, L. (1988). *When theology listens to the poor*. Harper & Row.

Bonikowski, B., & DiMaggio, P. (2016). Varieties of American popular nationalism. *American Sociological Review, 81*(5), 949–980. https://doi.org/10.1177/0003122416663683

Bourdieu, P. (1977). *Outline of a theory of practice*. Cambridge University Press. (Original work published 1972)

Bourdieu, P. (1984). *Distinction: A social critique of the judgement of taste*. Harvard University Press. (Original work published 1979)

Brandeis, L. D. (1915). *True Americanism*. Louis D. Brandeis School of Law Library. https://louisville.edu/law/library/special-collections/the-louis-d.-brandeis-collection/business-a-profession-chapter-22

Brennan Center for Justice. (n.d.). *Dark money*. https://www.brennancenter.org/issues/reform-money-politics/influence-big-money/dark-money

Brewster, F. (2019). *Archetypal grief: Slavery's legacy of intergenerational child loss*. Routledge.

Britannica Encyclopedia. (n.d.). *Sanatana dharma*. https://www.britannica.com/topic/sanatana-dharma

Brooks, E., Parker, C., Lin, N., Spievack, N., & Oxholm, P. (2022). *The structural racism remedies repository*. Othering & Belonging Institute. https://belonging.berkeley.edu/structural-racism-remedies-repository

Brown, D. A. (2021). *The Whiteness of wealth: How the tax system impoverishes Black Americans and how we can fix it*. Crown.

California Department of Education. (2021, February). *Current expense of education*. https://www.cde.ca.gov/ds/fd/ec/currentexpense.asp

Case, A., & Deaton, A. (2020). *Deaths of despair and the future of capitalism*. Princeton University Press.

Cashin, S. (2021). *White space, black hood: Opportunity hoarding and segregation in the age of inequality*. Beacon Press.

Center for Humane Technology. (n.d.). *Home page*. www.humanetech.com

Chetty, R., Friedman, J., Hendren, N., Jones, M. R., & Porter, S. R. (2018, October 1). *The opportunity atlas: Mapping the childhood roots of social mobility*. Opportunity Insights. https://opportunityinsights.org/paper/the-opportunity-atlas/

Chotiner, I. (2020, August 3). Why Stuart Stevens wants to defeat Donald Trump. *The New Yorker*. https://www.newyorker.com/news/q-and-a/why-stuart-stevens-wants-to-defeat-donald-trump

Clark, H., & Knowles, C. (2013). *Resolution in memory of Helga Burnham Watson*. Scott County Democratic Executive Committee.

Coates, T. (2017). *We were eight years in power: An American tragedy*. One World.

Cobb, J., & Zocalo Public Square. (2018, April 4). *Even though he is revered today, MLK was widely disliked by the American public when he was killed.* Smithsonian Magazine. https://www.smithsonianmag.com/history/why-martin-luther-king-had-75-percent-disapproval-rating-year-he-died-180968664/

Cokley, K. O. (2022). *Making Black lives matter: Confronting anti-Black racism.* Cognella Academic Publishing.

Communication Theory. (2014, July 10). *The Johari window model.* https://www.communicationtheory.org/the-johari-window-model/

Covey, S. R. (1989). *The seven habits of highly effective people: Restoring the character ethic.* Simon & Schuster.

Cronquist, K. (2020). *Characteristics of SNAP households: FY 2019.* U.S. Food and Nutrition Service. https://www.fns.usda.gov/snap/characteristics-snap-households-fy-2019

Dankasa, J. (2015). Developing a theory in academic research: A review of experts' advice. *Journal of Information Science Theory and Practice, 3*(3), 64–74. https://doi.org/10.1633/jistap.2015.3.3.4

Darity, W. A., & Mullen, K. A. (2020). *From here to equality: Reparations for Black Americans in the twenty-first century.* University of North Carolina Press.

David, E. J. R. (2013). *Brown skin, White minds: Filipino -/ American postcolonial psychology.* Information Age.

Davis, A. (2016). *Freedom is a constant struggle: Ferguson, Palestine, and the foundations of a movement.* Haymarket Books.

Davis, F. (2019). *The little book of race and restorative justice: Black lives, healing, and US social transformation.* Good Books.

Dearman, S. (2007, November 15). Ronald Reagan speech, Neshoba County Fair, 1980. *The Neshoba County Democrat.* https://neshobademocrat.com/stories/ronald-reagans-1980-neshoba-county-fair-speech,49123

DeGruy, J. (2005). *Post traumatic slave syndrome: America's legacy of enduring injury and healing.* Joy DeGruy Publications Inc.

Delpit, L. (2006). *Other people's children: Cultural conflict in the classroom*. New Press.

Deranty, J. P. (2016). Exploited: Exploitation as a subjective category. *The Southern Journal of Philosophy, 54*(S1), 31–43. https://doi.org/10.1111/sjp.12185

Diangelo, R. (2021). *Nice Racism: How Progressive White People Perpetuate Racial Harm*. Beacon.

Diangelo, R. J. (2018). *White fragility: Why it's so hard for White people to talk about racism*. Beacon Press.

DiMaggio, P. J. (1995). Comments on "What Theory Is Not." *Administrative Science Quarterly, 40*(3), 391–397. https://doi.org/10.2307/2393790

Dollard, J. (2010). *Caste and class in a southern town*. Yale University Press. (Original work published 1937)

Domhoff, W. G. (2017). *Studying the power elite: Fifty years of who rules America?* Taylor & Francis.

Doyle, W. (2001). *An American insurrection: The battle of Oxford, Mississippi, 1962*. Doubleday.

Editors of Encyclopedia Britannica. (n.d.). *Philosopher's stone*. https://www.britannica.com/topic/philosophers-stone

Fahle, E. M., Reardon, S. F., Kalogrides, D., Weathers, E. S., & Jang, H. (2020). Racial segregation and school poverty in the United States, 1999–2016. *Race and Social Problems, 12*(1), 42–56. https://doi.org/10.1007/s12552-019-09277-w

Fanon, F. (2004). *The wretched of the earth*. Grove Press. (Original work published 1961)

Fanon, F. (2008). *Black skin, White masks*. Grove Press. (Original work published 1952)

FBI History. (1964). *Mississippi burning*. https://www.fbi.gov/history/famous-cases/mississippi-burning

Feuerstein, G. (1989). *The yoga-sutra of Patanjali: A new translation and commentary*. Inner Traditions.

FindLaw. (n.d.). *What does "caveat emptor" mean?* https://www.findlaw.com/consumer/consumer-transactions/what-does-caveat-emptor-mean-.html

Fishkin, J., & Forbath, W. E. (2022). *The anti-oligarchy constitution: Reconstructing the economic foundations of American democracy.* Harvard University Press.

Floyd, I., Pavetti, L., Meyer, L., Safawi, A., Schott, L., Bellew, E., & Magnus, A. (2021, August 4). *TANF policies reflect racist legacy of cash assistance: Reimagined program should center Black mothers.* Center on Budget and Policy Priorities. https://www.cbpp.org/research/family-income-support/tanf-policies-reflect-racist-legacy-of-cash-assistance

Foner, E. (2019). *The second founding: How the Civil War and Reconstruction remade the Constitution.* Norton.

Fortin, J. (2021, November 8). Critical race theory: A brief history. *The New York Times.* https://www.nytimes.com/article/what-is-critical-race-theory.html

Freire, P. (1970). *Pedagogy of the oppressed* (M. Bergman Ramos, Trans). Herder and Herder.

Gates, H. L., Jr. (2019). *Stony the road: Reconstruction, White supremacy, and the rise of Jim Crow.* Penguin Books.

Gates, H. L., Jr. (Ed.). (2021, December 20). *Maya Rudolph reacts to family history in Finding Your Roots | Ancestry.* www.youtube.com; Ancestry.com | Finding Your Roots. PBS. Host, Henry Louis Gates, Jr., Season 3 Episode 3, Clip. https://www.youtube.com/watch?v=WpkYo8YLeH8

George, J. (2021, January 12). *A lesson on critical race theory.* American Bar Association. https://www.americanbar.org/groups/crsj/publications/human_rights_magazine_home/civil-rights-reimagining-policing/a-lesson-on-critical-race-theory/

Ghaemi, N. (2017, July 24). The ghost of Barry Goldwater and the censorship of American psychiatrists. *Washington Monthly.* https://washingtonmonthly.com/2017/07/24/the-ghost-of-barry-goldwater-and-the-censorship-of-american-psychiatrists/

Giddings, P. (1984). *When and where I enter: The impact of Black women on race and sex in America*. William Morrow.

Glaude, Jr., E. S. (2017). *Democracy in Black: How race still enslaves the American soul*. Broadway Books.

Glaude, Jr., E. S. (2020). *Begin again*. Crown.

Goldberg, P. (2010). *American Veda: From Emerson and the Beatles to yoga and meditation: How Indian spirituality changed the West*. Harmony Books.

Goyette, K. A., & Lareau, A. (2014). *Choosing homes, choosing schools: Residential segregation and the search for a good school*. Russell Sage Foundation.

Graham, J. (2021). *Plantation theory: The Black professional's struggle between freedom & security*. Mynd Matters Publishing.

Gramsci, A., Buttigieg, J. A., & Callari, A. (2011). *Prison notebooks* (Vols. 1–3). Columbia University Press.

Graves, E. M., & Savage, S. A. (2015). *Promoting pathways to financial stability: A resource handbook on building financial capabilities of community college students*. The Federal Reserve Bank of Boston. https://www.bostonfed.org/publications/one-time-pubs/financial-capabilities-handbook.aspx

Greene, A., & Greene, A. (2015, January 20). Flashback: Neil Young covers "Sweet Home Alabama" in 1977. *Rolling Stone*. https://www.rollingstone.com/music/music-news/flashback-neil-young-covers-sweet-home-alabama-in-1977-186638/

Guénolé, F., Marcaggi, G., & Baleyte, J.-M. (2013). Do dreams really guard sleep? Evidence for and against Freud's theory of the basic function of dreaming. *Frontiers in Psychology, 4*. https://doi.org/10.3389/fpsyg.2013.00017

Gutiérrez, G. (1988). *A theology of liberation: History, politics, and salvation*. Orbis Books. (Original work published 1971)

Hannah-Jones, N., & New York Times Company. (2021). *The 1619 Project: A new origin story*. One World.

Harris, F., III, & Wood, J. L. (2021, February 12). Racelighting: A prevalent version of gaslighting facing People of Color. *Diverse: Issues in Higher*

Education. https://www.diverseeducation.com/opinion/article/15108651/racelighting-a-prevalent-version-of-gaslighting-facing-people-of-color

Height, D. (2003). *Open wide the freedom gates: A memoir.* Public Affairs.

Helms, J. E. (2020). *A race is a nice thing to have: A guide to being a White person or understanding the White persons in your life.* Cognella.

Herbers, J. (1964, August 9). Neshoba County Fair unclouded by murder of rights workers. *The New York Times.* https://www.nytimes.com/1964/08/09/archives/neshoba-county-fair-unclouded-by-murder-of-rights-workers.html

hooks, b. (1989a). *Feminist theory: From margin to center.* South End Press.

hooks, b. (1989b). *Talking back: Thinking feminist, thinking Black.* South End Press.

hooks, b. (1996). *Teaching to transgress: Education as the practice of freedom.* Routledge.

hooks, b. (2001). *Salvation: Black people and love.* William Morrow.

hooks, b. (1996). *Killing rage: Ending racism.* Henry Holt and Company.

Hope, D., & Limberg, J. (2020). *The economic consequences of major tax cuts for the rich.* https://eprints.lse.ac.uk/107919/1/Hope_economic_consequences_of_major_tax_cuts_published.pdf

Isenberg, N. (2016). *White trash: The 400-year untold history of class in America.* Viking.

Jaccard, J., & Jacoby, J. (2020). *Theory construction and model-building skills: A practical guide for social scientists.* Guilford Press.

Janney, C. (n.d.). The lost cause. *Encyclopedia Virginia.* https://encyclopediavirginia.org/entries/lost-cause-the

Jones, R. P. (2020). *White too long: The legacy of White supremacy in American Christianity.* Simon & Schuster.

Kelly, J. T. (2012). *Framing democracy: A behavioral approach to democratic theory.* Princeton University Press.

Kendi, I. X. (2019). *How to be an antiracist.* One World.

King, M. L., Jr. (1967). *Beyond Vietnam: A time to break silence.* Common Dreams. https://www.commondreams.org/views/2018/01/15/beyond-vietnam-time-break-silence

King, M. L., Jr. (2010). *Why we can't wait.* Beacon Press. (Original work published 1963)

Klein, E. (2020). *Why we're polarized.* Avid Reader Press.

Kornfield, J. (2008). *Guided meditation: Six essential practices to cultivate love, awareness, and wisdom* [Album]. Sounds True.

Kozol, J. (1991). *Savage inequalities: Children in America's schools.* Crown Pub.

Krathwohl, D. R. (2002). A revision of Bloom's taxonomy: An overview. *Theory Into Practice, 41*(4), 212–218. https://doi.org/10.1207/s15430421tip4104_2

Kuhn, M., Schularick, M., & Steins, U. I. (2020). Income and wealth inequality in America, 1949–2016. *Journal of Political Economy, 128*(9), 3469–3519. https://doi.org/10.1086/708815

Ladson-Billings, G. (2006). From the achievement gap to the education debt: Understanding achievement in U.S. schools. *Educational Researcher, 35*(7), 3–12. https://doi.org/10.3102/0013189x035007003

Lakoff, G. (1996). *Moral politics: What conservatives know that liberals don't.* University of Chicago Press.

Lareau, A. (2011). *Unequal childhoods: Class, race, and family life* (2nd ed.). University of California Press.

Lee, B. X. (2019). *The dangerous case of Donald Trump: 37 psychiatrists and mental health experts assess a president: Updated and expanded with new essays.* Thomas Dunne Books, an Imprint of St. Martin's Press.

Lee, J., Sleeter, C., & Kumashiro, K. (2015). Interrogating identity and social contexts through "critical family history." *Multicultural Perspectives, 17*(1), 28–32. https://doi.org/10.1080/15210960.2015.994426

Leonardo, Z. (2005). *Critical pedagogy and race.* Blackwell.

Leonardo, Z. (2009). *Race, Whiteness, and education.* Routledge.

Leonardo, Z. (2013). *Race frameworks: A multidimensional theory of racism and education.* Teachers College Press.

Levitsky, S., & Ziblatt, D. (2018). *How democracies die*. Crown.

Manji, I. (2019). *Don't label me: An incredible conversation for divided times*. St. Martin's Press.

Mann, M. (2012–2013). *The sources of social power (Vol. 1–4)*. Cambridge University Press. (Original work published 1986)

Marsh, C. (1997). *God's long summer: Stories of faith and civil rights*. Princeton University Press.

Martin, M. (1987). *The Jesuits: The society of Jesus and the betrayal of the Roman Catholic Church*. Linden Press.

The Martin Luther King, Jr. Center for Non-Violent Change. (2022). *The beloved community: The fierce urgency of now* [Video]. https://www.youtube.com/watch?v=aujrJRFyI34

McDavid, I. R., Jr., & McDavid, V. G. (1969). The late unpleasantness: Folk names for the Civil War. *The Southern Speech Journal, 34*(3), 194–204, https://doi.org/10.1080/10417946909372004

McGhee, H. C. (2021). *The sum of us: What racism costs everyone and how we can prosper together*. One World.

Menand, L. (2018, January 18). Lessons from the election of 1968. *The New Yorker*. https://www.newyorker.com/magazine/2018/01/08/lessons-from-the-election-of-1968

Metzl, J. M. (2020). *Dying of Whiteness: how the politics of racial resentment is killing America's heartland*. Basic Books.

Miller, J. H. (1996). Kudzu eradication and management. In D. Hoots & J. Baldwin (Eds.), *Kudzu: The vine to love or hate* (pp. 137–149). Suntop Press.

Mills, C. W. (1956). *The power elite*. Oxford University Press.

Mills, C. W. (2000). *The sociological imagination*. Grove Press.

Mills, K. (1993). *This little light of mine: The life of Fannie Lou Hamer*. Dutton.

Mounk, Y. (2018). *The people vs. democracy: Why our freedom is in danger and how to save it*. Harvard University Press.

Newkirk, P. (2019). *Diversity, Inc.: The failed promise of a billion-dollar business*. Bold Type Books.

Nichols, J. (2010, November 11). The long goodbye. *The Economist*. https://www.economist.com/united-states/2010/11/11/the-long-goodbye

O., P. (1995). *There's more to quitting drinking than quitting drinking*. Sabrina Publishing.

O'Brian, E. G. (2018). *The jewel of abundance: Finding prosperity through the ancient wisdom of yoga*. New World Library.

Ownby, T. (2017). *Mississippi Action for Progress (MAP)*. Center for Study of Southern Culture, Mississippi Encyclopedia. http://mississippiencyclopedia.org/entries/mississippi-action-for-progress/

Painter, N. I. (2011). *The history of White people*. Norton.

Park, S. C. (2018). The Goldwater rule from the perspective of phenomenological psychopathology. *Psychiatry Investigation*, *15*(2), 102–103. https://doi.org/10.30773/pi.2018.01.25

Parmar, A., & Kaloiya, G. (2018). Comorbidity of personality disorder among substance use disorder patients: A narrative review. *Indian Journal of Psychological Medicine*, *40*(6), 517–527. https://doi.org/10.4103/IJPSYM.IJPSYM_164_18

Parry, M. (2019, November 8). The trouble with Ole Miss. *The Chronicle of Higher Education*. https://www.chronicle.com/article/the-trouble-with-ole-miss/

Phillips, A. (2022, June 27). The sex-trafficking investigation that's zeroing in on Matt Gaetz, explained. *The Washington Post*. https://www.washingtonpost.com/politics/2022/01/27/sex-trafficking-allegations-matt-gaetz/

powell, j. a. (2015). *Racing to justice: Transforming our conceptions of self and other to build an inclusive society*. Indiana University Press.

powell, j. a. (2017, August 29). Othering and belonging: An embodied spiritual practice. *Deep Times: A Journal of Work That Reconnects*. https://journal.workthatreconnects.org/2017/08/29/othering-and-belonging-expanding-the-circle-of-human-concern/

powell, j. a., Menendian, S., & Ake, W. (2019). *Targeted universalism: Policy & practice.* https://belonging.berkeley.edu/sites/default/files/targeted_universalism_primer.pdf

Reich, R. B. (2019). *The common good.* Knopf.

Reich, R. B. (2021). *The system: Who rigged it, how we fix it.* Vintage.

Rev. (2021, June 23). *General Milley, Secretary Austin answer critical race theory questions from Matt Gaetz testimony: Transcript.* https://www.rev.com/blog/transcripts/general-milley-secretary-austin-answer-critical-race-theory-questions-from-matt-gaetz-testimony-transcript

Richardson, H. C. (2020). *How the South won the Civil War: Oligarchy, democracy, and the continuing fight for the soul of America.* Oxford University Press.

Roediger, D. R. (2018). *Working toward Whiteness: How America's immigrants became White: The strange journey from Ellis Island to the suburbs.* Basic Books.

Rohter, L. (1998, April 3). 4 Salvadorans say they killed U.S. nuns on orders of military. *The New York Times.* https://www.nytimes.com/1998/04/03/world/4-salvadorans-say-they-killed-us-nuns-on-orders-of-military.html

Rubin, V., & McAfee, M. (2021, September 9). Decentering Whiteness: Building for the movement tasks ahead. *Nonprofit Quarterly.* https://nonprofitquarterly.org/decentering-whiteness-building-for-the-movement-tasks-ahead/

Sadoff, J. H., Sadoff, R. L., & Needleman, L. (2011). *Pieces from the past: Voices of heroic women in civil rights.* Tasora Books.

Salvador, J. (2022, February 15). Dr. Dre asked about Eminem taking a knee during the Super Bowl halftime show. *Sports Illustrated.* https://www.si.com/extra-mustard/2022/02/15/dr-dre-says-nfl-had-no-problem-with-eminem-taking-knee-super-bowl-halftime-show

Satz, R. (1986). The Mississippi Choctaw: From the Removal Treaty to the federal agency. In S. J. Wells & R. Tubby (Ed.), *After removal: The Choctaw in Mississippi* (p. 7). University Press of Mississippi.

Scott County Times Online. (2018). Slaughter Legacy honored: Forest Alderman W. L. And Mrs. Olivia Kelley Slaughter honored (posthumously) by Jackson

Tougaloo Alumni Club. *Scott County Times.* https://www.sctonline.net/front-page-slideshow-features/slaughter-legacy-honored#sthash.74ptwXBg.dpbs

Shontell, A. (2013, September 11). The last gift Steve Jobs gave to family and friends was a book about self realization. *Business Insider.* https://www.businessinsider.com/steve-jobs-gave-yoganandas-book-as-a-gift-at-his-memorial-2013-9

Sifton, E. (2003). *The serenity prayer: Faith and politics in times of peace and war.* Norton.

Sleeter, C. (n.d.). *Home page.* https://www.christinesleeter.org/critical-family-history

Sleeter, C. E. (2011). Becoming White: Reinterpreting a family story by putting race back into the picture. *Race Ethnicity and Education, 14*(4), 421–433. https://doi.org/10.1080/13613324.2010.547850

Sleeter, C. (2015). Multicultural curriculum and critical family history. *Multicultural Education Review, 7*(1–2), 1–11. https://doi.org/10.1080/2005615x.2015.1048607

Sleeter, C. E. (2018). *The inheritance: A novel.* Sleeter Publishing.

Sleeter, C. (2020). Critical family history: An introduction. *Genealogy, 4*(2), 64. https://doi.org/10.3390/genealogy4020064

Sleeter, C. E. (2021). *Family history in Black and White: A novel.* Brill Sense.

Sleeter, C. (2022). Federal education policy and social justice education. In T. K. Chapman & N. Hobbel (Eds.), *Social justice pedagogy across the curriculum: The practice of freedom* (2nd ed.). Routledge.

Smiley, T., & West, C. (2012). *The rich and the rest of us: A poverty manifesto.* Smileybooks.

Stanford University Law School. (2021). *ABA women trailblazer's project.* Robert Crown Law Library. https://abawtp.law.stanford.edu/exhibits/show/constance-i-slaughter-harvey/biography?_ga=2.110698829.914675179.1597941222-1936040103.1597615574

Steele, C. (2010). *Whistling Vivaldi: And other clues to how stereotypes affect us.* Norton.

Stevens, S. (2020). *It was all a lie: How the Republican Party became Donald Trump.* Knopf.

Stewart, S., III, Chui, M., Manyika, J., Julien, J. P., Hunt, V., Sternfels, B., Woetzel, J., & Zhang, H. (2021). *The economic state of Black America: What is and what could be.* https://www.mckinsey.com/~/media/mckinsey/featured%20insights/diversity%20and%20inclusion/the%20economic%20state%20of%20black%20america%20what%20is%20and%20what%20could%20be/the-economic-state-of-black-america-what-is-and-what-could-be-f.pdf

Stoute, B. J. (2017). Race and racism in psychoanalytic thought: The ghosts in our nursery. *The American Psychoanalyst, 51*(1). https://apsa.org/apsaa-publications/vol51no1-TOC/html/vol51no1_08.xhtml

Sullivan, C. (2002). *Rescuing Jesus from the Christians.* Trinity Press International.

Sullivan, C. (2004). *Why Beulah shot her pistol inside the Baptist Church.* NewSouth Books.

Sutton, J. (2008, November 11). *San Antonio Independent School District v. Rodriguez and its aftermath. Virginia Law Review.* https://www.virginialawreview.org/articles/san-antonio-independent-school-district-v-rodriguez-and-its-aftermath/

Takaki, R. T. (2008). *A different mirror: A history of multicultural America.* Back Bay Books.

Tan, A. S. (2021). *Who is racist? Why racism matters.* Cognella Press.

Tarasoff v. Regents of Univ. of Cal. 13 Cal. 3d 177, 118 Cal. Rptr. 129, 529 P.2d 553 (Cal. 1974).

Tatum, B. D., (2007). *Can we talk about race? And other conversations in an era of school resegregation.* Beacon Press.

Taylor, E., Gillborn, D., & Ladson-Billings, G. (2009). *Foundations of critical race theory in education.* Routledge.

The Nature Conservancy. (2019). *Journey with nature: Kudzu.* https://www.nature.org/en-us/about-us/where-we-work/united-states/indiana/stories-in-indiana/kudzu-invasive-species/

Toporek, R. L., & Ahluwalia, M. K. (2021). *Taking action: Creating social change through strength, solidarity, strategy, and sustainability.* Cognella Press.

Truth and Reconciliation Commission. (1998). *Final report.* https://www.justice.gov.za/trc/report/execsum.htm

University of Southern Mississippi Wesley Foundation. (n.d.). *Our history.* https://www.usmwesley.org/our-history

U.S. Department of Justice. (2021). *The U.S. Marshalls and the integration of the University of Mississippi.* U.S. Marshall Service. https://www.usmarshals.gov/history/miss/02.htm

U.S. Office of Energy Efficiency & Renewable Energy. (2016). *Fact #915: March 7, 2016 average historical annual gasoline pump price, 1929-2015.* https://www.energy.gov/eere/vehicles/fact-915-march-7-2016-average-historical-annual-gasoline-pump-price-1929-2015

Vespa, J., Medina, L., & Armstrong, D. (2020). *Demographic turning points for the United States: Population projections for 2020 to 2060 population estimates and projections current population reports.* U.S. Census. https://www.census.gov/content/dam/Census/library/publications/2020/demo/p25-1144.pdf

Villanueva, E. (2018). *Decolonizing wealth: Indigenous wisdom to heal divides and restore balance.* Berrett-Koehler.

Vitali, A. (2016, February 29). *Alabama's Jeff Sessions becomes first senator to endorse Trump.* NBC News. https://www.nbcnews.com/politics/2016-election/alabama-s-jeff-sessions-becomes-first-senator-endorse-trump-n527661

W, B., & Alcoholics Anonymous. (2019). *Alcoholics anonymous: The big book: The original 1939 edition.* Ixia.

Wakefield, J. C. (2015). DSM-5 substance use disorder: How conceptual missteps weakened the foundations of the addictive disorders field. *Acta Psychiatrica Scandinavica, 132*(5), 327–334. https://doi.org/10.1111/acps.12446

Wall Street Journal. (2016, November 15). Henry Louis Gates discusses ideological divides among Black Americans. https://www.wsj.com/video/henry-louis-gates-discusses-ideological-divides-among-black-americans/77306EFF-CDD0-425A-B47A-E07737846D57.html

Ward, L. (2020). *America's racial karma: An invitation to heal*. Parallax Press.

Watson, W., Esquivel-Swinson, A., & Montemayor, R. (2018). Collaborative impact and professional development: Effective student services for immigrant populations amid growing inequality. *Community College Journal of Research and Practice, 42*(11), 778–782. https://doi.org/10.1080/10668926.2018.1448727

Weber, M., & Tribe, K. (2019). *Economy and society a new translation*. Harvard University Press. (Original work published 1921)

Wells, S. J. (2014). *After removal: The Choctaw in Mississippi*. University Press of Mississippi.

West, C. (1994). *Race matters*. Beacon Press.

West, C. (2005). *Democracy matters: Winning the fight against imperialism*. Penguin Books.

Wilkerson, I. (2016). *The warmth of other suns: The epic story of America's great migration*. Random House.

Wilkerson, I. (2020). *Caste: The origins of our discontents*. Random House.

Williams, C. R. (2020, June 26). Opinion | You want a confederate monument? My body is a confederate monument. *The New York Times*. https://www.nytimes.com/2020/06/26/opinion/confederate-monuments-racism.html

Williams, P. (2020). The changing meaning of the American flag under Trump. *The New Yorker*. https://www.newyorker.com/news/us-journal/the-changing-meaning-of-the-american-flag-under-trump

Wilson, W. J. (2010). *More than just race: Being Black and poor in the inner city*. Norton.

Winter, W. F., & Mullins, A. P. (2006). *The measure of our days: Writings of William F. Winter*. William Winter Institute for Racial Reconciliation.

Wise, T. (2009). *Between Barack and a hard place: Racism and White denial in the age of Obama*. City Lights Books.

Wise, T. J. (2011). *White like me: Reflections on race from a privileged son: The remix*. Soft Skull Press.

Wise, T. (2020). *Dispatches from the race war*. City Lights Books.

Witness for Peace. (n.d.). *Home page.* https://www.witnessforpeace.org

Wolff, T., Minkler, M., Wolfe, S., Berkowitz, B., Bowen, L., Butterfish, F. D., Christens, B. D., Francisco, V. T., Himmelman, A. T., & Lee, K. S. (2017, January 9). Collaborating for equity and justice: Moving beyond collective impact. *Nonprofit Quarterly.* https://nonprofitquarterly.org/2017/01/09/collaborating-equity-justice-moving-beyond-collective-impact/

Yogananda, P. (2008). *Autobiography of a yogi.* Self-Realization Fellowship. (Original work published 1946)

Yogapedia.com. (n.d.). *What is Aham Brahmasmi?* https://www.yogapedia.com/definition/8231/aham-brahmasmi

Zaragovia, V. (2014, October 1). *Cajuns are fiercely proud of their culture, but they're divided over the word "coonass."* The World. https://theworld.org/stories/2014-10-01/cajuns-are-fiercely-proud-their-culture-theyre-divided-over-word-coonass

Zehr, H. (2016). *The little book of restorative justice.* Langara College.

Zinn, H. (2015). *A people's history of the United States.* HarperPerennial.

Zwiers, M. (2018, May 25). Eastland, James O. *Mississippi Encyclopedia.* https://mississippiencyclopedia.org/entries/james-oliver-eastland/

INDEX

A

A.A. Grapevine, Inc., viii
Abednego, 153
ability/inability, 118
acceptance, 148–150, 161, 168, 188
addiction recovery. *See* recovery
African American college, 154–155
aggressions, 153–154
agricultural economy, 59
agricultural success, 7
Aham Brahmasmi, 160
ahimsa (nonviolence), 172–184
Ahluwalia, M. K., 145
alcohol, 19
　behavioral reinforcement, 162
　as deadly problem, 33
　overrelying on, 21
　for smallness beholders, 108
　as solution, 23
　tolerance, 93
　for vastness beholders, 108
alcoholics, xxxi–xxxix
　broken beholderometer, 110
　defiant and resentful, 32
　devolving capabilities, 5
　first step of, 19
　heroic instinct, 92
　life cycle, 33
　loses capacity, 34
　mind games, 33
　recovering, 34, 70, 73, 123, 126, 128–129, 169, 174–175, 201

Alcoholics Anonymous (AA), 99
　believe, 31–39
　effectiveness of, 41
　problem-solving principles, vii, 112, 195, 200
　rigged advantage, 18–30
　stories in, 149
Alcoholics Anonymous Publishing, viii
alcoholism, 4–5, 103, 108, 110
　codependent system, 11
　deadly dysfunction of, 51
　dysfunction of, 111
　progresses, 34
　as self-spiraling phenomenon, 162
　as SUD, 36
　terror of, 162
　tragedy of, 93
alternative facts, 171
American dream, 114
An American Insurrection, the Battle of Oxford Mississippi (Doyle), 94
American Psychiatric Association, 35
America's Racial Karma (Ward), 186–187
ancestral slavery, 114
anonymity, vii–viii
anti-Americanism, 93
anti-Blackness, 29, 37, 46, 52, 66, 77, 94, 103, 116, 131, 137, 154
anti-Negro thunder, 102
Aspen Institute, xxxvi
asteya (nonstealing), 172–184
Atkins, C., 101

235

atonement, 16, 136–137, 152, 160
Augustus, 76
Autobiography of a Yogi (Yogananda), 174
autocracy, 15, 29, 62, 64

B

Baldwin, J., v, lii–liii, lv, lviii
bamboozle/bamboozling, 12–13, 15, 46, 51, 61–62
  convictions, 47
  power Whites, 46
  technique, 16
  theater, 80, 82
Barnett, R., xv, 16, 94
Basquiat, J.-M., 55
The Beatles, 174
beholder parents, 107
beholding, 107
belonging.berkeley.edu, 119
Biden, J., 95
Big Chris(t), xxxiii–xxxiv
Bill W., 34, 134
Biloxi, 41
Black Americans, 10, 24, 30, 78, 113
  abandon for, 158
  as "Others," 177
  benefits to, 17
  citizenship in the United States, 11
  deadly consequences, 157
  democratic citizenship, 30
  family memory for, 60
  households, 171
  marginalized expense of, 60
  presumption of whereabouts authority over, 176–178, 182, 184
  property for, 60
  remedy to, 113
  slavery. *See* slavery
  wealth inequality, 116
  whereabouts of, 104–105
  Whiteness calculation, 156
Black Panther Party, xvi–xvii, 64
Boff, L., 167
Brandeis, L. D., 194
Brown v. Board of Education, 176, 179–180, 183–184
bullied child, 138
Buren, M. Van, 58–59
Burnham, J. R., 9, 58
Burnham, Mama, xxviii, 9
Burnham, N. E., 59
Bush, George W., 44
Butlers, 58–59
Butts, C., 23

C

Cajuns, 42–43
Canaan-land, xlv
career in higher education, 144
Carter, J., 102
case study
  restorative justice, 81–83
  truth, 79–81
cedes to addiction, 21
Chaney, xvi, lii, 14, 101
changes, 98–105
Charlie P., xxi
Chetty, Raj, 120
Choctaw, 58
Christ consciousness, 54
Church and State, 182
civil rights, 104
  movement, 59, 173
  violence, 118
  working, 58
Civil Rights Act, 1964, 23, 101–102

Index | 237

Civil War, xvii
class, 23
class and race, 176–184
Colfax, 118
colonial ventures, England, 7
Columbus, 56
comorbidity, 36
competitive meritocracy, 144
complementary steps. *See* governing and complementary steps
confederate monument, 6, 24, 59
Confederate States of America (CSA), xlvi, 8–9, 12, 25, 59
confession, 74–75, 86, 124
connase, 42
consequences, 19–20, 34, 92
content, xxvii
contextualized family history assessment, 69
Continuum of Ideological Impermeability, 197–199
Coushatta, 118
critical legal theory, 13
Critical Race Theory (CRT), 13, 17, 63–64
culturally embedded entitlement, 177
Culture War Fight Club, 16
culture wars, 181

D

deaths of despair, 37
decision, 40–48
Delpit, L., 139
delusion, 65
democracy, vii, xv, xix, xxiii, xxv, xxx, xxxix–xl, xlii–xliii, xlix–lii, 6, 11–12, 15–17, 21, 30, 36, 39, 47, 55, 60–62, 68, 72, 75, 77–78, 88, 90, 94–97, 100, 104–105, 112, 122, 125, 129, 131, 137, 144, 158, 160, 170, 178, 180, 182–183, 186, 194–195, 198–202
Democratic National Convention, 100

denial, 33, 51, 113
Deranty, 67
Diagnostic and Statistical Manual of Mental Disorders (DSM-5), 36
discoveries, 55, 86–87, 150
displacement *versus* projection, 67
Divine Right of Kings, 30, 62
Dixiecrats, 100
domestic violence, 66
Doyle, W., 94
drawing the circle, 184–187
Dr. Bob, 34
drinking, 5, 20. *See also* alcoholism
    driving and, 1
    history of, 134
    identity, 21
    next morning after, 109
    social, 197
dual diagnoses, 36
Duchamp, M., 55
dysfunctional adaptations, 51

E

Eastland, James O., 165
East Mississippi Legal Services, xvii
economic competitiveness, 117
education, 143
    adequate system, 180
    Brown v. Board of Education, 179–180
    debt, 144
    design, xxxix
    enterprise, 140
    funding, 180, 183–185
    goals, 140, 143–144
    iceberg, 139
    opportunities, 180–181
    outcomes in, 29, 66, 119
    Rodriguez on, 180

educator, xxxix–xli
ego-dystonic, 67
ego-syntonic, 67
Elders of Zion, 64
elite Whites, 7, 11, 26, 47, 182
Elizabeth I, 7
Emancipation, 80
Encyclopedia Virginia, 8
England
   colonial ventures, 7
   Virginia, 23
enslavement, 59, 104–105
entitlement of Whiteness, 24
entitlements, 177
equal protection, 179–180
Evers, Medgar, xviii–xx
explicit problem, 49–70
exploitation, 67, 135
   debased, xxvii
   group, 28, 64
   in rigged advantage theory, 48
   of Whiteness, 12
   sadistic, xxv
   subjective, 65–67, 77, 150, 178
   subjective experience of, 64
exploited Whites, 65–66, 160
   co-opt, 28, 65
   delusional mechanism, 29
   displacement *versus* projection, 67
   power Whites, 46–47, 64, 67
   in Rigged Advantage Theory, 66, 178

F

Fact magazine, 35
fair competition, l–li
family consciousness, 59
Faulkner, W., xv, xix, lii
FBI's COINTELPRO operation, 64

Federal Reserve Bank Survey of Consumer Finances, 116
Finding Your Roots, 22, 150
The Fire Next Time, v, lii
Floyd, G., xxx, lviii, 10
Forest (Mississippi), xvi, 42, 78
Frankenthaler, H., 55
Free Breakfast Program, xvii
freedom and justice, 197–198
Freire, P., 167
"The Friendship Oak," 42
French Quarter, 43–44, 164
Fugitive Slave Act, 10

G

Gandhi, M. K., 75, 172–173
Gates, H. L., Jr., 22, 150–151
genetic predisposition, 135
geo-political lines, 57
Georgia senators, 16
Ghaemi, N., 36
Glaude, E. S., Jr., 47, 160
Goldwater, B., 35
Goldwater rule, 35–36
Goodman, xvi, lii, 14, 101
governing and complementary steps, lvii–lviii
Grant's Tomb, 25
Guanahani, 57
Gulf of Mexico, 42
Gulf Park, 42
Gutierrez, G., 167

H

Haas, R. D., 119
Hamer, F. L., xv, 100–101
harm, identification of, 106–120
harm reduction, 36
Harper, B., xliv

Harperville, xxxiv, xliv, 24, 118
Harperville Baptist Church, xxxiv, lii
Harvard Law School, 79
Harvard Medical School, 36
Hattiesburg, xxxiii, 149
Hawkins, L., 22
Head Start, xvi, xix
Hebrews, 54
Heraclitus, 54
higher education
    boutique, 144
    career in, 144
    community colleges, 180
    equity-minded practitioner in, xxxvii
    vantage point of, 84
Hillsboro, 9
hitting bottom, lviii, 92, 126
Hobbes, Thomas, 76
home, 42
homophobic, 9
honkytonk, xxix
human spirit, 92, 135
humility, 86, 99, 191–192
Hurricane Camille, 41, 43
Hurricane Katrina, 43–44

I

identification of harm, 106–120
ideological permeability, continuum of, 197–198
ideological rigidity, 197
ideology in modern life, 24–25
"I Have a Dream" (King's speech), 172
Illinois Republican State Convention, 76
Indian Removal Act, 58
inequality, 11, 44–47, 96, 112, 116–117, 159–160
inheritance, 30, 62, 68, 104, 114, 140
injury, 111

integrity, liv, 201
intentional *versus* unintentional beliefs, 97
"I Saw the Light," xxxiv
It Was All a Lie (Stevens), 101, 183, 199

J

Jackson, A., 58
Jesus, 54, 76, 163–164
The Jewel of Abundance (O'Brian), 184
Jim Crow segregation, 46, 118, 177
Joe Camel, xxiv
Joe M., xli
Johari window, 86
juke joint, xxix, xliv
junkyard dog, xxvi, 147, 153–154
justice and freedom, 197–198
justice system, xlv
justification, 33

K

Kandinsky, W., 55
karma, xxix, 186
kazoo, xlii
Kemp, B. E., Jr., 42
Kennedy administration, 94
Kennedy, J. F., xv, 94, 104
Kennedy, R., xv, 94
killing, 57
King, M. L., Jr., 23, 64, 172–174
kriya yoga, 174
Kudzu, 88–89
Ku Klux Klan (KKK), xvi–xvii, xxviii–xxix, lii, 14–15, 24–25, 101–102

L

Lady Warrior, xviii–xix
Lake Pontchartrain, 44
language, 54

Lauderdale County, xvi
learning enterprise, 140
learning outcomes, lviii–lx
Lee, Robert E., 9
Le Fleur's restaurant, xvii
legacies
   civil rights, xxx, xxxvi
   of Gandhi, 172
   of kriya yoga, 174
   of plantation control, 9
   of plantation economy, 23
   of plantation slavery, 182
   racial, 15
   of slavery, xliv, 6, 9, 11–12, 15–16, 46, 66, 77, 88, 94–98, 116, 137, 144, 152, 176–177, 184, 196–197
   victors, 7
liberty free from rigged advantage, 194–202
logos, 54
Long Beach, 41–42
lost cause movement, 8
"Love Lifted Me," xxxiv–xxxv
loving kindness meditation, 187–188
Loyola University, xxi
lynching, 118

M

MacArthur Foundation, 120
Maccabees, 163
making sense of things, 53
Malcolm X, 64
managing impressions, 109
mandala. *See* practice mandala
March to the Sea, 9
Mardi Gras, 42
marginalization, 25, 51, 63, 65, 69, 84, 187
market forces, l

Marxist indoctrination, 63
McCabes, 59
McGhee, H., 78
McKinsey and Company, 119
media consolidations, 96
median wealth, 171
meditation, 187–188
"membership privileges," 14
mental health/illness, 35–36
mentally disordered megalomaniac narcissist, 12
Meredith, J., xv, 94–95, 104, 204
meritocracy *vs.* rigged advantage, 32
Meshach, 53
message, xlvii–lx
messenger, xxxi–xlvii
Miller, J., 89
Milley, General, 79–80, 82
Mississippi Action for Progress, xvi
Mississippi Burning, xvi
Mississippi Freedom Democratic Party, 100
Mississippi Gulf Coast, 41–42
Mississippi Institute for Hopeful Futures, 20
Mississippi National Guard, xv
Mississippi's Giant House Party, 101
Montana, Joe, xli, 149
Moses, B., 100
multiple sclerosis, 141

N

NAACP, xviii–xix
narcissism, 110
narcissistic personality disorder, 110
national dysfunction, 38
National Equity Atlas, 120
nationalequityatlas.org, 120
Nebuchadnezzar, xxx, 53

Neshoba County, xvi, 101–102
Neshoba County Fair, 101
Neshoba County Fairgrounds, 102
New Orleans, 44–45
The New York Times, 102
Niebuhr, R., 38
Nighthawk Rednecks, xxxiv
Nixon, Richard, 179
niyamas (practices to do), 173
nonstealing. *See asteya* (nonstealing)
nonviolence. *See ahimsa* (nonviolence)

O
Oak, Rowan, xv
Obama, Michelle, xxvi
O'Brian, Ellen Grace, 166, 184
Old Testament, 174
Ole Miss. *See* University of Mississippi
Opportunity Atlas, 120
otherness, 46
Other People's Children (Delpit), 138
"Others," 177
overt and covert violence, 24

P
Paine, Thomas, 76
Panama City, 42
Pantanjali, 173
Pass Christian, 41
Pasteur, L., 56
Patrick, K., 14
Paul O., 149
Pearl Harbor, xxxiv
Pedagogy of the Oppressed (Freire), 183
personality disorder, 36
Philadelphia Centennial Exposition, 88
Philo, 54
plantation behavior, 24–25

plantation system, Virginia, 8
Plessy v. Ferguson, 177
PolicyLink, 120
political campaigning, 101
political enthusiasm, 101
poverty, 44
powell, john a., 26, 119
power Whites, 46, 64–65
practice mandala, lvi, lvii
presumption of whereabouts authority (PWA), 24, 176–178, 182, 184
Price, Leontyne, xv
problem drinkers, 32
problem-solving, 72–74
  in language, 3
  principles, 112
  process, 123–124, 130
  sequence, 112
  steps, 2
problem-solving principles, vii
process stability, xxvi–xxvii
projection *versus* displacement, 67
Pronto Pups, 101
property, 58
Prosperity Now, 120
Prudhomme, Paul, 42
psychotherapist, xli–xliii
Putin, B., 104

R
race, 23, 170
  and class, 176–184
  consciousness, 14–15
racial difference, 23
racial habits, 160
racial segregation, 176–184
rationalization, 33
Reagan, R., 102, 104

Reconstruction, xlii–xliii, 9, 117, 177
recovering alcoholics, 34, 70, 73, 123, 126, 128–129, 169, 174–175, 201
recovery, 86–88, 190–191
   from rigged advantage, 194–202
   hard work and, 191
   miraculous work of, 50
   onset of, 37
   principles, 16, 34, 88, 116
   self-assessed path, 86
   tradition, 38, 116
   treatment plan, 4, 37
registered coon ass, 42
repairing harm, 133–146
repentance, 136
replacement narrative, 110
Requiem for a Nun, xix
Rescuing Jesus From the Christians (Sullivan), 164
resolution, 74, 124–125
restorative justice, 82
reverence, 161–188
   ahimsa (nonviolence), 172–184
   asteya (nonstealing), 172–184
   drawing the circle, 184–187
   loving kindness meditation, 187–188
   telescoping, 169–171, 174
   we *vs.* me, 171–172
Rhodes Scholar at Oxford, 139
Riders, F., 64
rigged advantage, 6, 52, 64
   Alcoholics Anonymous (AA), 18–30
   application to, 73–74, 123–124, 131
   competitiveness of, 83
   dysfunction, 111
   in democracy, 88
   junk of, 154
   liberty free from, 194–202
   meritocracy *vs*, 32
   norm of, 37
   operates a Whiteness collusion, 154
   problem of, 75, 117
   slavery, 23
   threatens, 37
   White-affiliated, 105
   Whiteness coalition, 11
Rigged Advantage Theory (RAT), 61–67
Rogers, Carl, xlii
Romero, Archbishop Oscar, 166
Romero, Oscar, 166
Rudolph, M., 150–153

S

Sammy, 109
San Antonio v. Rodriguez, 176, 179–181, 183–184
Sanatana dharma, 173
San Francisco State University, xxi
sanity, 32
San Mateo County, 180–181
scaffolding, xxxix, li
Schwerner, xvi, lii, 14, 101
Scott County, xvi, xlv, 9, 101
Scott County Improvement Association, xvi
Seale, Bobby, xvi–xvii
segregation. *See* racial segregation
serenity prayer, 38
Sergeant Pepper's Lonely Hearts Club Band (The Beatles), 174
Sessions, J. B., III, 103
Sessions, S. J., 102
7 Habits of Highly Effective People (Covey), 200
shackles, 2, 5–6, 11
Shadrach, 53
Sherman, General W. T., 9

Shipley Donuts, 109

Shoney's, xxxiii

Silicon Valley, 141, 155

Six Cees Superette, xvi

Slaughter-Harvey, Constance, xv–xix

Slaughter, Olivia Kelly, xvi

Slaughter, W. L., xvi

slave catchers, 10

slavery, xliv, 6, 9, 11–12, 15–16, 23, 46, 66, 77, 88, 94–98, 114, 116, 137, 144, 152, 176–177, 184, 196–197

slaves, 59

Sleeter, C., 69

smallness beholders, 108

smallness children, 108

smoldering exploitation of Whiteness, 12

The Social Dilemma, 1

SNCC-Student Non-Violent Coordinating Committee, 100

social justice mastery, 159

social media, 12, 96

societal dysfunction of racial oppression, 37

socio-economic status, 119

southern strategy, 182

spiritual awakening, 187–188, 190

spiritual discipline, 169, 195–196

spirituality, xxiii–xxvi

Stanford Educational Leadership Institute, xxxvi

state-sanctioned violence, 29, 66

states rights, 102–103

Stevens, S., 101, 103, 183, 199

St. John's Lutheran Church, 109

Stoute, B. J., 67

Student Non-Violent Coordinating Committee (SNCC), 100

Student Violent Coordinating Committee, 64

subjective exploitation, 65–67, 77, 150, 178

substance use disorder (SUD), 36–37

suicidal ideation, 109

Sullivan, Clayton, 163–165

The Sum of Us (McGhee), 78

Sutton, Jeffrey, 179–180

systemic collusion, 11

T

Taino, 57

Taking Action (Toporek and Ahluwalia), 145

Tallabogue Creek, xliv

Tangipahoa Parish, 42

Tarasoff v. Regents of Univ. of Cal., 35

telescoping, 169–171, 174

There's More to Quitting Drinking Than Quitting Drinking (Paul O.), 149

Thibodeaux, 24, 118

Thich Nhat Hahn, 186

13th Amendment, 10

3D power: dominance, defense, and deliverance, 55

Time, 141

tobacco industry, xlix–1

Toporek, R., 145

tragedy, 57

Trail of Tears, 59

Treaty of Dancing Rabbit Creek, xlv

triumvirate mastery, 159

Trump, D., 102, 104

truth, 6, 16–17

Truth and Reconciliation Commission, 81–83

Tulsa Massacre, 82

Tutu, Archbishop Desmond, 81, 83, 146

U

ugliest instinctual aggressions, 153–154

Ukraine, 104

unintentional beliefs, 97

United States competitiveness, xiv, li, liii–liv, 1, 48, 60, 62, 71, 75, 83–84, 116–118, 121–123, 145, 157

United States of America, 2, 30, 116
- alcoholism's etiology, 5
- Black Americans citizenship in, 11
- constitution of, 7
- culture, 13
- democracy of, 30, 61
- history of, 7–8
- household wealth in, 26
- inequality in, 45
- patriotism, 7
- rigged advantage in, 3, 7
- shackles, 6
- slavery, 25
- slavery economy, 8

United States security, xiv, li, liii–liv, 1, 16, 48, 60, 62, 71, 82–83, 116–118, 121, 139, 145, 157, 183

United States Supreme Court, xv, 10, 25, 94, 117, 179–180, 184

University of California, Berkeley, 119

University of California, Los Angeles (UCLA), xvi

University of Mississippi, xv–xvi, 94

University of Mississippi School of Law, xvi

University of Southern Mississippi, 42

untreated alcoholic, 34

Upanishads, 108

USC Equity Research Institute (ERI), 120

U.S. Department of Agriculture, xxviii

U.S. Forest Service, 89

U.S. Soil Conservation Service, 88

V

value gap, 160

"vandals at the gate," 13, 17

variables, 135

vastness beholders, 108

vastness children, 108

Vicar of Christ, xlix

Vietnam War, 173

vigilant, remain, 147–160

violence
- as tool, 10
- civil rights–era, 118
- domestic, 66
- overt and covert, 24
- state-sanctioned, 29, 66

violent retribution, 24

Virginia, 7–8, 23, 26, 80

Virginia Law Review, 179

voter registration drives, xvi–xvii, xix, lii, 14, 100

voter suppression, 29, 46, 66

Voting Rights Act, 1965, 23

W

Ward, Larry, 186–187

Warhol, A., 55

Warren, Earl, 179

Watson, Helga Burnham (Mother), xv, xviii–xix, xxviii–xxix, xxxiv–xxxv, xlvi, 15, 58–59, 100, 150–151

Watson, Hubert (Father–Daddy), xv, xvii–xviii, xliv, 100, 114, 163

wealth/wealth gap, xlv, 6, 11–13, 15, 17, 23, 26–27, 29, 44, 47, 66, 102, 104, 116–119, 159, 171, 179–180, 184

Wesley Foundation, 166

we *vs.* me, 171–172

White absconding wealth, 117

White Americans, 26, 38, 113
- characteristics, 114
- culled, 25
- delusional mechanism, 29
- elite, 47, 95
- exploited, 11, 25, 60

in power, 95
nonelite, 11
rigged, 27
rigged advantage threatens, 37
White cold = Black flu, 37
Whiteness, 38, 64, 83
affinity, 48
derivative benefits of, 112
entitlement of, 24
masquerades, 28
political coalition, 46
relation to, 156
White race, 177–178, 181
White Southern, xliii–xlvii
White supremacist terrorists, 114
White supremacy, 37, 46, 52, 65–66, 77, 94, 102–103, 137, 178
White working class, 22–23
Why Beulah Shot Her Pistol in the Baptist Church (Sullivan), 165
widening inequality, 96. *See also* inequality
Williams, Hank, xxxiv

Wilmington, 24, 118
Wilson, J., 42
Winfried L., xxi
Winston cigarettes, xxiv
Witness for Peace, 167
W. K. Kellogg Foundation, 120

X
X, Malcolm, 64

Y
yamas (practices to avoid), 173–174
Yellow-Dog Democrat, xix
yoga, 173–174
Yogacharya Ellen Grace O'Brian, xxii, 166, 184
Yogananda, P., 54, 174, 184
The Yoga Sutra (Pantanjali), 173
yoke, 186, 195–196

Z
Zinn Education Project, 120
zooming perspectives, 57

www.ingramcontent.com/pod-product-compliance
Lightning Source LLC
Chambersburg PA
CBHW060944230426
43665CB00015B/2054